The Shadows and Lights of **Waco**

INFORMATION *Series*

Series Editor
Paul Rabinow

The Shadows and Lights of **Waco**

MILLENNIALISM TODAY

James D. Faubion

PRINCETON UNIVERSITY PRESS

PRINCETON AND OXFORD

Copyright © 2001 by Princeton University Press
Published by Princeton University Press, 41 William Street, Princeton, New Jersey 08540
In the United Kingdom: Princeton University Press, 3 Market Place, Woodstock,
Oxfordshire OX20 1SY

All Rights Reserved

Library of Congress Cataloging-in-Publication Data

Faubion, James D., 1957–
    The shadows and lights of Waco : millennialism today / James D. Faubion.
        p.   cm. — (In-formation series)
    Includes bibliographical references and index.
    ISBN 0-691-08997-3 (alk. paper) — ISBN 0-691-08998-1 (pbk. : alk. paper)
      1. Koresh, David, 1959–1993. 2. Branch Davidians. 3. Waco Branch Davidian
    Disaster, Tex., 1993. 4. Cults — United States. 5. United States — Religion — 1960–
    I. Title. II. Series.

    BP605.B72 F38 2001   2001027845

This book has been composed in Sabon with Futura Display

Printed on acid-free paper. ∞

www.pup.princeton.edu

Printed in the United States of America

10 9 8 7 6 5 4 3 2 1

10 9 8 7 6 5 4 3 2 1
(Pbk).

To Amo Paul Bishop Roden

WOMAN OF SPIRIT

Contents

Acknowledgments

I WOULD LIKE to thank the librarians of the Texas Collection at Baylor University in Waco, Texas, for accommodating my somewhat irregular presence among them and aiding me in exploring their invaluable archives. I would also like to thank Mary Murrell, Fred Appel, Jennifer Backer, and the other editors at Princeton who have helped me render my manuscript into a proper book. I owe a great deal to friends and colleagues who have tolerated my moods, listened to my grand (and less than grand) postulations, challenged my positions, and read and commented on my prose over the past six years. I would like to thank those students and professors of the Rice Department of Religious Studies who have so gracefully tolerated the outsider they have found in their midst. I am immensely grateful to the students, staff, and faculty of the Rice Department of Anthropology for their enduring curiosity and congeniality, and I want especially to thank my chair, George Marcus, for his many modes of support. Throughout this project, as in the past, Paul Rabinow has lent me his ear and mind, cajoled and coached me, and never allowed me to indulge my self-pity to anything approaching the point of permanent self-distraction. Dr. Sandra Barton has graced me with her relentless skepticism, without which I might have dared to become self-satisfied on more than one occasion. Claire Fanger applied her scholarly and poetic gifts to a reading of what I mistakenly thought to be my final draft; I have taken from her more than she knows, and more than I can adequately return. Robert Bellah offered me singularly acute criticisms of my venture into an anthropology of ethics. He will not be satisfied with that venture as it now stands, but has made me well aware that, fully formed, it will require a book of its own. William

ACKNOWLEDGMENTS

Pitts brought his considerable expertise in the history of Christianity and the Davidian and Branch Davidian movements to the manuscript and, much to my relief, did not find it terribly wanting. Victoria Mukerji did not hate the manuscript, which I consider no mean feather in my cap. The University of Chicago and University of California Presses allowed me to reproduce excerpts from articles I published previously with them. Finally, W. R. Dull, who took all of the photographs in this volume, would undoubtedly like me to list, one after another, all the contributions he has made to my project from start to finish, but I resist indulging him. The list would in any event be far too long — a veritable book in its own right. Without Amo Paul Bishop Roden, the project would have lacked force and life and much of what wisdom it might contain.

Prolegomena

HAVE UNDERTAKEN what I would like to think of as an anthropological inquiry and have given it the form of what I would like to characterize as an anthropological essay. The subtitle of the latter is a half-stolen twist on the title of another such essay, written some four decades ago, which we know in English as Claude Lévi-Strauss's *Totemism*. French readers would know it more accurately as *Le totémisme aujourd'hui*, "totemism today." I am not returning to totemism, of course, but like Lévi-Strauss, I would insist that the topic, the theme, the phenomena that concern me are not insular, not autonomous, not a system unto themselves. I would—I do—insist that they can be understood only against the wider backdrop of our social, cultural, and historical lives; that they are inseparable from those lives, within them, and so, however much we would beg to differ, within us as well. Again with Lévi-Strauss, I make ample use of the work of my colleagues, past and present, in anthropology, history, philosophy, and religious studies. I exploit their research; I review, I applaud, I criticize their analyses. I take them seriously. I presume my license to do so to be an anthropological license, the license of an intellectual discipline of dirty hands and of that vulgar daring to wrest the question of human nature from the arena of aprioristic speculation and pitch it instead upon the muddier soils of our actual works and days. I have relegated many of the more technical of my scholarly commentaries to endnotes that the less pedantic of readers will surely be happy to ignore. Much complexity nevertheless remains in the body of my text. It is inescapable. It is a reflection of the complexity of the topic, the theme, the phenomena I address.

Departing from Lévi-Strauss's precedent, I have grounded my inquiry in my own fieldwork, which I have conducted intermittently but regularly over the course of the past five and a half years. I might call what I have done "ethnographic," save for two reasons. The first is that I have no wish to stake the claims I make on my authority as an ethnographer. Though the great majority of my fellow anthropologists still hesitate to admit it, they know as well as I do that, the real epistemological virtues of fieldwork aside, ethnographic authority cannot stand on its own. Or to put it more carefully, it has no distinctive authority of its own. As method, it belongs to the far broader domain of eyewitnessing, of historical second sight, of journalistic investigation, of practical know-how (or coming to know who). It is often more thorough than its methodological cousins, or at least more resolutely eclectic; cultivating its eclecticism, the ethnographer is able to engage in a self-monitoring, a cross-checking, that methodologically more pure research may not allow. It is a rational method. It is also a pathic method and in its "pathology" engages (and changes) the fieldworker's mindful body not merely analytically but also intuitively, affectively; it is a way at once of being and of feeling (the) human. Hooray for ethnography. Any assessment of the adequacy of a particular course of fieldwork, however, always hinges on its contribution to the resolution (if not the solution) of the questions that the fieldworker sets out to explore or encounters as he or she proceeds. Its design, even its vaunted density, can legitimately vary in light of those questions. Conversely, if the fieldworker's questions are themselves without authority — pointless, or confused, or otherwise not to be taken seriously — no amount of fieldwork will make them so. Authority rests with a discipline (and so is often neither timeless nor innocent — but that is simply the fate of disciplinarity).

Of the two most general questions from which I proceed, one is old and often revisited: What is this thing we call "religion"? The other is inevitably timely: What has become of religion today? Their authority — such as it is — rests with anthropology. Here, once again, I am Lévi-Straussian and perhaps place myself among the anthropological rear guard as a consequence. In any event, I do not agree with those of my colleagues who think that anthropology has lost whatever authority it might have once commanded. I still take its observational perspective seriously. I remain convinced that it can still yield a good question or two. For all this, I would place myself nearer the front guard (and at odds with Lévi-Strauss) in at least one respect: I doubt fundamentally that the social or human sciences can lay claim to any methodological directive a priori, any categorical imperative, that would establish the goodness of fieldwork independently of the specific questions that provide it with its always necessarily specific rationale. What I would claim for my own fieldwork, which unfolded in part as a life-historical profiling, is that it was good enough to bring into resolution (though by no means exhaust) the anthropological questions I was pursuing.

My second reason for putting a distance between ethnography and the text I have written is less meta-methodological than simply conceptual. In brief, the text does not have an ethnos as its referent, its object. For the ancient Greeks, an ethnos was a community of people who might share a common label, a common marker of identity, but who had no polis of their own. For us, an ethnos is (roughly speaking) a culture. Neither my fieldwork nor my text has a culture as its object. Its units are practices; the practical and semiological currents I term "traditions"; and millennialism, which in its always particular enactment and expression is a gnosis, a spiritual knowing, a Wisdom that is (as I shall argue) trans-traditional. No ethnography here, then — only the social, and the cultural, and their inevitably complex entanglement.

In the text proper, I deploy three voices or, better, three modulations of voice. One modulation is that of the anthropologist. Another is that of his principal interlocutor, Amo Paul Bishop Roden (whose words appear in italics throughout). The third speaks for me. None of these voices is altogether distinct. The anthropologist is (very much) a part of me but also some part of Ms. Roden, as I am of her and as she is of me. If the anthropologist and I are successful, we will persuade our readers that we are all — Ms. Roden decidedly included — part of them as well, that we are all others, that we are all intersubjects, that the alterity we share is what we have in common. We are not, for all of that, identical. If I have chosen to incorporate the difference between the anthropologist and Ms. Roden, and between Ms. Roden and me, into the form of my text, if I have highlighted modulations of voice, I have done so in large part to highlight our mutual irreducibility. I have also done so to lessen the imperiousness of the anthropological voice itself. I do not pretend nor do I aspire to achieve "polyphony." Such beautifully equalitarian music *might* be possible in the utopia of free-floating fiction, but it is not possible in the heterotopia of the academic monograph, in which such people as anthropologists function also as editors, cullers and connoisseurs, orchestrators and arrangers, and then append their signatures to what — concretely in the end — they have wrought. Such people nevertheless have their limits — of voice, of insight, of judgment, of being. They might at least produce texts that testify explicitly to those limits of which they are aware (and leave readers to point out the rest). So the anthropologist and I have tried to do and, in the attempt, have also tried to allow Ms. Roden at least occasionally to speak for herself. In any event, she is capable of speaking for herself, and it would frankly have been difficult for either the anthropologist or I altogether to have silenced her even had we made the effort.

Tricks, devices, experiments — they are all fine and well, but this is also an inquiry into that specific mode of religion, or religiosity, known as millennialism, into what it is, and into what has become of it today. It is yet another inquiry into millennialism, though there have already been so many, especially of late. It is the result of my having indulged something of an intellectual (and not merely intellectual) passion, to be sure. But its occasion is a conflagration, the flames of which have, even after more than eight years, yet to die and the outbreak of which was in no small part due to the widespread refusal to acknowledge even the faintest glimmer of reason in millennialism itself. Anthropologists are hardly to be accused of having aided and abetted such a refusal; they are not read widely enough to have influenced it at all. Yet for all their professional charity they have tended more often than not to relegate millennialism to the realm not merely of alterity but instead of sheer Otherness, to the ex-otic (and ex-pathic). Social and cultural historians tend to be less well behaved but perhaps more honest: they often diagnose the millennialist consciousness as a false consciousness; or they sneer at the preposterous extravagance of its interpretations of the past and present and future; or they condemn its arrogant hypocrisy; or they fall in with the prevailing psychological manuals in declaring it the incoherent symptomatology of depressive or paranoid aberrations. It was not always this way. Indeed, measured on the scale of the *longue durée*, it was not this way until recently. I have accordingly undertaken a genealogical sketch of the abrupt rise of the irrationalization of millennialism that will have fulfilled its purpose if it unsettles the complaisant exclusivism of even one reader even remotely as much as it has unsettled my own.

I have also set out to accomplish a more constructive end. The millennialist consciousness as arrogant and hypocritical; the same consciousness as symptomatic, aberrant, out of control: these vividly opposed diagnoses are merely one substantive example of an ambivalent and unstable polarity that continues to afflict our theoretical and practical regard of human commitment generally. On the one end, all that we profess and all that we do appear to be the manifestation of our decisions, our choices. On the other end, all that we profess and all that we do appear to be the manifestation of external causes, of forces beyond our control. Moral philosophers know this opposition as the opposition between freedom and determinism. Social scientists more often know it as the opposition between agency and structure. A few diehard extremists aside, most moral philosophers and most social scientists are prepared to admit that human commitment, whether ideational or practical, falls somewhere in between its mutually repellent charges. The all-too-familiar strategy that amounts to nothing more than concocting commitment out of some mixture of the two—a cup of freedom here, a tablespoon or two of determinism there—is nevertheless spent. Commitment has a chemistry in its own right. Seeking to comprehend it, I have taken up and gone some way toward developing a frame, a model that at least has the virtue of being familiar. Casually put, it is a model of "education." Anthropologists will recognize it as a model that incorporates both "socialization" and "acculturation." I call it "pedagogy" and do my best to apply it to the dynamics of religious commitment, from conversion, through gnosis, to ethical self-cultivation. Its terminological keystone is neither choice nor coercion but instead *poiēsis*, the Greek for "making" or "producing" or "creating." One of the points that I care most to emphasize is that were pedagogy—any pedagogy—to be judged only in light of its "boot camp," its "basic training," it would always deserve our indignation. Initially, pedagogy—any and every pedagogy—is violent, disempowering, a curtailment of possibilities. What is or what ought to be more crucial—for those who would judge—is whether it remains so, whether it ultimately renders its students and charges nothing more than the slaves of their masters. Here, many a religious, many a millennialist pedagogy might well prove suspect—but suspect because of their design, their ratio, their reason, not suspect because of the absence of it. Hence, I could characterize what I have concocted as a critique of millennialist reason, which is certainly an impure reason, but then again, hardly less pure, hardly less infused with passion and the practical, than my own—than our own.

PART ONE

A Conversion

IT CAME TO HER unexpectedly — not unwelcome but still unsought. *I had moved to Texas in December of 1980, and I stayed at a farm . . . and it just came over me as I was here in all this beautiful, peaceful country that I owed God a lot, and I said, "O.K., God, take the rest of my life."*[1] William James would perhaps have found in such an inkling of transcendence one of those "original experiences" of which he thought all religions to be born.[2] Yet its resonant gratitude, its sigh of relief, had a past — and would have a future.

Amo Paul Bishop Roden, who refuses the anonymity usually accorded ethnographic subjects, was born on 20 January 1943 in Fort Marsh, Florida.[3] She shares her given name (the Latin "I love") with her mother and her daughter. Her middle name honors her maternal grandfather.[4] She has an elder brother and is the oldest of three sisters.[5] She spent her childhood winters in Florida, where her mother's parents lived and where her father found seasonal work in the shipyards.[6] When not in Florida, her family and she resided in Maine. Ms. Roden notes nothing remarkable in such transhumance; she neither speaks nor writes of any sense of uprootedness, any sense of drift. She does, however, refer to her family as *extremely dysfunctional*. She mentions sexual tensions and sexual errancy.[7] She mentions sibling rivalries. Hence, among other things, her lackluster academic record: *I was an underachiever. My brother was a year older, and there was a rivalry between us, and I dealt with it just by becoming an underachiever. That's as simply as I can explain it.*[8] She nevertheless reports that she was a National Merit Scholarship semi-finalist and that she received a partial scholarship from the University of Maine, from which she earned a degree in mathematics, *with a minor in psychology.*[9]

Ms. Roden's maternal great-grandfather was a minister. Her parents followed another path. *My father's basically an atheist, and my mother is a Christian, but she's kind of what you call a lukewarm Christian.* Her siblings *are very psychically gifted,* but their gifts *not aimed at religion.*[10] Nor, as a child, were her own. She attended a Protestant church of short-term ministries and eclectic doctrines. Her attendance was regular but more a matter of habit than passion, querulousness, or fascination.[11]

In college, the focus of her conscience, and of her anxieties, was political. *I have been told by an FBI source that a file labeling me subversive exists. And the March on Washington to protest the war in Vietnam is my best guess as to how they first got my name. I booked a seat from Boston to Washington in my own name.*[12] *At the end of the sixties, I was so distressed . . . that I left the country and went to Canada. When I was in the country before I went to Canada, I was a very normal kind of person. I just had regular jobs, and I went to work, and I watched t.v. All the things that normal people do, you know.*[13] While in Canada, Ms. Roden met the man who would become her first husband, and with whom she would have her first child, a son. Several years later, their marriage would end in divorce. *And I spent ten years in Canada being a normal person, and very out of touch with the United States, because it got so much worse between the late sixties and when I returned in '80.*[14] Her son accompanied her on her move south.

As it turned out, the relief that initially came to her was short-lived. A few short months later: *I felt a call from God to go to a church, and I went to a Pentecostal church out on Robinson Road—I'm not sure I can remember the name of it; I think it's called the Calvary Assembly of God—and I met a woman there, . . . and basically, I was so ignorant. . . . It was in '81, I guess. I would have been a little short of forty, and she taught the Bible some, and she took my hand that first day and talked me into going right down and being saved, taking communion there.* Two years beyond, in the summer of 1983, *I began to have visions.*[15] By autumn, she had decided to distribute an urgent letter to her family, and to several individuals whom she thought to be of local prominence:

> *Dear Sir: My name is Amo B. I am a systems analyst by profession. Although both my mother's parents' families have a history of precognition or clairvoyance, incidents of this kind have been infrequent in my life. Nonetheless, when I dreamed of a nuclear war in November,*[16] *I was concerned enough to watch the news for warning signs. Some items did seem particularly relevant, leading me to do a feasibility study of a surprise nuclear attack this fall using a Russian point of view.*

I found the bottom line alarming, so I prepared the attached for your review. Would you please study it carefully.

Although I can't predict what the Russians will do, I felt the need to warn people in Waco to prepare. You are one of a few people I felt could help to quietly spread the word as your acquaintance should touch a broad segment of the community.

If you are willing to help would you please make copies of the enclosed study and distribute it to your friends, family, neighbors, and workmates. If you feel you can't be involved in this effort, would you please put this letter, envelope and all, in tomorrow's mail so that I may attempt to replace you.

I will be sending some comments on how to survive radiation exposure shortly (when I finish them). If you have any questions you may reach me at . . .

Best regards . . .

P.S. In an effort not to worsen a grave situation would you please keep this study away from the press.

The argument Ms. Roden offered ran as follows:

1. The United States under Ronald Reagan has a hostile and aggressive attitude toward Russia; this will likely continue another five years with his re-election.

2. Arms-reduction talks have produced no result beyond political posturing; indeed, while Reagan announces new proposals, the United States Secretary of Defense discusses arms sales to China.

3. The United States is reinitiating the arms race with an economic recovery and a huge budget. Historically, the United States has dominated such competition.

4. The recent grain deal allows Russian stores of grain to be maximized before [the] onset of hostilities.

5. The country which initiates the war, particularly if by surprise, has numerous advantages: (a) [a] few missiles targeted at major missile emplacements could, with their multiple warheads, substantially reduce counter-attack; (b) key people and technology can be safeguarded; (c) the choice of time of attack during daylight hours in Russia would reduce casualties.

6. The following military considerations apply: (a) Pershing missile deployment will substantially increase Russian casualties; (b) the United States' lead in laser targeting was confirmed with successful testing of bomber defense lasers (five anti-aircraft missiles were destroyed from the B59 they were chasing in sixty seconds). Obviously the United States will equip its long-range bombers with this technology immediately; (c) with improved laser targeting (a marriage of two fields the United States appears to dominate, radar and computerization), a defense against nuclear weapons will shortly be reality. With its deployment, the United States could fight nuclear war with relative impunity.[17]

She received no reply, no return — or rather, the return made was very different from what she had expected it to be. *I was so naive back then.*[18]

Social and cultural historians have ready evidence that the prospect of nuclear holocaust has exercised a diverse array of religious imaginations in the United States for several decades. In a recent survey, Paul Boyer traces a stream of commentary and concern about "the bomb" and what it might portend flowing with equal vigor through popular and more esoteric theologies from the destruction of Hiroshima to very near the present (1992: 115–51). Among the majority of the established or "mainstream" denominations, orthodoxy has licensed drawing no more than moral lessons from the ghastly instrument that had somehow found its way into human hands.[19] Among the New Denominations, however, eschatological speculation acquired increasing urgency, and the "final days" increasing imminence, as the race between the United States and the Soviet Union quickened in pace. In the 1970s, Jerry Falwell, Pat Robertson, and Billy Graham were merely the best known of a new wave of evangelists exhorting their audiences to expect a thermonuclear gigantomachia (Boyer 1992: 137–39). Hal Lindsey's *Late, Great Planet Earth* proffered a similar "Armageddon theology" (cf. Halsell 1986; Kierulff 1991). Published in 1970, it had sold nine million copies by 1978 and ranks as the premier nonfiction best-seller of the decade. It had sold twenty-eight million by 1990, a year before its release in a revised edition.[20] All the while, the congregations of the New Denominations continued — and still continue — to grow at the mainstream's expense.[21]

Of course, none of this implies that the worries of our recently atomic era have given rise to Ms.Roden's religiosity any more than they have given rise to that of even the most anxious of her contemporaries. Much less does it imply that religious sentiment or religious commitment has its general source in fear, whether of the known or of the unknown. The emotional tenor of what — borrowing a phrase from Marshall Sahlins (1985: 150–51) — could be called the "symbolic interest" of the bomb is in any event complex. Bleak distress is frequently of a piece with relieved confidence. So, for example, influential evangelist M. R. DeHaan could assure the auditors of his "Radio Bible Class" and the readers of his several exegetical treatises that it was precisely the unprecedented horrors of military technologies that confirmed the promise of the imminent salvation of the faithful.[22] So, too, Lindsey, whose contemplation of the conflicts and cataclysms of the future is, as Michael Barkun has noted, unflaggingly exuberant (Barkun 1985: 24; cited in Boyer 1992: 128). Like DeHaan, indeed, Lindsey expresses every confidence that, for the faithful, the story he tells has a "happy ending."

The prevailing state of mind might simply seem incongruous—and perhaps would be, if it rested merely in the ironical observation that the very invention that had saved the "free world" has also unleashed the specter of planetary ruin. Yet, for Lindsey as for his eschatological company, the bomb is not genuinely an irony. It commands awe; it provokes terror, humility, and resignation. It attracts the most grand and grotesque of descriptive language. It is a figure of power and often resonates with all the hyperbolic excess proper to the sublime—or, more often, the countersublime. An allegorist could easily enough fit it out as a demon. For most latter-day eschatologists, however, the bomb remains a machine. Its emplotment renders it sublime or countersublime only as a metonymic stand-in, as a sickle might stand in for the reaper who wields it. The reaper—the real god, or demon—lurks elsewhere.[23]

Scholars of Christianity generally classify the type of emplotment at issue as "premillennialist." It allows for further subdivision, and for an indefinite number of variations, but its poetic architecture remains relatively constant.[24] The prophets of both the Old and the New Testaments refer occasionally to the "last days" (for example, Isa. 2:2; Mic. 4:1) or the "time of the end" (Dan. 11:40) of the world, a historical culmination that Timothy pronounces "perilous" (2 Tim. 3:1) and Daniel "a time of trouble, such as never was since there was a nation, even to that same time" (Dan. 12:1). The author of the final book of the New Testament, Revelation, prophesies its tumultuous course in considerable if often cryptic detail. He tells of the ascent of a succession of "beasts." The eighth in their line (Rev. 17:11) has a powerful dragon at his service, the distinguishing mark of "six hundred threescore and six" (Rev. 14:9–10), and no earthly rival. Those who worship him prosper. The faithful remnant of God—some "hundred forty and four thousand"—suffer torment and retreat to Mount Zion to receive the Lamb, who appears at last in their midst (Rev. 14:1). The beast and his forces inscribe a line of ultimate battle at "a place called in the Hebrew tongue Armageddon" (Rev. 16:16). In the engagement, the faithful suffer, but the army of God prevails. Among its members is "an angel come down from heaven, having the key of the bottomless pit and a great chain in his hand." He captures the dragon, "which is the Devil, and Satan," and binds him "a thousand years," and locks him within the bottomless pit, "that he should deceive the nations no more, till the thousand years should be fulfilled" (Rev. 20:1–3).

7

This thousand years is the "millennium" on which all Christian millennialisms dwell. In his youth, Saint Augustine seems to have been something of a millennialist himself. His later thought, especially the thought of *The City of God*, is resolutely antimillennialist (Desroche 1969: 56; cf. Funkenstein 1986: 258–59). He had come to understand Revelation's imagery—not least, its temporal imagery—to be largely allegorical and its real story the tale of the success the church would ultimately enjoy in bringing all the world's peoples into its fold (1952 [413–426]: book 20, chaps. 7–17). His opinion has remained canonical for Catholicism and finds no challenge from Eastern Orthodoxy. Among Protestants, postmillennialists can agree with Saint Augustine that the church must be the agent of the cleansing and conversion of the world, but they locate themselves near the close of the process and expect the literal return of the Christ in its immediate aftermath. Premillennialists deem the agent of cleansing and conversion to be none other than the Christ and await his (or her) return all the more anxiously the more they are convinced that the extraordinary troubles of the last days of the world are, indeed, their own. At this juncture, the bomb joins the roster of an already dense biblical catalog of troubles, which includes "the dragon" but also earthquakes, thunder and lightning, plagues, predatory animals, the blood of the dead, lakes of fire fuming with brimstone, and Peter's apocalypse of the "day of the Lord" as a day "in which the heavens shall pass away with a great noise, and the elements shall melt with fervent heat, the earth also and the works therein shall be burned up" (2 Pet. 3:10).

Thus emplotted, such monstrosities and misfortunes are doubly evocative. If tropes of power, they are more precisely tropes of a power that looms as a transcendent threat, an implacable and encroaching doom. In sights and sounds and odors and unbearable physical pain, they sensuously encode the practical sense of danger, of the body in peril. Nor is that body merely material, nor merely individual. It is also social, a body of persons interacting and communicating with one another. It is also political, the body of subjects and those who rule over them. In all its dimensions, it is a body ill at ease, a body of suspect integrity. Yet what it experiences, what it anticipates, is not simply the visitation of evil, not even as a test. In the Bible itself as in so many of its premillennialist elaborations and extrapolations, the catalog of troubles is replete with devices that might equally serve Satan or God. Like such Old Testament prophets as Jeremiah and Ezekiel, the author of Revelation in fact has far less to disclose of the devices of Satan's corruption than of the devices of God's wrath and retribution. Nor is Satan the deity's only victim. So, too, is the body of those whom he has corrupted—the body of idolaters, of the lapsed and the errant, of all those who are mired in sin.

I remember a dream that must have come to me in 1962 or 1963, when I was six or seven. In it, I was watching a tiny dot in the distant sky. As it neared, I was able to see that it was an airplane flying at a spectacular speed. It released something from its belly — another dot, which rapidly grew larger in its fall and soon took on the dimensions of a zeppelin, as imposing as the Hindenberg. It, too, opened its belly, the contents of which, a veritable peasant arsenal of pitchforks and spears and boiling oil, rained down from the sky in an endless, lethal train. I awoke terrified. My older brother was soon blamed for having poisoned my imagination with gruesome explications of the news of the day. I took comfort in the accusation, however unjust, and soon returned to sleep. The nightmare passed, or gave way to others. Yet, I do, after all, still remember it; and at the droning sound, or sight, of a zeppelin, still feel the slight but distinct nausea of dread.

As we know, there is always more to a dream than the dream itself. So perhaps the wars, hot and cold, of my childhood and adolescence left their imprint more indelibly than I can now discern. I vaguely recall the controversies over Cuba. I remember John Kennedy's funeral procession, televised over and over again like the refrain of a dirge; Walter Cronkite's sober, nightly recitation of body counts during the Vietnam War; and the announcement over the intercoms of my elementary school of the assassination of Robert Kennedy (but not of Martin Luther King). What I remember most vividly is a tense day I spent during my senior year of college in the stuffy rooms of an inescapable skyscraper with more than a dozen fellow candidates anticipating advancement to the national finals of a competition for a prestigious graduate scholarship. The initial round of interviews had generated no obvious winners. During the second round, the panel in charge of the interviews told me that recipients of the scholarship were expected to have a special role in "fighting the good fight." They asked me what I thought might especially qualify me for such a battle. I have no retrospective idea of what I actually said. I recall only my scornful thought that if the panel hoped for an earnestly missionary response, I would be happy to be among the losers — which, none too happily, I was.

In fact, it was only in retrospect that Ms. Roden came to identify her dream as a "call to prophecy." *God had started giving me visions, heart-wrenching knowledge of the time of trouble . . . [but] I was ignorant of the Bible; so was my family. In the end-time God will pour his Spirit on many people. I know that now, but I didn't then.*[25] Her letter went unanswered. It was not, however, entirely ignored. *I suspect that I was reported to the government by my landlord, but that's just a hunch. The day after I gave him a copy, I was under surveillance. My food was*

9

poisoned, my house was sprayed with chemicals, people who hid their faces from me started fishing in my landlord's pond. Alarmed, I told my family. . . . Between the visions, and the concern that someone was trying to kill me and my reputation for honesty, I was easy prey.

The deputy sheriff arrived within minutes after my sister . . . and took me to the mental health ward of Providence Hospital. . . . I spent forty-five minutes denying what I could and explaining the rest. The doctor . . . advised further treatment, and I signed an agreement to attend twelve therapy sessions. I was strong-armed by two people to consent to court order, but I wasn't about to sign. . . . I did not attend the therapy sessions I signed up for. . . . That left me without a mental health record.[26] The government of this country feels that it is necessary for anyone remotely suspected of being subversive to have a mental health record. . . .

The persecution started again in June 1984. This time I didn't tell anyone. Again my food was poisoned and my house sprayed, and this time intimidation was added. One of my carving knives was left in the dishwater with its blade broken in half. Finally, I moved down to my farm, where I was to build a house. It was fine summer weather, but there was little shelter, and the persecutors had a great day.[27]

Her son remained with her. *Something hot to the touch was sprayed on our clothes and bedding. Airplanes flew over, and when we hid under a wet sheet under the bridge from the hot stuff, the water got hot. [My son] saw a man through the sheet throwing something into the water. Mostly, I was busy scooping water from the bottom of the pond up around my son. He was getting burned by the water, and it scared him, so I kept bringing up cold water from the bottom. I saw my dog, Buddy, take a drink from the pond, and he lay down at once. I started yelling, "They murdered my dog! They murdered my dog!" He didn't move for twenty minutes; then he got up and walked away.[28] After awhile the airplane went away, and the water cooled down, and I got out and fed [my son] and put him to bed. When I lay down, the sheet under me made my back burn, and I realized that they might come after me to kill me and kill [my son], too. I wasn't thinking too clearly, but I felt that keeping him with me was endangering him, and I was afraid that the hot stuff was radiation. I got him up, sent him into the pond to wash, and went in myself. I didn't dare put his clothes back on; I didn't know what was on them. I sent him naked to a neighbor's house. I didn't bother with my clothes, either. I sat down on the bridge and waited for the government to finish its job.[29]*

Two deputies arrived; I ducked down when they arrived, then stood up as they approached with flashlights. I asked one for a blanket, and he gave me one. I took them to the rented house and tried to get them to take samples of the food, but they weren't interested. The deputies took me to a hospital, and I was examined, and two people harassed me to sign forms. When I arrived at DePaul Mental Hospital, I snapped, and stated my opinion of the Texas mental health industry in a very loud voice. I was prepared to die rather than spend more time with these fools. One hypodermic wasn't enough to shut me up once I started; I'd been through too much. It took two. . . . After six days, they cut me loose. The court record shows that no mental health services were ordered.[30] *They lied to me, as the social worker's statement confirms. They told me I had to attend therapy sessions until the doctor released me.*

When I was released from the hospital, my sister . . . took me to my lawyer's office.[31] *[The lawyer] gave me a document to sign, stating that if I signed this, [my son] would go directly into his father's custody; otherwise he would have to spend two months in a foster home. I signed it without reading it. I feared to keep [my son]. I wasn't admitting that people were trying to kill me, but I wasn't going to endanger him anymore. The thought of him in a foster home appalled me. [The lawyer] was my legal representative. Would she set me up and lie to me? Turns out she would. The inner pages of this agreement contained an admission of child abuse and neglect. However, not only does the court no longer have a copy, [the lawyer] claims she doesn't, either. She would be without custody of her son for two years. He came back loving me, but thinking I was insane.*

And was she? Is she? One can only guess at what those who received her letter must have thought: that she was "a crackpot," perhaps; or, more gently, that she was "letting her imagination run away with her." But what she wrote, what she actually put down in words, was hardly unreasonable. On the contrary: it was very much in accord with all those more or less official pronouncements that had driven so many concerned citizens in the 1950s and 1960s to stockpile necessities, to construct or to finance the construction of underground shelters, and to identify and label local structures sturdy and impervious enough to offer them safe refuge — or so, mistakenly, they believed — if and when the bomb finally fell. By the early 1980s, shelters had largely gone out of fashion, though less because the fear of nuclear assault had abated than because the very idea of finding safe refuge in the face of nuclear assault had been ever more forcibly unmasked as a fantasy. Ms. Roden was, moreover, evidently as well versed as any other ordinary citizen in current strategic affairs. She was not setting out to repeat the obvious. She was instead setting out to subvert or, in any event, to contravene it. The official rationale for the ongoing investment in nuclear development at the time was precisely contrary to what her own analysis had compelled

11

her to conclude. She saw what the Reagan administration put forward as the optimal means of containing Soviet "aggression" as the optimal means of stimulating it. One can imagine that some of her readers would have disagreed. Even those who found her argument plausible might nevertheless have found the depth of her implicit distrust of the political order somewhat odd. They might have found her implicit conviction that she had somehow won the privilege — and thanks to a dream, of all things — of divulging a horrible and dangerous secret to be somewhat odd as well. They would no doubt find her reports of persecution odder still.

Ms. Roden, who rarely refrains from giving voice to what remains on the tips of more polite tongues, has this to say about her condition: *I believe that my experience with the government is by no means unique; as a way to deal with people thought to be politically destabilizing it is so successful that it has probably been widely used. That the* Encyclopedia Americana *records American paranoids to be generally better integrated than other psychotics is likely a symptom of our police state.*[32] The anthropologist does not dispute her sincerity but seeks a broader structural context, and finds an approach to it in what would seem to be a most unexpected source. Emile Durkheim plainly did not have the paranoiac in mind when he formulated his definition of the "social fact." Seeking a positive, an empirical ground for a social science, he appealed to what he evidently presumed to be a virtually universal human experience: that of a "force" imposing itself "coercively" and as "constraint" from without (Durkheim 1938 [1895]: 1–4). He would much later argue that the sense of the sacred had its original and enduring wellspring from the same experience (Durkheim 1995 [1912]: 195–216). Pierre Bourdieu, among others, has suggested that the social, thus delimited, is virtually "empty" (Bourdieu 1977: 23). At a first reading, Durkheim indeed seems to conflate a variety of modalities of coercion that are experientially distinct: that of the conclusion validly derived from its premises with that of moral duty; that of moral duty with that of such practically inescapable conventions as driving on one or the other side of the road; that of convention with that of punishment; that of punishment willingly suffered from that of punishment unwillingly suffered; and so on. But, some of these conflations are surely intentional.[33] Whether or not intentional, they bring to light a number of structural relationships that intuition may hesitate to entertain.

With the addition of only a single variable, Durkheim's experiential model of the social fact yields an experiential model of paranoia. Intuition may incline toward positing that what the sense or sensation of being subject to an external coercive force lacks in order to be paranoid is a "reality check." But not only is such an addition extra-experiential, it is also insufficient, even for as secure a sociological realist as Durkheim, who would have to admit with the rest of us that even paranoiacs occasionally have real enemies. What the experience of the social lacks in order to pass as paranoid is simply that additional sense, or sensation, of "election" — positive or negative from one "case" to the next. If positive, the paranoid sense of election often finds its symbolism in the imagery of the messenger or messiah, in the symbolism of a sometimes burdened but distinctive blessedness that psychomedical discourse casts as the "delusion of grandeur." If negative, the paranoid sense of election often seeks out those symbologies of the scapegoat and sacrificial victim that psychomedical discourse takes as the stuff of a "persecution complex." Nor are the values mutually exclusive: the sense of election can be negative and positive at once.

The phenomenological proximity of social and paranoid experience does not merely suggest that paranoia is itself a social, not a psychological, phenomenon. It further suggests that each of the two modalities of experience implicates the other, as presence implicates absence or, better, as one pole of a continuous scale implicates the opposite pole of the same scale. The difference between the two seems, in other words, to be merely a matter of degree, not genuinely one of kind. Durkheim hints at their fundamental unity in noting that, at its most social, social experience goes unnoticed. Or at least it passes for something else: having been internalized, having become an aspect of the habitus, external coercion has the feel of personal inclination (Durkheim 1938 [1895]: 2). At such an extreme lie those practitioners of Bourdieusian theory for whom "the conditions of the production of the habitus and the conditions of its functioning are identical or homothetic" (Bourdieu 1990: 63) and who thus reproduce the schemas of perception and patterns of action that have made them who and what they are without knowing or needing to know what they are doing. The palpable externality and coerciveness of the social both increase, however, with even the slightest failure of the reproductive circuit, with even the slightest lessening of structural investment. The tension between duty and desire (between what one is obliged to do and what one wants to do) occupies the structural interstices, the little rifts that thus appear in the practical web, as do its closest sentimental companions — the half-surprised, half-scornful tingle that comes when *fusis* (nature) is unveiled as mere *nomos* (convention); the egoistic irritation that comes with unnecessary burdens, the slightly aggressive resentment that comes with distrust, the hollow cheer that comes with skepticism.

Such skepticism, in turn, finds its readiest and perhaps most pure methodological instrument in what might be called a *sémiotique du soupçon*, a semiotics of (the) suspicion, of the inkling, clue, or trace.

The author of the Book of Revelation posits a limit, at once logical and historical, at which that semiotics would no longer have any methodological rationale whatever: "the days of the voice of the seventh angel, when he shall begin to sound, [and] the mystery of God should be finished" (10:7). Beyond its threshold, all signifiers would be fully adequate to their referents; a condition of absolute semiotic clarity and absolute semiotic transparency would hold sway. The evidential relationship would be delivered of all its semantic poverty and pragmatic insouciance. "Theory" would be nothing more than idle speculation. Or it would revert to its Aristotelian — which, in modern parlance, would have to be deemed either its "pre-theoretical" or its "post-theoretical" — modality.[34] No longer sustained by phenomenal or factual indeterminacy, theory could be nothing more (nor anything less) than the synchronous contemplation of the real. It would demand no specialization, no research, no expertise. Like critique in Marx's communist society, it would be radically popular. A semiotics of suspicion is a semiotics for a far less perfect world, less crystalline and less crisply visible, like so many reflections in a dark mirror. In such a world — in our world — signifiers are likely to distinguish their referents crudely at best, or even to have no referents. Both semantic and pragmatic obscurity are constant and often incorrigible. Intentions are often articulated vaguely even when they are not actively being disguised.[35]

A semiotics of suspicion is a semiotics, in short, for a world that cries out — just so long as it cries out — for interpretation. It is thus peculiarly well suited to the still imperfectly revealed world recounted in the Bible, and especially to the biblical world of Erich Auerbach's *Mimesis*, in which every pivotal historical moment is the "figure," the always suggestive but always partial figuration of yet another later historical moment, and in which history itself, "with all its concrete force," thus "remains forever a figure, cloaked" and so forever inviting and forever in need of the final disclosure, the final demystification, of which the author of the Book of Revelation dreams (Auerbach 1953: 58; cf. Lambropoulos 1993: 11). Auerbach's habit of identifying the biblical view of the historical process with the Judeo-Christian view should, however, be resisted (1953: 73; cf. Lambropoulos 1993: 14). It is at the very least ethnologically uninformed, all the inspiration that the Bible has provided to millennialists and theorists of conspiracy alike — especially during the past two centuries — notwithstanding.[36] As Vassilis Lambropoulos has pointed out, it also constitutes the first principle of an anti-Hellenic celebration of Judeo-Christian tolerance and Judeo-Christian relativism against an allegedly Homeric and allegedly pagan attraction to "everything sceptic, static, autocratic, absolutist" (1993: 14). Lambropoulos might have suggested more forcefully that it further constitutes an equally prejudiced refusal to acknowledge the myriad semiotic obfuscations on which the central events of both the *Iliad* and the *Odyssey* (among many other texts in the Greek corpus) turn. Or perhaps one might better and more accurately write less of prejudice than of self-deception. Auerbach, a fierce critic of Nazi tyranny, was compelled to cast himself and his readerly enterprise as direct heir to a Judeo-Christian legacy of epistemological fallibilism, epistemological openness. Was he thus compelled to suppress all that his enterprise owed to the precedent of the godly point of view adopted and consecrated by so oracular and so wry a poet-interpreter as Homer—whoever he, or they, might have been—himself?

Some two centuries ago, Friedrich Schiller declared ancient Greek poetry, and with it the ancient Greek sensibility, "naive"—semiotically untroubled, perhaps even semiotically self-satisfied (1965 [1794–95]). Long before Auerbach, Schiller may thus have been the first modern Occidental thinker to turn away from what might well have been an uneasy, somewhat unflattering, and somewhat too revealing encounter with the ancient hypostasis of the interpretive craft. Aristotle's epistemological self-confidence aside, the Greeks certainly knew of both the necessity and dangers of interpretation. Their theology suggests indeed that they knew of both all too well. Hermes was among the first order of their gods, though not the equal of Zeus—law-giver and the hand of justice. Hermes' special domain was that of the *metafora*, the "transference" or "haulage" but also "change," as of one phase to another, also "metaphor." Divine messenger, Hermes also presided conjointly over boundaries, crossings, and journeys. He was the master of commerce; the master, too, of *logos*—of communication, of speech and writing and eloquence. And who, after all, but the god whose distinctive virtues were those of making and securing connections should also be able to boast of that complementary virtue, that accessory power or talent called *deinōtēs*, "cunning" or "guile," but also "marvelousness," "awesomeness"?

One must accordingly be struck by the symbolic overdetermination of that gesture through which a group of conspirators (whose identity was never firmly established) undertook one March night in 415 B.C.E. to cast a pall over the success of what the good citizens of the Athenian assembly had agreed to be a most timely invasion of Sicily. Throughout the Athenian city-state, Hermes stood in small stone effigies, "Herms," registering and attesting to the limits of lots and parcels of private property. He bore most often only what might be thought of as his barest essentials: the formal, smiling face of the benign host or patron; and an erect penis, the ubiquitous ancient icon at once of the power of continuity and the power of transgression. The conspirators, who seem to have

15

gone undetected in spite of the noise their chisels must have made, mutilated what Thucydides carefully specifies to be "the faces" of the Herms.[37] Other commentators have insisted that the mutilations were more thorough.[38] Partial or more complete, the widespread desecration amounted to a slap in the face of a democratically adjudicated policy, and so in the face of the Athenian democracy itself. But the scandal was not merely political. It was also moral and religious, a matter of what ancient wisdom continued to regard as a cardinal sin. The conspirators had committed *hubris*, the "outrage," the "overweening arrogance" of having done insult to a presence to whom they should only have done honor. Even worse, in having sought to spoil through their own devices the divine auspices under which the Sicilian expedition could have been expected to sail, in having thus taken the matter of the blessedness or cursedness of the expedition into their own hands, they had not merely dishonored Hermes. They had — the very quintessence of hubris — presumed to dethrone him, to put themselves in his place.

Whoever they were, the conspirators managed to inaugurate an enduring tradition. Their epigones appear again in the Renaissance. Some are Neoplatonist mystics; others are alchemists. They are united in their dedication to the Egyptian god Thoth, whom they presume to be a more original, more pure, and more mighty incarnation of the Greek Hermes and whom they accordingly call Hermes Trismegistus, Hermes "Thrice-Great." Pious, perhaps, but there is little question that these "Hermeticists," as they called themselves, were hardly content merely to honor the divinity whose cunning gave him special entry into the realm of the secret, the mysterious, and the occult. There is little question that they also sought to acquire his secrets from him. And if not heirs to theirs, then to whose example are "we" — secular and modern semioticians of suspicion — proper heirs? Do we not — almost conspiratorially — strive to dissemble, by appeal to such secular pieties as those of "scientific rigor" and "methodological restraint," the actual ambitions that come almost to light especially when we refer to ourselves by that most precious of our occupational titles: "hermeneut"?

Or should I really speak, not for whom I presume the majority of my readers to be, but instead only for myself? So be it, then. I certainly found Ms. Roden's letter odd. I am inclined to believe that there is now an FBI file dedicated to her but doubt that it came into existence as early on as she claimed that it did. I found her tales of persecution quite incredible — and a counterinterpretation ready enough at hand to be virtually spontaneous. Yet, what could I have brought forward to justify my suspicious opinions? What evidence could I claim to possess that would have proven her wrong? What did I know that she did not? I am not privy to the archives of the FBI. I was not witness to any of the events she reported, nor acquainted with anyone else who might have had evidence sufficient to warrant a different, contrary report. My sole "proof" lay merely in the fact that she was telling me such things, that she herself seemed sure of their veracity. Nor would even that proof have functioned as such, much less functioned quite so spontaneously as such, had I not long ago absorbed, and come to apply with all the unreflective reproductivity of the best Bourdieusian practitioner, a psychomedical behaviorism that at once permitted and impelled me to conclude that, like any other person who would tell me such things—and so avidly—Ms. Roden must be mad. The taking of such interpretive liberties was, moreover, all the more extravagant (or hypocritical?) in my particular case, since I prefer to posture myself a critic of psychomedical behaviorism, even among its most unremitting skeptics. But there is skepticism, it would seem, and then there is skepticism. My own is tempered far more rigidly than I once realized by all the investments that—proud marginal though I be (or posture myself)—I nevertheless retain. The psychomedical model still belongs to my world: modern, secular, and "scientific" (if in a broad sense of that term). Whatever doubts I might harbor about it do not reach far enough to undermine my conviction that it still must be taken seriously—even when it leads to error or injustice. Nor, a fortiori, do my doubts reach far enough to undermine at least my abstract trust in the potential benignancy of the politico-economic orders within which secular science has become so comfortably settled. I can of course expound on the "evils of capitalism"; I can shake my head in libertarian and democratic disgust at the internal and external imperialism of my government. But Ms. Roden has made me acutely aware how much, unreflectively and reproductively, I have continued to have faith—my own little civil religion, or some decrepit version of one. I simply could not believe that the government would do to any of its citizens what Ms. Roden claimed its agents to have been doing to her; I just could not imagine it. I wonder if I can genuinely imagine it even now. What I can at least entertain is the thought that, deprived of the bulwark of my good burgher's assurance that in the ultimate analysis my world is the lesser evil, I would have nowhere else to drift, semiotically or imaginatively, but toward increasing darkness.

Ms. Roden is not a good burgher and so partakes of virtually none of his comforts. She is much farther from the pole of unreflective reproduction than from its opposite, from the extreme of Weber's charismatic leader and his, or her, radically revisionary slogan: "It is written; but I say unto you" (M. Weber 1946: 250). In the company of the charismatic, standing nearer or farther away, are those like-minded souls who, for no doubt widely variable reasons, find themselves inclined to listen, perhaps to realize their own election, negative or positive (or both) from one case to the next. Here, paranoia has its structural *agora*, its structural forum.[39]

Though Durkheim would probably have chosen a different label, the extremes at which paranoia thrives can well enough be deemed — and have often been deemed — extremes of "alienation." But from what? Not from the social itself, for even such extremes stop short of the boundary that divides "deviance" or even resolute enmity from actual anomie. Nor do paranoiacs stand altogether beyond or leave altogether behind the realm of the cultural. They are not preoccupied with meaninglessness, with the Absurd. They are rather preoccupied with mysteries. They are aware of the sometimes terrible ironies of ignorance. But the aura of the uncanny that abides in even the most abstract of paranoid revelations stems from an anxiety over more than mere ignorance. The paranoid are the inheritors of Cassandra's curse: their suspicions meet with bemused dismissals; their knowledge falls on obstinately deaf ears. It is not truth from which they are alien but from what Michel Foucault has called the "regime of truth," or what might more broadly be called the "regime of signification" — the social organization of the production and the distribution of the truth, of epistemic authority, of intellectual and moral legitimacy, which also might provide for secrets to be harbored, plots to be hatched, and deceit to flourish like a parasitic vine behind any number of hermetic doors.[40]

Even the rare paranoiac who entertains no thoughts whatever of conspiracy still often speaks of some warp or perversion that has placed both power and truth beyond human managing. At its paranoid extremes, alienation leaves the personal, the political, and the social body equally ill at ease. Whatever the political or social status of the body who suffers it, such alienation would appear to have the sense of election, positive or negative, as its most common and spontaneous externalization. Whatever its precise sources, which are surely multiple, its objective measure lies in the gap between the personal body — its embodied subjectivity — and that political and social subjectivity most finely adjusted to use and to serve the steering mechanisms of the political and social regime in which it subsists.[41]

Such considerations are unlikely to give pause to our contemporary legion of psychic workers. However, they at least aid in the clarification of what is at stake in the perpetration of an exclusively psychomedical model of paranoia and in the consequent codification of the paranoiac as a psychomedical "case." If Hegel and Marx could, for once, agree, that was perhaps because they were simply registering the obvious: the

18

alienated are rarely ardent devotees of the status quo ante; potentially at least, they constitute instead the forward guard of its overthrowers. From the vantage of the status quo ante, alienation is indeed the seed of subversion. Against it, the psychomedical model seems to operate retroactively, guiding intervention in the aftermath of the manifestation of a symptomatology that has already proven too persistent and too telltale to ignore any longer. In fact, it also has a proactive function, for in effecting the reduction of what might be defined as a structural situation into an internal, perhaps organic syndrome, it endows its patient or client not merely with a disease but also with a constellation of susceptibilities and habits that require a veritable lifetime of monitoring, treatment, insulation, protection, and therapeutic mollification. As Erving Goffman and Foucault have endeavored to show, the psychomedical model casts the alienated body not simply as a suffering body but further as a suffering subject, whose anxieties and pains and delusions are clues of less visible debilities, less visible handicaps or wounds.[42] Hence, the alienated body emerges as an abnormal subject and its abnormality as a matter of what it cannot accept, or cannot tolerate, cannot bring itself to do or not to do (cf. Foucault 1997 [1975]). Its stigma is the stigma of incompetence (cf. Goffman 1963: 128–29). (Not to say that our psychic workers should thus either be suspected or accused of conspiracy; that would indeed be paranoid.)

Following the neo-Lacanians, one might describe what is personally at stake in such a reduction, or casting, as a descent into "abjection."[43] Yet, however degrading the stigma of mental illness might still be, the psychomedical also has its comforts, its compensations to offer suffering subjects, whose suffering, which may sometimes well be due to one or another organic syndrome, is itself very real.[44] As the moral champions of deinstitutionalization learned somewhat awkwardly during the campaigns of the 1970s, at least some thought the asylums to which they had been confined genuinely worthy of the name and had no wish whatever to be freed.[45] Nor have the events of the subsequent two decades entirely undermined their wisdom. If, moreover, neurosis consists as it does for Lacan in the patient's incapacity to construct and embrace a coherent and unbroken narrative of his or her life, psychomedical discourse itself provides ample symbolic curatives to those who would be or become its subjects. It is, after all, replete with narratives that explain the etiology and the dynamics of suffering, which make sense of suffering in attaching it to a genetic legacy or traumatic past and render it all the more bearable in promising at the very least that every effort will be made to lessen it in the future.[46] From the paranoiac, what such narratives require in return is a single concession: that what he or she believes to be true is in fact false; that his or her suspicions are groundless; and that his or her experience is nothing more than a symptom, nothing more than the invalid effluence of a pitiable and common mutation.

That Ms. Roden struggled against and sought to distance herself from her psychomedical subjectivation should not be ascribed to anything so deliberate and calculative as "choice." What will, what judgment came to bear in carrying her along her way allows for no precise determination. It must suffice to note that she was in any event never entirely bereft of alternatives. She was never entirely without friends and mentors. She was never entirely emptied of the force of her passions.

Beyond her family and the other recipients of her letter, Ms. Roden told at least one other person of her dream: the woman she had met at the church she attended several months before. *She put me onto Bible studies because she said if it was true, it would be in accordance with Scripture. And so that's how I got into Bible study . . . I hadn't ever read it, and I started heavily studying it. Hard-core Bible study for four years . . . I found the visions in the Bible. It was like being given a key.*[47]

But, the key was slow to turn. Upon her release from De Paul Hospital, deprived of her son, Ms. Roden *was lonely. I attended six group therapy sessions, said I had a breakdown (true enough, if not the whole truth; I was physically exhausted and suffer from chronic anemia even now as a result of the chemical warfare) and helped other patients with their problems. I suppose the therapists were glad to get rid of me. They released me after the six sessions. [The wife of the presiding physician] remarked that I had a good understanding of my problems and didn't need therapy. I began to meet people again. Among them was [the man] who shortly became my second husband. Between us we built my house. [My husband] had severely damaged his liver making illegal chemicals and abusing drugs and alcohol. He grew strong while he was eating the high-protein, organic vegetarian diet that I lived on. After awhile I realized that he was compulsively abusive; when I complained about one form of abuse, he shifted to another. He only actually hit me twice. Both times he claimed were accidents, but it stopped when I refused to accept the accident theory. When he could no longer abuse me, he began to abuse himself. I couldn't stop him, and after awhile I couldn't watch. Despite repeated stomach hemorrhages, he continued to drink and abuse drugs. In March of 1985, he died of liver failure at the age of thirty-two.*[48]

Several months would pass before she would finally meet George Roden: *son of Ben and Lois Roden and elected president of the Branch Davidian Seventh-day Adventists.*[49] George had offered to help her in transporting the frame of a small house from the property of the acquaintance who had bestowed it upon her to her own property, several miles away. George *made a Branch Davidian of me in an hour, just talking about V[ictor] T. Houteff's message — he was preaching Houteff's message of the Davidian kingdom, and certainly from everything he said, I knew it was biblically true, biblically correct. And so I started reading Branch Davidian literature, and studying that.*[50] Nor was George's appeal merely doctrinal. *Somewhere in the middle of moving the house, I realized that we were becoming emotionally very close, and I asked him about his family and discovered that he had a wife. At which point I started backing off.* But the two *agreed to study the Bible together, and he suggested that I come up and get water from his well, because I require quite a pure drinking water. I came here to Texas for my health; I find that the chemicals in the water trouble me. This is an extremely pure water. At least it was; the well was destroyed in '93.*

So we were seeing each other a couple of times a week, and talking about religion. Eventually, he came up to the farm one afternoon and asked me to marry him. He said he'd divorce his wife. His wife had moved to Israel a year before. He came, and he said that he'd called her up and asked her to come home for their thirtieth wedding anniversary, and she refused. And so he came and asked me to marry him.[51]

She accepted his proposal. She soon moved to George's home, a seventy-seven acre tract of land known as New Mount Carmel, or simply Mount Carmel. *Throughout the history of Israel, God has used Mount Carmel to teach men respect for himself, his prophets, and priests.*[52]

"Conversion" derives from the Latin verb *converto* — to turn back or around, to change, to translate, to turn in a particular direction, to direct, to devote. Its canonical example is that of Saul of Tarsus, a "Pharisee" who left behind his "zealous persecution" of the Christian church (Phil. 3:5–6) after witnessing an epiphany of Jesus. The author of Acts recounts the episode with compelling vividness:

> And Saul, yet breathing out threatening and slaughter against the disciples of the Lord, went unto the high priest, and desired of him letters to Damascus to the synagogues, that if he found any of this way, whether they were men or women, he might bring them bound unto Jerusalem. And as he journeyed, he came near Damascus: and suddenly there shined round about him a light from heaven: and he fell to the earth, and heard a voice saying unto him, Saul, Saul, why persecutest thou me? And he said, Who art thou, Lord? And the Lord said, I am Jesus whom thou persecutest: it is hard for thee to kick against the pricks. And he trembling and astonished said, Lord, what will thou have me to do? (Acts 9:1–6)

After passing three days in blindness, without food or water, Saul arrived at Damascus. Shortly afterward, the Lord sent a certain Ananias to restore his sight, baptize him, and inform him that he had been ap-

21

pointed to bear Jesus' name "before the Gentiles, and kings, and the children of Israel" (Acts 9:15). Thus, the commencement of the apostolate of Saint Paul.

Scholars appropriately observe that not every experience or every confession of conversion conforms to that of Saint Paul. Suggesting a vaguely dialectical relationship between any such experience and those available paradigms or motifs that channel expectations of what conversion is and should be like, John Lofland and Norman Skonovd acknowledge the Pauline as the Christian prototype (1981: 375–77). But, they count it as only one of six motifs that might shape conversion (or at the very least, its narration, whether in the first-person of the convert or the third-person of the analyst). The Pauline is the "mystical" variant — perhaps solitary, always relatively brief, passive, emotionally and cognitively intense, and the prelude to "participation in the ritual and the organizational activities" of the religion thus revealed (1981: 378).[53] The "intellectual" variant of conversion might similarly be wrought in solitude, but it is of more extended duration and less a passion than a quest for "illumination" (1981: 376).[54] Here, doctrinal conviction largely precedes congregational or denominational affiliation. With the "experimental" variant, in contrast, the would-be convert "tries out" the religion to which he or she would belong well before believing what it espouses or finding meaning in the rituals it prescribes (1981: 378).[55] With the "affectional" variant (which Lofland and Rodney Stark first identified as such in 1965), "personal attachments or [a] strong liking for practicing believers" is the primary stimulant of conversion; social pressures have a role, "but more as 'support' and attraction than [an] 'inducement'" (1981: 380).[56] The intellect cedes priority to sentiment, as it does with the "revivalist" variant, for which the pressures and the emotional ecstasies of the crowd are the motor of the turning of the individuals engulfed within it (1981: 380–81). Pressures are the exclusive premium of the "coercive" variant, in which the deprivation of liberty, isolation, frequent exhaustion, torture, and humiliation together compel the infidel toward the convictions of his or her masters (1981: 381–82). Lofland and Skonovd conclude that even if their typology proves eventually to be obsolete, it at least has the virtue of registering conversion as a process whose prevailing motifs might be expected "to differ significantly from one historical epoch to another, across societal boundaries, and even across subcultures within a single society" (1981: 383).

Conversions do, of course, differ from one another across such dimensions and divides. The documentary evidence is overwhelming; only the normative imposition of a distinction between the authentic and the inauthentic, the genuine and the spurious, could license the inference

22

that conversion is really only one and not many different things. In the most comprehensive synthesis of scholarship on conversion to date, however, Lewis Rambo places equal emphasis on another of the aspects of conversion: that more often than not, it is many things at once, partaking of plural motifs, of a typological mixed bag. Rambo accordingly grants the heuristic utility of Lofland and Skonovd's synopsis but pursues the construction of a model that renders typologically "simple" conversions the limit cases of what is usually a multifaceted process. The model at which he arrives specifies seven stages of that process. It allows for some measure of sequential flexibility; but what in any event must always already be in place is the context in which or out of which any conversion must emerge (Rambo 1993: 20–41). Rambo is rigorously inclusive and accordingly fashions a context that is simultaneously macroscalar and microscalar, simultaneously social, cultural, religious, and psychological. In general, though, he draws most systematically from theorists who, in the footsteps of Anthony Wallace, deem most productive of conversion those contexts most rife with "stress" and "strain" — whether structural, personal, or (at their most dynamic) both.[57]

The second of Rambo's stages — "crisis" — encompasses Lofland and Skonovd's mystical motif but sensibly ranges over a much broader sweep of experiences, from illness and recovery to the yearning for transcendence, which might sometimes (as with Saint Paul) provoke or trigger conversion but more often act as the catalyst of the budding believer's ensuing "quest" to give sense to and make sense of what he or she has seen or undergone.[58] The latter constitutes an additional processual stage: an initial response to a crisis experience, the intellectual or imaginative current within conversion, an intensification of the quotidian search for meaning which Rambo, like Lofland and Skonovd, assumes most often to have the character of an active engagement rather than that of a passive reaction or surrender to indoctrination (1993: 56–57). The quest assumes the character of an interaction once it brings the seeker to an encounter with the advocates of an established church (or once such advocates come calling, as they often do). Following Thomas Beidelman, Rambo recognizes the advocate as the agent not merely of interpersonal but of structural change (1993: 69; cf. Beidelman 1982). Invoking the accounts of the missiologists, he nevertheless emphasizes that the encounter between potential convert and advocate most often unfolds as a mutual negotiation, and that the "influence" of the one on the other is often mutual as well (1993: 67). In light of such encounters, the potential convert may at last arrive at "commitment" (1993: 124–41), and with it, be left to face the "consequences" (1993: 142–76).

One might object to a certain establishmentarian excess in Rambo's model. Highlighting those conversions that result in the seeker's incorporation into an already institutionalized church, it may unduly neglect others, less routine and perhaps more critical or more radical in their inventiveness.[59] It gives little regard to "ultimate origins." It gives even less regard to that "internalization of authority" that Robert Bellah claimed to be among the most salient hallmarks of distinctively "modern" religion and often churchless "modern" religiosity (1972 [1964]: 46–50; cf. Greer and Roof 1992). One might further object to Rambo's psychological catastrophism. The remarks with which he closes his study are especially telling: "Conversion is personal and communal, private and public. It is both passive and active. It is a retreat from the world. It is a resolution of conflict and the empowerment to go into the world to confront, if not to create, conflict. Conversion is an event and a process. Conversion leaves us devastated — and transformed" (1993: 176). In discussing the details of their "experimental" variant of conversion, Lofland and Skonovd warn against inferring that "a dramatic change of life orientation" could only be the result of experiences and forces equally dramatic, equally "deep" and "strong." They see in such an inference an instance of what they call "the fallacy of the uniformly profound" (1981: 379).

To be fair, Rambo does not treat every instance of conversion as uniformly profound or devastating. His model, however, betrays a preference for the more devastating over the less. Perhaps precisely for this reason it proves to be strikingly consonant with the stages of Ms. Roden's own transformation, her own turn to devotion. Even so, it would do Ms. Roden an injustice to leave her within the dualisms — of personal and communal, private and public, passive and active, retreat and confrontation, internal and external — that have long infected the hermeneutics of conversion as a whole. Rambo's particularly forthright dualism stems in part from his very effort at hermeneutical synthesis. It stems additionally from a holism that inhibits him from assigning greater interpretive weight to any one of the stages or moments of his model over any other. There is much to admire in his synthesis and in his caution. Yet, as Harold Bloom has pointed out, dualism is the imagistic way of metaphor, and metaphor a trope that dissipates meaning even as it seems to foster it (1975: 100–101). The humanist might be content to let conversion be not just many but virtually all things at once. A practical woman in her way, Ms. Roden demands — of herself and of her interpreters — greater resolution.

One has her testimony. Her dreams and visions set her apart; they left her ready to act but uncertain what precisely to do. Not until she met George Roden was she able to begin to clarify the exception that she had become, the name and the stigma that she would subsequently wear as her own: *Branch Davidian.*[60] One has the testimony of the author of Acts. Saul's vision on the road to Damascus had its effect on him, to be sure. It left him blind, unable to eat or drink, a veritable dead man for three days. It was not until the arrival of Ananias that "there fell from his eyes as it had been scales: and he received sight forthwith, and was baptized" (Acts 9:18). It was not until Ananias informed him of it that he understood his mission and went "straightaway" to preach "Christ in the synagogues, that he is the Son of God" (Acts 9:20). In his letters to the early Christian congregations, he would never use his Jewish but rather always his Roman name: Paul. The anthropologist might notice the traces of a familiar pattern in both these testimonies. The vision isolates, separates the visionary from the "ordinary" life to which she or he had formerly been accustomed. It is the prelude to a period of uncertainty, of disorientation, of the suspended animation of the self. The time is troubled indeed but culminates in a pivotal inspiration that is itself the prelude to a renascence, to the reentry of a self revived and rechristened into something of the same — if by no means entirely the same — life from which she or he had been removed. The pattern is of course that of the classic rite of passage — but I shall return to this point later. At this juncture, only the pivot of the pattern, its transformational fulcrum, needs scrutiny. In neither testimony — the Branch Davidian's or Saint Paul's — does that fulcrum consist merely in an "encounter" between the seeker of definition and the advocate of a revelatory lexicon. Nor does it hinge on "mutual negotiation," on diplomatic conversation or barter. Its structure is instead pedagogical; its scene, a pivotal scene of instruction.

There are, perhaps, virtually as many pedagogies as there are ways of conversion and virtually as many techniques and apparatuses of instruction as there are criteria for charting the progress and graduation of the convert. The primal scene of instruction must, however, be public, or in any case social, for many of the same reasons that Wittgenstein adduced in arguing that language itself must be public, or at least derive from interactive "games" and "forms of life." Educational progress and graduation must permit assessment and so must permit palpable expression — the production of the correct answer, the right gesture or response, the appropriate move or procedure. Criteria of rectitude must also be stable, or at least stable enough to be palpable in practice and as practice. Criteria are not always rules or laws, however widespread the civilizational (and social scientific) penchant for reifying them into rules or laws might be. They are instead touchstones, which usually offer only indirect and partial evidence of the capacity or competency to which they attest. They owe what stability or regularity they have to the necessary regularity of capacities and competencies themselves. Criteria might be decreed by arbitrary fiat, but they cannot function as criteria without undergoing conventionalization or, as Weber would have it, "routinization."

The portrait of the solitary reader in her carrel is thus pedagogically misleading.[61] Detached from the scenes in which the arts of decryption and comprehension must first have been acquired, it makes a fetish of the reader and her library alike. Gadamer's picture of hermeneutical inquiry is more complete. But its depiction of a reader who brings his tradition along with him to his meeting with a text is still pedagogically truncated; it relegates too far to the background the scenes in which tradition is received and absorbed. Even Aristotle's sketch of pedagogy in the *Nicomachean Ethics* fails to be exhaustive, but the scene it evokes has a sort of skeletal adequacy about it that can hardly be surpassed. For Aristotle, pedagogy directs an *askēsis*, a program of exercise or training in both the characterological and the intellectual *aretes* — "virtues," but also skills or fluencies. At its most minimal, it requires only the pedagogue; his repertoire of recipes and principles and primers; and a student, whose absorption of his lessons would one day be realized as and in *eupraxia* — "practicing well," or being good at what he does. Bloom locates a more ancient and, to his mind, more primal pedagogy in the *askēsis* of ritual communion. H. Wheeler Robinson's *Inspiration and Revelation in the Old Testament* is his point of departure:

> [I]n his study of Old Testament inspiration, [Robinson] moves toward the trope of a Scene of Instruction when he sees that while oral tradition rose to interpret written Torah, written Torah itself as authority replaced cultic acts. The ultimate cultic act is one in which the worshipper receives God's condescension, his accommodating gift of his Election-love. Election-love, God's love for Israel, is the Primal start of a Primal Scene of Instruction, a Scene early displaced from Jewish or Christian into secular and poetic contexts.[62]

The constellation remains triadic: God as pedagogue; the materialization of his love in the teachings of the Covenant; and his beloved, Israel. If substantively of narrow scope, it has myriad structural iterations: in Aristotle's "secular" alternative; in the relation among prophets, their prophecies, and their audiences; and in the relation among charismatic leaders, their visions and revisions, and their followers the world over.[63]

Missing from both Aristotle and Bloom is that particular dualism that would impose a strict separation between the education of the body and the education of the soul, or spirit, or mind. That it is missing is doubly advantageous: first, because analysis is thus freed from the terms and the sides of long-standing but civilizationally particular debates (over the essence of faith and freedom, for example) that are probably incorrigibly moot; and second, because analysis is thus free to proceed immediately to the lineaments of conversion as practice or, more precisely, as a reorientation in and of practice. The ancient Greek for "convert," *prosēlutos* (whence the English "proselyte"), broadly denotes someone who lives as a foreigner, or who has gone to live in a foreign city or foreign land. It more specifically denotes someone who has gone to Israel, or "gone over" to Judaism. Hence, one of the most outstanding lineaments of conversion as practice: it transpires as a displacement and as a replacement. Nor is the Greek too literal; it is merely too literally geographical. The practical convert need not alter her residence. She must instead alter (or suffer the alteration of) that "structured set of structuring dispositions" that constitute the habitus itself (Bourdieu 1990: 52; cf. Mauss 1973 [1934]). Such an alteration may be more or less extreme, but it must in any case involve more than the riddance of an extraneous opinion or the cultivation of an isolated taste. It must be systematic because the habitus itself is systematic. It is a replacement that is also always a reintegration, and not merely that reintegration of the "consciousness" that hermeneutical or phenomenological inquiry might raise. The lessons that the convert might at first consciously absorb must ultimately seep into his very body. So he must give himself, or be granted, time enough for what he has acquired to be realized as what Bourdieu calls "a practical *mimesis* (or mimeticism) which implies an overall relation of identification and has nothing in common with an *imitation* that would presuppose a conscious effort to reproduce a gesture, an utterance or an object explicitly constituted as a model" (1990: 73; emphasis in original). The story of Saint Paul's conversion is in this respect highly condensed; if not that, his conversion is, in its extreme brevity, astonishing enough in itself to merit his sanctification. The ordinary convert must change, and the change become him, at a much slower pace, with much "backsliding," as Ms. Roden might put it, and with far less assurance and—it would seem—far less confidence than Saint Paul had that one would become a legend not merely in one's own time but also in times to come.

The exercises of practical conversion must thus be exercises of reembodiment, of a disciplined self-renovation. Their full sequence can and often does include reflexive sessions—exercises that the self performs by itself upon itself. But, the frequent services of the master, the coach, the advisor at even these sessions once again suggest the semiotic and pragmatic insecurities of excess privacy. The original agent of discipline must in any case always be external to the self, must always be another (or others). Were it not, the self would itself already have to be in possession of sufficient savoir-faire, of sufficiently activated virtue, to be its

27

own pedagogue—*per impossibile*, at least if Aristotle's view is largely correct. The implication is somewhat discomforting, but inescapable, and may as well be stated baldly now and qualified later: education is inherently oppressive (or suppressive, or repressive, or all of these at once) and remains so even at its most reflexive, even when the self exerts control entirely by itself only over itself. Or as Antonio Gramsci observed rhetorically:

> In education one is dealing with children in whom one has to inculcate certain habits of diligence, precision, poise (even physical poise), ability to concentrate on specific subjects, which cannot be acquired without the mechanical repetition of disciplined and methodical acts. Would a scholar at the age of forty be able to sit for sixteen hours a day at his work-table if he had not, as a child, compulsorily, through mechanical coercion, acquired the appropriate psychophysical habits? (1971: 315)

He would, one might say, only if, with the practical convert, he could somehow garner the means of disciplining himself anew.

Only a dualistic diremption of body from mind would, moreover, prevent Gramsci's comments on habituation from applying mutatis mutandis to belief. The discipline of embodiment and reembodiment is also a discipline of informing and reinforming, or is an aspect of it, the giving form or another form to that which is, in rough but regular parallel, becoming informed or reinformed. Before dualism, or beyond it, Bourdieu's own rhetoric loses some of its materialist brutality but retains a hard, Gramscian edge:

> [H]ow can one fail to see that decision, if decision there is, and the "system of preferences" which underlies it, depend not only on all the previous choices of the decider but also on the conditions in which his "choices" have been made, which include all the choices of those who have chosen for him, in his place, pre-judging his judgements and so shaping his judgements. The paradoxes encountered by the endeavor to conceive belief in terms of the logic of decision show that the real acquisition of belief resolves [them] in practice. Genesis implies amnesia of genesis. The logic of the acquisition of belief, that of the continuous, unconscious conditioning that is exerted through conditions of existence as much as through explicit encouragements or warnings, implies the forgetting of acquisition, the illusion of innateness. There is therefore no need to invoke the last refuge of dignity and the freedom of the person, "bad faith" in the sense of a decision to forget decision and to lie to oneself, in order to account for the fact that belief, or any other form of cultural acquirement, can

28

be experienced simultaneously as logically necessary and socially un-
conditioned. (1990: 49–50)

With an even harder edge, Bourdieu further asserts that "practical belief
is not a 'state of mind,' still less a kind of adherence to a set of institutional dogmas and doctrines ('beliefs'), but rather a state of the body"
(1990: 68). Once again, however disconcerting, the implication must be
drawn. The discipline of what appears to be remembering is always also
a discipline of forgetting. The training of the wit is also a training in
being unwitting. The will—even the will to convert—is the student of
its conditions, of its structural impetuses, its often hidden and often
impersonal, or suprapersonal, disciplinarians. The body that is its own
is not its own, after all.

Nor is this true of the converted body—the body already practiced,
the body already believing—alone. It is true of the body in crisis as
well. The point is not that the "objective conditions" in which one or
another body finds itself allows the analyst to infer its being in crisis
without further inquiry. As Michael Barkun has come to admit, the objective structural disasters he once identified as the causes of the millennialist revivalism that swept the northeastern United States in the
decades preceding the Civil War are not as determinative as he was
initially inclined to argue (Barkun 1974). He would still insist that disasters are a necessary condition of the sociogenesis of millennialism.
But, he would further point to disaster as a "mental construct which
can be linked not only to observable death and destruction but events
that symbolize the loss and control of meaning" (1986: 153–54).[64] He
thus avoids reducing the perception or experience of disaster to the
merely psychological—as many other scholars of millennialism have
been inclined to do (for example, Brummett 1991: 28). Concomitantly,
he moves toward the trope of a scene of instruction that makes up for
what it may lack of the primeval in suggesting that what Rambo would
identify as the pretext of conversion is no less the object of pedagogical
scrutiny and pedagogical interchange than the quests and the encounters to which it leads. Or to put the point more directly, the solitary
reader in her carrel is no less analytically misleading that the solitary
Saul on his way to Damascus; the psychologization of disaster is no less
misleading than the psychologization of epiphany or crisis. Paul's epiphany—as epiphany—is not removed from the scene of his instruction but
already a part of it. Contrary to what Rambo's model of stages would
seem to imply, what constitutes a crisis—as opposed to hard times or a
momentary lapse or a mere rebuff or a merely personal trauma—is itself a matter of pedagogical scrutiny and pedagogical interchange. It is a
matter of intersubjective legitimation—with which God has little to do,

or so the anthropologist — professional infidel, inevitable vulgarian —
would be inclined to press.

I would be guilty of the worst sort of deception were I to perpetrate yet
another dualism, to feign too great a divide between the anthropologist
and me. However, I was forced to confront the difference in considering
my reaction upon first meeting Ms. Roden and forced to confront it
repeatedly as the reaction persisted, with an eerily fresh spontaneity, for
several years. I had come upon her by accident (though she would likely
dispute that). In February 1993, I was teaching at Reed College, and
preparing a lecture on early Christian millenarianism for a first-year
course in the humanities. Two or three days before the lecture was due,
I heard the news of the eruption of violence at the Branch Davidian
compound, about ten miles northeast of the center of Waco, Texas.
What I had to say gained little in topicality because few students in the
course bothered to attend to the news. I was nevertheless struck by the
coincidence and subsequently followed the events at the compound
more assiduously than I might otherwise have been inclined to do. In
early April, I was unexpectedly offered the position at Rice which I
continue to occupy. On 19 April, the compound burned — the ghastly
climax, but by no means the end, of what would later come to be
known, and rendered iconic, as the Branch Davidian "fiasco." By August, I had moved to Houston, but it was not until the following summer, after all the explanations and retractions, the accusations and
counteraccusations, the social commentaries and psychological commentaries, and the arrests and trials had already begun to bore the media, that I decided to join a steady stream of curiosity seekers, pilgrims,
and tourists of disaster and visit the compound myself. The staff of the
Waco Visitor's Center provided directions to the site discreetly, but graciously, upon my request.

The site, Mount Carmel, lies in a slight depression of the open prairie, an expanse of ranches and farms, sparsely populated, verdant in the
summer with grasses and wild sunflowers. When I arrived at it, the
ruins of the compound were surrounded by a wire fence, inside of
which security guards kept a twenty-four-hour watch and bulldozers
ploddingly scraped charred wood, broken concrete, blackened shards of
metal, and soil into the twisted piles of a gruesome sculpture garden. A
quarantine was in effect; the ground had been contaminated with lead.
Visitors could not pass through the fence, at the foot of which was a
collection of seared and mangled tricycles and other toys, and on the
front of which hung a long row of small, white crosses commemorating
the dead.

Above the ruins, nearer the road, Ms. Roden was keeping her vigil.

From the scraps of the compound, she had constructed a small hut, which a sign identified as the office of the Seventh-day Adventist Branch Davidians. There were a great many other signs and postings in the vicinity — quotations from Ezekiel and Jeremiah, "before" and "after" photographs of the compound, reprints of the writings of the former leaders of the church, photocopies of the deed to the Mount Carmel property. Ms. Roden also had photocopies of her own writings on display — biblical exegeses, a denunciation of the government and its courts, a timely reinterpretation of the *"mene, mene, tekel, u-phar sin"* of the fifth chapter of the Book of Daniel, and a brief history of her church and of the fiasco, which she had arranged as a list of answers to questions she had evidently been asked a great many times. She was nevertheless happy to continue talking and answering questions, as still another sign proclaimed, and was talking to a curiosity seeker, or pilgrim, or tourist of disaster when I first saw her. The conversation went on at such length that I confined myself to an introduction, a short outline of my interest in "the comparative study of religion," and the fixing of an appointment for an interview several days thence.

Ms. Roden is striking: slim but by no means frail; very fair, her long hair bleached even more blonde under the prairie sun, her skin tanned and sere, her eyes liquid and always watchful. Our interview — the first of many interviews and conversations — went well, I thought, though I learned shortly later that she had already produced written expositions of virtually every query I had raised. Even so, she was never impatient with me. On the contrary: I found her astonishingly forthright, sparklingly bright, and of a delightfully wry humor. I have never ceased to admire the courage of her convictions and the fortitude that has sustained her through what would have proven to me to be insufferable hardship, many times over. I have never ceased to admire her charm. Our acquaintance would extend and deepen. Yet, nearly three further years would pass before I was able to leave behind, to assign to the past, a distress that was at first the constant companion of my preparations for every new journey to Mount Carmel, and on several occasions the cause of their disbanding. It would begin as a knot in the stomach, or a tightening of the chest, then a loss of appetite, sleeplessness, fatigue, an urge for solitude — the unmistakable psychosomatology of fear.

I would still like to be able to claim that the object of that fear was Mount Carmel, the site itself. It is certainly disturbing: a scar roughly scratched in a placid landscape, only all the more raw and indelible since a regional militia financed the planting of a memorial grove of crape myrtles, each shading a stele etched with the name of one of the dead; a ghost of holocaust, which can only conjure up other holocausts, and the possibility of still others in the future. Nor did all violence die

31

out with the flames themselves. Mount Carmel is a property under dispute, and among its claimants are representatives of three schismatic factions of the Branch Davidian church: one loyal to David Koresh, the messiah in residence throughout the fiasco, and dead at its climax; another loyal to no one after George Roden's mother, Lois; and Amo, who continues to press her husband's legal entitlements even though he, too, is now dead. All appear to have adhered consistently to the adage that possession is nine-tenths of the law. Of late, they seem (largely) resigned to coexist. Formerly, a few of them, Ms. Roden among them, had occasional resort to weapons, now and then for intimidation, now and then for self-protection. I was consequently relieved that I do not drive and so never had even to consider visiting Mount Carmel alone. The antagonisms in the air soon led to my opting against focusing on the Branch Davidian "community" in favor of focusing on Ms. Roden. I did not, however, seriously believe that I would ever have to endure anything more damaging than mild hostility from any of her adversaries, and I rarely had to endure even that. I found Mount Carmel a bit eerie; I was afraid of Ms. Roden herself.

Auto-analysis has gradually uncovered an experiential mélange, composed in one part of the uncanny and in the other of ambivalence. So far, I have made much of my differences from Ms. Roden, even if I have cast them only as differences of degree. Yet what made her uncanny to me was that, our obvious differences notwithstanding, she reminded me so much—too much—of myself. In her political and semiotic suspicions, in her alienation, in her passion for making sense, in her scholarly devotions, I could not but recognize emphatic expressions of my own. What made me ambivalent toward her was her very being, a self whose courage, whose singleness of missionary purpose, whose fierce enactment of dedication to its calling stood concretely before me as a seductive but forbidden alter ego, a self I might even yearn to be but could become only with the transgression of all the standards of my thoroughly secular upbringing, and of the standards of the undersecretary of secular rationalism that I now am, and—because I am not, after all, so radically alienated from what I like sometimes to tout as the manifold absurdities of the temporal order I inhabit—have no compelling wish to surrender being. But again, the hiatus between the two of us has always only been one of degree, not of kind. Of course, if I thought myself thus to be confessing to an idiosyncrasy, I would not confess at all. To declare what could, at this point, probably go without saying: I think that I am far from alone, and think instead that a subjectivity similar to my own lurks in a considerable number of others who have decided—if decision there was—to pursue careers in the academy, especially careers in its hermeneutical sectors and subsectors, anthropology prominent among them.

I have argued for such a position at greater length elsewhere and will not repeat my argument here (Faubion 1999). I will merely adduce one of its corollaries. Too much of the scholarship on religious activism, and far too much on millenarianism, now seems to me to be infected analytically and textually with the same defensive strategy that I have so often felt impelled to deploy: a strategy of distancing, which would seek to disguise what is in fact familiar, all too familiar, in the costume of the far-flung exotic. Some of its devices are transparent: rationalist mockery, bemused or belittling, which is content to dismiss as foolish or infantile whatever might threaten to reflect back to it the extra-rational grounds of its own complaisance; and that sort of behavioral scientism that rapidly weaves the feathery headdress of a psychopathological profile to crown whoever might threaten to reflect back to it the most arbitrary of those social conventions that saturate its schemas of perception and diagnosis. Other devices are more subtle. Among them, I am inclined to include a frequently sympathetic historicism that manages to stitch an uncanny or forbidden religiosity seamlessly to the past of a tradition that is somehow never the historicist's own. Anthropologists have needed even less sleight of hand when they have sought to ensconce "cultists" once again within the unique and insular mythologies of their ancestors. Yet, however venerable such ethnographic particularism may be, it has always run the risk of delivering difference over to the realm of the absolute, of reifying alterity into an Otherness that belongs nowhere better than among the exhibits in a believe-it-or-not museum — or, though anthropologists might protest, in an asylum; or in that place that seems well on its way to resuming its former double duty as asylum, the prison.

The particularists, however, seem at least to have realized that their project cannot abide by the hermeneutical standard. It cannot be one of somehow incorporating the "cultic" Other into their own horizons, of showing the Other to be really the Same. Nor can it quite be the Geertzian project of translating the unfamiliar into the more familiar. For me, it has rather been one of holding on to a resemblance, a dark mirror, that I have had every temptation to let slip and shatter. It has demanded not translation — there was no "foreign language" for me to gloss — but *metafora* — transference, change of phase, frequent appeal to metaphor.

PART TWO

A Gnosis

ALIENATION, it must be granted, is little more than an experiential and motivational placeholder. If, at its political and semiotic extremes, it frequently resolves experientially into a sense of election, its motivational resolutions are far more diverse, their distribution covering the whole gamut from quietistic passivity or withdrawal to revolutionary rebelliousness. It is by no means the certain path to religious conversion. Furthermore, the alignment of practical or mimetic conversion with the process of (re)education does little more than establish a structural commensurability, an analogical universe within which comparisons might plausibly be made. Beyond that, it has only the barest substance. It includes no rigorous distinction between the religious and the nonreligious and so between types of conversion and types of education that the great majority of concerned contemporary citizens, inside and outside of the academy, would rush to separate. Much less does it indicate either the practical requirements or the practical outcomes of converting to or of being (re)educated into Branch Davidianism.

Although the Branch Davidian Seventh-day Adventists were never part of the Seventh-day Adventists (their predecessor church, the Davidian Seventh-day Adventists, left the Seventh-day Adventists in 1929), the churches all share many core beliefs. Among them are the following:[1]

That Yashua (Christ's Hebrew name, which means "God's salvation") has the same nature and essence as the Eternal Father. While retaining His divine nature, Christ took upon Himself the nature of the human family, lived on earth as a man, exemplified in His life the

37

principles of righteousness, attested His relationship with God by mighty miracles, died on the cross for our sins, was raised from the dead and ascended to heaven, where He makes intercession for us (John 1:1, 14; Heb. 2:9–18; 8:1, 2; 4:14–16; 7:25).[2]

That every person must experience a new birth in order to obtain salvation; this new birth is a transformation of life and character by the power of God and the faith in Christ (John 3:16; Matt. 18:3; Acts 2:37–39).

That the Holy Bible was given by inspiration of God, and contains an all-sufficient revelation of God's will to men, and is the only unerring rule of faith and practice (2 Tim. 3:15–17).

That Baptism is an ordinance of the Christian church and should follow repentance and forgiveness of sins. The proper form of Baptism is immersion (Rom. 6:1–6; Acts 16:30–33).

That the will of God as it relates to moral conduct is the ten commandments, which are great, unchangeable precepts.

That the fourth commandment requires the observance of the Seventh-day Sabbath, as a memorial of creation and a sign of sanctification (Gen. 2:1–3; Exo. 31:12–17; Heb. 4:1–10).

That the followers of Christ should be a godly people, regulating their conduct as becomes a follower of the meek and lowly Master (1 Cor. 3:16, 17; 9:25; 10:31; 1 Tim. 2:9–10; John 2:6).

That God has placed gifts of the spirit in His church for the work of the ministry, and that these gifts include healing, prophecy and spiritual discernment, and are to bring forth apostles and prophets and pastors and teachers (1 Cor. 12; 1:5–7; Eph. 4; Rev. 12:17; 19:10).[3]

That the second coming of Christ is the great hope of the church (Luke 21:25–27; 17:26–30; John 14:1–3; Acts 1:9–11; Rev. 1:7; Heb. 9:28; James 5:1–8; Joel 3:9–16; 2 Tim. 3:1–5; Dan. 7:27; Matt. 24:36, 44).[4]

That God will warn His people of impending judgment, and that this is the work of the angel messengers in Rev. 14 (Amos 3:6–7).

Additionally, most Branches also believe:

That there are seven angel messages in Rev. 14. So far, five messengers are recognized by all Branch Davidian congregations.

Rev. 14:6–7: "And I saw another angel fly in the midst of heaven, having the everlasting gospel to preach unto them that dwell on the earth, and to every nation, and kindred, and tongue and people. Saying with a loud voice, fear God and give glory to Him; for the hour of His judgment is come: and worship Him that made Heaven and Earth, and the sea, and the fountains of water."[5]

Historically, William Miller founded the Advent Church, anticipating the return of Christ at Atonement in 1844. Because Christ did not come, this is referred to as the Great Disappointment. Ellen White, who loudly proclaimed the next message, comments that Miller was correct about the time, but not the event. Miller based his dates on the prophecy of Dan 8:14: unto two thousand and three hundred days; then shall the sanctuary be cleansed. The cleansing of the sanctuary at Atonement is described in Leviticus 16. The decrees of Artaxerxes to rebuild the temple issued in 457 B.C. is the starting-date of this prophecy; this is consistent with the starting-date of other prophecies in Daniel relating to the first advent of Christ. According to Ellen White, because the earthly sanctuary was destroyed in 70 A.D., this event takes place in the heavenly sanctuary. Christ entered the heavenly sanctuary on Atonement, Oct. 22, 1844, and began the process of judging the dead. Either their sins were blotted out of the book of their deeds, or they were blotted out of the Book of Life. Either way, their sins no longer profane the temple.

Rev. 14:8: "And there followed another angel, saying, Babylon is fallen, is fallen, that great city, because she made all nations drink of the wine of the wrath of her fornication."

Ellen White announced that the churches had fallen as a result of refusing the first message. A prolific writer, White's message covered much of the ground of the messages after her.

Rev. 14:9–11: "And the third angel followed them, saying with a loud voice, if any man worship the beast and his image, and receive his mark in his forehead, or in his hand, the same shall drink of the wine of the wrath of God, which is poured out without mixture into the cup of His indignation; and he shall be tormented with fire and brimstone in the presence of the holy angels, and in the presence of the Lamb: and the smoke of their torment ascended up for ever and ever: and they have no rest day or night, who worship the beast and his image, and whosoever receiveth the mark of his name."[6]

The third messenger, V.T. Houteff, was a great light on the Bible, particularly explaining the judgment and the harvest of the world, and calling people to become part of the 144,000. He preached that the Kingdom of God would be founded to preserve God's chosen people during the destruction of the wicked.[7]

Rev. 14:12–13: "Here is the patience of the saints: here are they that keep the commandments of God, and the faith of Jesus. And I heard a voice from Heaven saying unto me, write, blessed are the dead which die in the Lord henceforth: yea, saith the spirit, that they may rest from their labours; and their works do follow them."

These verses mark the transition from the judgment of the dead to the judgment of the living. Those who die during the judgment of the living, if they die in God, are written in the Book of Life with all of their sins blotted out. They are to be born anew in the Kingdom of God without seeing the time of trouble. The rest, like me, will have hard work before us. The Kingdom is earned.

Rev. 14:14: "And I looked, and behold a white cloud, and upon the cloud one sat like unto the Son of Man, having on his head a golden crown, and in his hand a sharp sickle."

Ben Roden, the fourth messenger, proclaimed the judgment of the living at the beginning of his ministry in 1955. He crowned himself king in 1970. The sickle shows that his is a slaughter message.

Rev. 14:15: "And another angel came out of the temple, crying with a loud voice to him that sat on the cloud, thrust in thy sickle, and reap: for the time is come for thee to reap; for the harvest of the Earth is ripe."

Lois Roden joined her husband in his work; that she comes out of the temple indicates that God's footstool has been established again on Earth. The first harvest is in the church. In 1977, Lois Roden was given her own spiritual message, the femininity of the Holy Spirit, and therefore, she was the fifth angel messenger.[8]

Rev. 14:16: "And he that sat on the cloud thrust in his sickle on the Earth; and the Earth was reaped."[9]

When V.T. Houteff died, his widow, Florence, claimed a deathbed appointment to lead the church. Ben Roden claimed that God had told him to call himself the Branch and take over the church. V.T. Houteff neither appointed a vice-president nor reappointed his executive council in the year of his death. He stated in the preface to his church law that his movement would merge into a greater one. As Florence Houteff fought Ben Roden for control of the church (and sold the church property when she lost), she and those in the church who refused Ben Roden's message were spiritually slaughtered.

Florence stole the tithe and married a man named Eakin (Hos. 2:14–15; Josh. 6:17–7:26).

Organizationally, then, the Branch Davidians have two proximate ancestors. The nearest is the Davidian church, which now has bases in Exeter, Missouri, and Salem, South Carolina. At yet another degree of generational remove is the Seventh-day Adventist (SDA) Church, formally established in 1863 and now among the most rapidly growing of the New Denominations emerging with it, slightly more than a century and a half ago, during the later decades of the Second Great Awakening.[10] Since its inception, the SDA Church has regularly convened General Conferences, during the course of which its members have reviewed and not infrequently revised or supplemented its statement of fundamental beliefs. The current statement continues to endorse baptism, but perhaps not the Baptist understanding of it. Its language is in any event no longer that of "new birth." It describes ritual immersion instead as a testament to the initiate's commitment "to walk in newness of life" (General Conference of Seventh-day Adventists 2000). In articulating her doctrinal legacy, Ms. Roden draws closely, if selectively, from an SDA credo in force in 1970 (cited in Damsteegt 1977: 306–9). She appropriates its Christology but not its Trinitarianism. She reproduces its doctrine of the sufficiency of the biblical revelation. She embraces its Pentecostal trust in the largesse of the Holy Spirit and its specific confidence in Ellen White's prophetic gifts. She nevertheless recognizes subsequent prophets. She reiterates the ritual program that the 1970 credo prescribes but omits its dietetics, which calls for complete abstention from "intoxicating drinks, tobacco, and other narcotics." Here, her own prescriptions (and proscriptions) are somewhat different. She affirms the doctrine of the second Advent but not the SDA reckoning of its imminence. Here again, she has a reckoning of her own. She further departs from the SDA avowal of justification "not by obedience to the law, but by the grace that is in Jesus Christ." Few other Branch Davidians would follow her quite so far, but she is herself less the heir of Luther than of Calvin, or at least of those of the Methodist epigones of Calvin who emphasized and have continued to emphasize that the justice, the righteousness, of the believer might come not merely through grace but also through his or her works. To repeat: *Those who die during the judgment of the living, if they die in God, are written in the Book of Life with all of their sins blotted out. They are to be born anew in the Kingdom of God without seeing the time of trouble. The rest, like me, will have hard work before us. The Kingdom is earned.*[11]

Like many other New Denominations, the SDA Church espouses a charter that leaves its institutional stability always potentially at risk. It is in principle a congregational democracy; it permits any of its qualified members to act as legislators of its vision and mission. Especially now that its enrollment is global, and well over a million strong, only a few members actually have the chance to do so. Its leading figures, moreover, have come increasingly to acquire their qualifications through routinized channels, among them any one of several universities that the church has itself endowed. Yet, from its establishment forward, and still today, it has consistently held that the genuine minister's first and most essential qualification rests with the gift he or she has received from the Holy Spirit.[12] Ministerial authority is thus fundamentally charismatic. It is manifest as extraordinary powers — of healing, teaching, self-sacrifice, charity, and, by no means least, prophecy. The church formally recog-

41

nizes Ellen Harmon White as its only prophetic authority but cannot pretend to have resolved the mystery of the divine pneuma, the Holy Spirit itself. It consequently leaves open at least the logical possibility that Ms. White will have successors, divinely anointed to deliver a truth more "present," and more final, than her own.[13] Every good functionalist knows the dangers of such a concession, however begrudging it might be. As Weber recognized some time ago, charismatic authority is inherently antithetical, often organizationally disruptive, and occasionally revolutionary in its effects. It is at best a dubious ally of the institutional manager. It is the constant companion of the schismatic (cf. M. Weber 1946: 245–52).

Charismatic authority is social, or in any event intersubjective, and so resides not in an individual but instead in the relation between an individual and an audience that acknowledges one or another of his or her skills or talents as the proof of anointment. Enter Victor Houteff, whose humble condition more likely helped than harmed him and whose imaginative exegeses of both the Bible and Ellen White's copious writings coalesced into a message the general tenets of which have been dear to schismatics everywhere. In 1907, at the age of twenty-one, Houteff immigrated to the United States from Bulgaria. In 1918, he renounced his native Orthodoxy for Seventh-day Adventism. A decade later, he was living in Los Angeles, selling appliances, and occupying himself with a review of the more prominent prophets of the Judeo-Christian past. In 1929, he began teaching at the Sabbath School of the SDA congregation to which he belonged. His studies had brought him to several conclusions that he believed himself obliged to promulgate. Two of them would prove to be especially controversial. The first was that the succession of the seven angels (or messengers) of the final days had begun with Martin Luther and culminated in his own person. The second was that all signs pointed toward the urgency of gathering of those 144,000 "Israelites" (cf. Rev. 4:7) divinely elected to support the returned Messiah in his fateful battle with anti-Christly forces at Armageddon and reestablish a Davidian kingdom with him in historical Palestine. Houteff's septad included Ellen White as its penultimate angel, but only at the expense of rendering her vision incomplete. Houteff's reckoning of the number of the messianic army was for its part scrupulously true to the original and the number itself considerably smaller than the aggregate SDA body of his day.[14] Nor did he let the discrepancy pass in silence. Reiterating the complaints of religious reformers through the ages, he instead accused his church of having grown too worldly, too accommodating, and devotionally much too lax.[15] Citing Ms. White's similar admonitions, he demanded purgation. In 1934, he found himself banished from the SDA fellowship. In 1935, with only a minimal entourage, he broke the ground for the millennialist way station he called "Mount Carmel Center" at a site now partially submerged beneath the waters of the city of Waco's municipal reservoir.

If antithetical, then, in both his rhetoric and his practice, Houteff is nevertheless far from being an unqualified incarnation of Weber's ideal-typical charismatic. His Mount Carmel community, which grew into the hundreds during the 1940s, was hardly the creation of a man prepared to make "a sovereign break with all traditional or rational norms" (M. Weber 1946: 250). It was an austerely disciplined missionary corporation, devoted to its printing press, internal economy, and daily routine of worship and religious study. Throughout, it remained consistent with SDA precedent not simply in its observance of the Saturday Sabbath but in its broader pursuit and elaboration of an ecclesiology of restoration, of a return to Mosaic law. The same ecclesiology in fact continues, with further elaborations, beyond Houteff to Ben and Lois Roden. In his role as the "Branch" whom God had anciently appointed to rebuild His temple (Zech. 3:8, 6:12), Mr. Roden urged his flock to adopt not merely the Commandments but the entirety of Jewish Orthodox ceremonialism. In his wake, his wife would seek to undergird the veracity of her own revelation philologically, bypassing the grammatically neuter pneuma of the Greek Septuagint for the grammatically feminine terms for the Holy Spirit in the original languages of the Bible.[16] Amo Roden is herself something of a restorationist. So, too, was (and still is) the man who was acting as priest during the celebration of what the slow-witted and still largely unversed anthropologist failed to recognize as Day of Atonement ceremonies at New Mount Carmel in 1994. Many years a Branch Davidian, he wore a prayer shawl and a yarmulke, and called his service to order by imitating the sound of a ram's horn bugle, a shofar.

One might thus speak of Branch Davidians as "conservative" or "traditionalist" religious reformers. But their ecclesiology of restoration is also an ecclesiology of teleological fulfillment or consummation that by no means entails that the future either will or should be an indifferent repetition of the past. In this last respect especially, they remain loyal to Ellen White—if not always to the letter, then at least in their exegetical methods. Ms. White in turn derives her methods most immediately from William Miller. Hence, a second proximate ancestry, whose apical patriarch was the most influential lay revivalist of the Second Great Awakening and the chief pedagogical architect of the period's premillennialist enthusiasm. Even so, Miller's biographers reveal a person made of his time more than a maker of it—and even farther from the Weberian charismatic than Houteff, at least until the end of his active religious career. Born in the "Burned-over District" of rural New York, young

William had the benefit of only the most cursory education, but he was bright and querulous. Though largely untutored, he read avidly and widely. Intellectually, he would always display something of the auto-didact's simultaneous insecurity and independence of opinion (cf. Barkun 1986: 47). Early in his adult life, he joined the better-educated elite in embracing deism but soon enough began to lose the strength of his convictions. His crisis perhaps came with the War of 1812, in particular with the battle of Pittsburgh, at which he stood. In Everett Dick's summary: "In this engagement fifteen hundred regulars and four thousand volunteers on the American side defeated fifteen thousand British troops. Before the battle, Miller and his comrades had felt that defeat was practically certain. The amazing outcome appeared to him as the workings of a power mightier than man" (1986: 4). By 1816, he had joined the Baptist Church but was still sensitive to deist ridicule of scriptural inconsistencies. "So he began a reverent study of the Bible, comparing passage with passage, to make it explain itself" (1986: 4).

The exegetical principles he brought to his efforts, first distributed in print in 1840, have come to be known as "Miller's Rules of Bible Interpretation" (Damsteegt 1977: 15–16). They specify that the Bible contains no superfluity; that it contains no doctrinal indeterminacy; that it is a coherent unity; and that it is its own authority. They exhort the exegete to have faith. Resting on the assumption that the text of the faith is also the text of the world, they direct the exegete to visions, figures, and parables as forecasts of a future beyond them. They delineate an epistemology of figuration itself. Thus, figural reading is the only alternative when the literal reading of a biblical term makes no sense, or does "violence to the simple laws of nature"; figural terms must never be read literally; and some figures are polysemic, as is "day," which might sometimes denote an indefinite period of time — sometimes a year, sometimes a thousand years.[17] These are the principles that guided Miller in his initial calculation that the Messiah would return in 1843. The "sanctuary" of Daniel 8:14 is a figure for the earth; its "cleansing," the final fulfillment of the parable of Noah's flood; and the "two thousand and three hundred days" after which that fulfillment would come figural of 2,300 years. Artaxerxes' decree to "rebuild the temple" (Ezra 7) is itself figural of a future restoration of Jerusalem "unto Messiah the Prince" (Dan. 9:25); and 2,300 years would have passed between its issuance in 457 B.C. and 1843 A.D.[18]

Or so, for awhile, it seemed. When 1843 passed without obvious incident, Miller and such loyal Millerites as Samuel Snow appealed to other calendars, other calculi, and more than a little crossing of fingers in arriving at a new, even more precise estimation of the Advent.[19] Hence, 22 October 1844, the date of the Great Disappointment and of the rapid fracturing of a movement that may have comprised as many as fifty thousand believers at its height.[20] Under the authority of Ellen White's vision, as Ms. Roden has reported, the SDA Church would subsequently embrace the date as marking Christ's entry not into the earthly but the heavenly sanctuary, there to begin the extended process of the judgment of the dead.

However, if the latter date is thus distinctively Millerite and Seventh-day Adventist, the former — 1843 — is not. Though rarely as the year of the Second Coming, it has special eschatological import for many of the British premillennialists who had found in the French Revolution what Ernest Sandeen has described as "a prophetic Rosetta stone" (1970: 7). Miller was the near contemporary of his British counterparts but perhaps had only passing familiarity with their writings.[21] In any event, neither his exegetical rules nor his exegetical results seem to have been extracted directly from any single prior source. As Sandeen has nevertheless appropriately noted, Miller and the British premillennialists held the majority of their hermeneutical instruments in common.[22] They addressed the same texts and the same prophecies. They were interested in the same dates and assigned them to the same historical events. They were jointly expecting the prophecy of the 2,300 days to "come to fruition in 1843 or 1844" (Sandeen 1974: 111). Sandeen accordingly regards them as revivalist "twins." Whitney Cross is less inclined to emphasize transatlantic family resemblances but characterizes Miller and the Millerites as elaborating on positions common to "the whole of American Protestantism" during the first half of the nineteenth century (1965: 320). Ruth Alden Doan characterizes them somewhat more circumspectly as "offspring" of the "evangelical culture" of the same period (1987b: 118–19; cf. Doan 1987a: 9–30).

For Sandeen, among others, the "biblicism" and the "literalism" of the Millerites are the wellsprings of what would widely come to be called "fundamentalism" in the 1920s (Sandeen 1970: ix–xii). That the Millerites were Biblicists — embracing the Bible as the locus of all moral, historical, and cosmological truth — is beyond dispute. That the Millerites were literalists is correct as far as it goes, but it also warrants qualification. P. Gerard Damsteegt finds in Miller's own hermeneutical writings an explicit and general acknowledgment of the "metaphorical" meaning of biblical "figures," from which moral and other homiletic lessons might always be drawn (1977: 18; citing Miller 1833: 3–4). Ellen White plainly shares his view; Victor Houteff and the Branch Davidians are connoisseurs of it. At the very least, then, Millerite (or Branch Davidian) literalism should not be confused with the general semiological dogma that would reduce meaning to reference, sense to denotatum. Sandeen labels it a "historicist" literalism, which is once again correct but still too imprecise (1970: 51). For Miller as for his hermeneutical successors, the Bible is indeed a record, an archive. Its persons are actual persons; its prophets are forecasters of actual events. That its dramatis personae, its narratives, and its prophecies are "figures" implies that its meaning is not self-evident, its facts not able to speak for themselves. Millerite semiotics is (once again) suspicious — and so among other things of ancient provenance. Millerite hermeneutics is itself ultimately the offspring not of the nineteenth or eighteenth century but of the centuries of the authorship of the New Testament, perhaps even of the centuries preceding them. Proximate genealogies are simply the terminal segments of a much longer train of begetting (see Goppelt 1982: 1–13).

Auerbach's "figure" is also Miller's. It derives from the Latin *figura*, but more specifically from "figura" as the Patristic gloss of the Greek *tupos* (*tupoi* in the plural) in a sense first attested in Saint Paul's epistles. At Romans 5:14, Paul writes that "death . . . reigned from Adam to Moses, even over them that had not sinned after the similitude of Adam's transgression, who is the figure [*tupos*] of him [that is, Moses] that was to come." At 1 Corinthians 10:6, he alludes to Old Testament narratives of sinful behavior as having been "our examples [*tupoi*], to the intent we should not lust after evil things, as they also lusted." At 1 Corinthians 10:11, he refers to the sinners' divine punishments as having "happened to them for ensamples [*tupoi*]: and they are written for our admonition, upon whom the ends of the world have come."[23] In the latter two instances, the explicit import of such *tupoi* is moral but implicitly also redemptive; *tupoi* are God-given lessons that the godly would heed. In the first instance, Adam's sins remain exemplary, but his person is also an *umbra*, a shadow or foreshadowing or prefiguration or prototype of the person who would finally expiate them. Here, Adam as umbra, as *tupos*, has Jesus as his *veritas*, his truth, and also as his *antitupos* (from the Greek for "counterblow," "impression," or "copy"). From the Patristic period forward, "typology" has endured largely as the hermeneutics of the relation between biblical "types" and their biblical and extrabiblical "antitypes."[24]

Quintilian wrote at length on the distinction between figura (translating the Greek *skhēma*) and *tropus* — the English "trope" (1978: 156–69). Tertullian, however, is the first to gloss as "figure" the proleptic or prophetic tupos, and it is after Tertullian that Auerbach writes of figural interpretation as " 'allegorical' in its widest sense, [but different] from most of the allegorical forms known to us by the historicity of both the sign and what it signifies" (1959: 53; cf. Brumm 1970: 25–27). The trope is mental or textual or linguistic. The figure as type is always a historical, actual hypostasis. Miller's much later distinction between "metaphors" and figures echoes the ancient rhetoricians and survives widely in the practices of hermeneutical Millerites, those of Ms. Roden included.[25] However, figures (whether as schemata or as types) are also tropic in and of themselves and so permit tropological parsing. Thus, the type is a metonymic distillation of the person, or corpus, or event, or sequence of events to which it refers. In Charles Peirce's terms, it is an icon (1982: 162–63, 243–45). The antitype might for its part also be, or function as, a type, a further foreshadowing of that which its precursor was already a foreshadowing; Moses as the antitype of Adam might thus also be read as a subsequent typification of the New Adam, of Jesus himself. As antitype, however, it is the metonymic hypostasis of its precursor. The antitype as antitype rematerializes the icon to which it is linked; it is a trope of reembodiment. As a "metonym of a metonym," it has all the attributes of what Harold Bloom has discerned in the trope of transumption or metalepsis—the reversal of cause and effect, or the inversion of temporal priorities (Bloom 1975: 101–3). If such a trope is still "mimetic," it is thus far from being merely a reproduction, a copy. It is not the trope of the eternal return. So, too, the referent of an antitype is not a reincarnation, clone, or second or third coming of the referent of its correlative type, with perhaps the single exception of the returned Christ. As the fulfillment, as the "increase" or consummation of its precursor, the antitype signifies the bringing of something new into the world, a novelty of which its correlative type was only an iconic anticipation (cf. Goppelt 1982: 17–18). The antitype signifies the realization of its correlative type. It is also a Peircean index or, more precisely, partakes of the dynamic reversion of icon to index, of Peircean "secondness" to Peircean "firstness" (Peirce 1961: 356–57; cf. Lee 1997: 111–13). The antitype reappoints the reference of its correlative type at the same time that it points to it, picks it out in its more complete historical actuality. It does so partially or imperfectly—unless it is the last in its series. Only of the truly consummate antitype might it be said that meaning and reference, sense and denotatum, are one. The typologist is an unmitigated literalist, then, only when history is altogether complete, altogether actual. Then, indeed, all suspicion will be dispelled and the mystery of God dispelled along with it.

That we should wait for such a day, that we should even expect its eventual arrival, is, however, another matter. In a monograph of remarkable intelligence and insight, Stephen O'Leary has sought the source of such expectation in the dramatic, narrative, and argumentative structure of apocalyptic. O'Leary casts apocalyptic as a "mythic" representation of "the perfection of the cosmos through the purgation of the principle of evil in a final eschatological Judgment through which the divine sufferance of evil will be justified" (1994: 51). It is thus at once an eschatology and a theodicy, within which the finitude of time is a constitutive topos or commonplace, and history itself the course of the career of evil in the world. Apocalyptic historicity expresses for O'Leary the logic of narrative, of a temporal progression that has a beginning and a middle but must also have an end (1994: 28–29). It is more specifically a tragic historicity, fateful, cadential, and closed.[26] The end of time, which also marks the final defeat of evil, is its climax; only beyond both does the divine comedy of an eternal paradise begin to unfold — and, of course, only for the survivor. This is perhaps more than enough to invite chronological speculation. If chronologically indeterminate, however, apocalyptic narrative lacks any mechanism that would lend it climactic immediacy. Hence, it is without any intrinsic practical urgency. The rhetor must accordingly intervene, must provide the necessary supplement. Apocalyptic fully itself must have dramatization. It must have a rhetor capable of rendering its tragicomic dualism present to an audience, capable of persuading his or her listeners or readers that its climactic epoch is their own epoch, that its drama is their drama, and its dramatis personae their rulers, their neighbors, themselves. The catalyst of personal gnosis, of transcendent self-identification, the successful rhetor is also the catalyst of a thoroughly practical anxiety that has its only adequate catharsis in chronological exactitude — even if it must be imported into the apocalyptic narrative either through revelation or some other means.[27] Having been convinced of their part in it, the actors in apocalyptic tragedy can only grow increasingly impatient for their final curtain. Should their director persist in refusing them a conclusive script, they can only underscore their demand for a deus ex machina. This was indeed Miller's fate; 22 October 1844 was consequently more a matter of numerological prestidigitation (and not all of it Miller's own) than Biblicist deduction. In O'Leary's judgment, "the critic may conclude . . . that charismatic manifestations are a predictable outcome of arguments that predict the End of time with a high degree of specificity" (1994: 115).

So cursory an overview of O'Leary's "psychology" of apocalyptic "form" can only do violence to its subtlety, but it can at least take note of some of its many virtues. Foremost among these is its emphatic reiteration — after Claude Lévi-Strauss, after Kenneth Burke and the new narratologists — that the stories we tell ourselves about ourselves are much more than the inert receptacles of our experience. They are machinic, the technological interface between raw feeling and formulable sentiment, between sensation and classification, between suspicion and its representation. They are at once transformational and generative, and as O'Leary appropriately insists, they stand inevitably in the way of any and every direct path between socioeconomic circumstances and ideological commitments (1994: 8–10). Deployed rhetorically, utilized as instruments of persuasion, they function as technologies of deliberation and decision, of practical reasoning. They are a doxic circulatory system, reservoirs of "common knowledge" but also its practical channels. Received indexically, understood as being applicable to the here and now, they are matrices of the transmutation of the possible into the actual, the matrices of both objectification and subjectivation.

O'Leary's syncretic theory of narrative is also a theory of hermeneutics, and so of typology itself, one method of biblical reception, one rhetorical supplement to the Bible among many others. As a rhetorical theory, however, it is not quite a pedagogical theory, not quite a theory of either narrative or hermeneutics as a technology of instruction. That it is not hints less at a weakness than at an excess of strength. On the one hand, O'Leary's general psychology of narrative — a liberal mixture of Aristotle, Burke, Weber, Paul Ricoeur, Joseph Campbell, and Mircea Eliade, to name only a few — might strike the less philosophical (and less humanist) of anthropologists as presumptuous. On the other hand, the practical privileges he accords to the dynamics of rhetor and audience suggests a construal of the scene of instruction as a scene of persuasion of restrictive scope. O'Leary is not an emotivist, yet he does tend to attribute the persuasiveness of even rational argumentation to the "formal satisfaction" or feelings of "certainty" that it engenders. His hypothesis that apocalyptic specificity characteristically gives way to "charismatic" justification is for its part plausible; his "heuristic" if "tentative" identification of pathos or Aristotle's "emotional proof" with "the qualities of Weberian charisma" runs the considerable risk of reducing the essentially performative proof of charismatic authority to the seductiveness of the charismatic leader. Such a reduction would be especially troubling as the paradigmatic underpinning of a theory of conversion — not because conversion is independent of pathos, but because it is only sometimes "enthusiastic" (as the sober *lumières* of the Enlightenment liked disparagingly to put it) and even more rarely "passive" or "pathetic" (as contemporary cult-busters disparagingly like to think of it). The scene of persuasion risks relegating the frequently long, arduous, and somber askesis of conversion too far to the wings.

O'Leary's analysis of apocalyptic narrative may also err in the direction of an exaggerated intellectualism. Its subsumption of apocalyptic soteriology under the ostensibly broader rubric of theodicy in any event invites the misleading impression that the most burning of apocalyptic problems is also among the most abstract. At the very least, it invites the misimpression that apocalyptic religiosity is more concerned with the puzzle of the divine tolerance of evil than with the puzzle of how, when, and whether there might be an escape from it. These puzzles are linked, of course, though it is far from obvious that the answer to the second must be derived from an answer to the first. The vast majority of historical (and ethnographic) evidence suggests, moreover, that apocalyptic religiosity itself has salvation as its primary preoccupation and the topos of election—of the chosen, or the saved—as its primary commonplace.[28] Or more cautiously, it assigns the topos of election to no lesser league than it assigns the topos of evil. O'Leary neglects, however, even to entertain election as an apocalyptic topos, an omission that is all the more surprising because so many of his predecessors—most famously Norman Cohn—have defined apocalyptic movements precisely as soteriological movements (see Cohn 1970: 15). The omission may stem in part from his not having found election among Campbell's or Eliade's rosters of putatively universal commonplaces. It may or may not be due to what would have to be deemed an all-too-doctrinaire presumption that only the rhetor can bring apocalytic soteriologically home. Whatever its rationale, it promotes a double oversight: of the incipient indexicality, the insinuation of indexicality, that already informs apocalyptic as narrative; and of the performative logic that informs apocalyptic soteriology not merely within the Abrahamic tradition but outside of it as well.[29]

Within the Abrahamic tradition and widely outside of it, the logic of election and redemption seems at a cursory glance to be that of a reciprocal exchange of favor, or favors, and so the logic of reciprocity and the gift. Henri Hubert and Marcel Mauss brought such a perspective somewhat more narrowly to sacrifice, though with less than definitive results (Hubert and Mauss 1964 [1899]). It might also be brought to bear on the relation between supplicant and saint in Catholic and Orthodox southern Europe or, more ambitiously, though perhaps more convincingly, on the ceremonial life of peoples as far-flung as the aboriginals of Australia and the pueblo dwellers of the North American southwest. The logic of reciprocity cannot be brought to bear on most apocalyptic doctrines of election and salvation—not, at least, without serious qualification—for two reasons. One is obvious: reciprocity is in principle recursive and infinitistic; it models a relationship that, barring disruption or violation, might never end. The second reason is in fact only a corollary of the first, but for any anthropologist who presumes the logic of reciprocity to be the original logic of social organization, considerably more startling: as a logic, it is more complex than the apocalyptic logic of salvation. It is possible, all the same, to move from the former to the latter—by elimination.

As is well known, Mauss defines reciprocity by appeal to three norms, three subliminal or sublimated obligations: to give; to receive; and to make return (1990 [1925]: 13–14). For all that has subsequently been written about gift giving, the definition remains standard. Yet, it might for its own part be more complex than necessary. Performatively, reciprocal exchange continues to conform to its Maussian triad, but it also conforms to a dyad; its performative force is that of two promises, simultaneously made, with the gift their common pledge. Received, the gift is a pledge to make a return; given, it is a pledge to accept a return. Were the gift merely a good, the logic at play would — or could — be contractual, the logic of a debt incurred and repaid. As a gift, however, its value is that of neither use nor exchange. It is instead social; its worth is the worth of the relationship of which it is the "promissory note" and, as Mauss observed, the "spirit" (1990 [1925]: 10–13, 14). Semiotically, it is thus metonymic, a representative part of the totality of a relationship that will endure indefinitely or, rather, will endure just so long as its common pledge is never fully redeemed, never fully reduced to its merely material substance, to which a utilitarian or market value could be assigned. Metonymic of the life of a relationship, the gift is also always a foreshadowing of another gift, of a return that is also a receipt, and so a reactivation of the double promise of sociality itself. So long as it remains metonymic of the life of a relationship, the gift in fact can never be anything other than a foreshadowing. Every instance of giving and receiving is the promise of another; every gift the virtuality of the one that will follow it.

In the apocalyptic native's point of view, election is itself consistently conceived as a gift and is the foreshadowing of what is with similar consistency conceived as the promise of redemption. The logic of election and redemption nevertheless differs from that of reciprocity in one definitive respect: divine largesse allows for no return. The gratitude that the elect express through their worship, through their obedience to divine commands and their fulfillment of divinely appointed duties, is not a counter-gift. It is not a token whose receipt would bind the divine to its promise. As every predestinarian has at least implicitly recognized, it is not even necessary. The errant elect may provoke divine displeasure and punishment. They may consequently find themselves wandering in the marketplaces of vanity far longer than they might have hoped. But if there is nothing they can do to extract the promise made to them, there is similarly nothing they can do to prevent its ultimate fulfillment. The divine can be neither compelled nor thwarted. The mystery of the promise of redemption is the mystery of Bataillean sacrifice, of the gift that is also abandon — in this case, divine abandon (Bataille 1976: 310–11). It is the mystery of a purpose or a will whose motives transcend any merely human comprehension, a love beyond merely human feeling, a grace beyond merely human powers. It is the mystery of an event that will come to pass because, and only because, the divine has given its Word.

Nor is its Word confined to a single pronouncement, a single parable or narrative episode. From the apocalyptic view that Miller and Ms. Roden share with Saint Paul, the promise of redemption is pledged everywhere, in all things. It is infused throughout the world as the Word in its material aspect.[30] It is infused throughout the Testaments as the inevitably flawed translation of the Word into merely human tongues. The logic of the Bible is thus the logic of the singular promise of redemption; its semiotics the semiotics of the pledge and the promise made and made good. Hence, the hermeneutics of type and antitype. Every "bibloseme" is a metonymic foreshadowing of the march toward redemption. Historically and narratively, the early bibloseme is inevitably less complete than the later one. All point to a climax that will take the form of a triple coincidence: human beings will suffer final judgment, salvation or damnation; historical time — which is the time of sin, of wandering, of the rupture of heaven and earth, of the agon of good and evil — will cease; and the divine will show itself forth in all its plenary presence, as eternal Sovereign and as eternally sovereign Word. "Lastness" will be not a restoration but the instauration of firstness, just as the (semiological) Trinitarian Peirce would have it.

For Ms. Roden, Florence Houteff deviated from the light of the church, but she was nevertheless a token in her way of the progress made in the march toward redemption. In the aftermath of her husband's death, Ms. Houteff assumed leadership of the executive council of the Davidian church. Among other things, she oversaw the completion of a project that her husband had already begun: the selling of the properties of Mount Carmel, which was suffering from increasing urban encroachment, and the relocation of the Davidian community to over nine hundred acres of still open prairie land.[31] This was the original expanse of New Mount Carmel. Reports vary on whether Ms. Houteff also put herself forward as a prophetic authority. With the other members of the council, however, she exercised an interpretive ministry and was particularly voluble in her rejection of Ben Roden's newly wrought typological proofs that he was Victor Houteff's true spiritual heir and proper leader of the next phase of the church's mission.[32] Perhaps further to discredit him, perhaps because the commonplaces of apocalyptic were exercising an influence of their own, Ms. Houteff would eventually come to announce, or in any event to endorse the announcement, that the cleansing of the earth (and the outbreak of war in the Middle East) would begin precisely on Passover, 22 April 1959.[33] By Passover eve, nearly one thousand faithful had gathered with her to await the predicted event, many of them having sold their homes and possessions and traveled hundreds, even thousands, of miles to do so. Like the Millerites before them, the Davidians would suffer disappointment. Ms.

Houteff would linger on for some three years, but in the spring of 1962, she voted with her council to dissolve the church and to sell all but the seventy-seven acres of New Mount Carmel on which Ben and Lois Roden would subsequently settle. She seems to have reserved at least some of the income from the sale and did indeed move to California. Though other sources are discreetly silent on the matter, Ms. Roden is certain that she also married "a man named Eakin." With perfect hermeneutical consistency, Ms. Roden looks for shadows wherever she can find them and finds this one in the wanton mother of Hosea 2, whom the Lord lures into the wilderness of the valley of "Achor"; in the thief's tale of Joshua 7; and in its thief, "Achan," the son of Carmi, the son of Zabdi, the son of Zerah, of the tribe of Judah.

But there is, of course, more — much more.

The fourth trumpet is Rev. 8:12: "And the fourth angel sounded, and the third part of the sun was smitten, and the third part of the moon, and the third part of the stars so as the third part of them was darkened, and the day shown not for the third part of it, and the night likewise."[34]

This prophecy is fulfilled symbolically in the fourth seal to the church and literally in the fourth seal to the world. Gen. 37:9–10 shows that sun, moon, and stars can symbolize a family, and many families were cut off by Ben Roden's message. In the literal slaughter associated with the fourth seal to the world, the destructions create thick clouds.

The message of the fourth seal is that Christ's return saves the righteous, and in mercy to the righteous, Christ will destroy the wicked. The seal has to do with knowledge of Christ; his new name is Branch.

The fifth message came from Lois Roden, who followed her husband in the leadership. The fifth angel message is Rev. 14:15: "And another angel came out of the temple, crying with a loud voice to him that sat on the cloud, Thrust in thy sickle, and reap: for the time is come for thee to reap; for the harvest of the earth is ripe."

Because the earthly sanctuary is the image of the heavenly sanctuary, the angel coming out of the temple in heaven is repeated by Lois Roden coming out of the temple on earth. Thus, this Scripture confirms that Ben Roden reestablished God's true church on earth. Lois Roden was a helpmeet to her husband in his work, but we must look elsewhere for her message, which came after his.

The messenger is described in Rev. 3:1–6: "and unto the angel of the church in Sardis write; These things saith he that hath the seven Spirits of God, and the seven stars; I know thy works, that thou hast a name that thou livest, and art dead. Be watchful, and strengthen the things that remain, that are ready to die: for I have not found thy works per-

fect before God. Remember therefore how thou hast received and heard, and hold fast, and repent. If therefore thou shalt not watch, I will come on thee as a thief, and thou shalt not know what hour I shall come upon thee. Thou hast a few names even in Sardis which have not defiled their garments; and they shall walk with me in white: for they are worthy. He that overcometh, the same shall be clothed in white raiment: and I will not blot his name out of the book of life, but I will confess his name before my Father, and before his angels."

Here, the seven spirits of God are brought forth, and rightly so, because Lois Roden's message concerns the femininity of the Holy Spirit, and her representative is found among the seven spirits of God. Lois Roden, despite her faults, is written in the book of life. Initially, she heard and received the message of David Koresh, who beguiles her. God rebukes her for this. Still, a few of her flock are undefiled by Koresh's corrupting message. These will walk among the saints.

The fifth seal is described in Rev. 6:9–11: "And when he had opened the fifth seal, I saw under the altar the souls of them that were slain for the word of God, and for the testimony they held: and they cried with a loud voice, How long, O Lord, holy and true, dost thou not judge and avenge our blood on them that dwell on the earth? And white robes were given to every one of them, and it was said unto them, that they should rest yet for a little season, until their fellow servants also, and their brethren, that should be killed as they were, should be fulfilled."[35]

This is a seal of martyrs, and, indeed, Lois Roden was martyred among them. The souls of the saints under the altar were to be joined by the martyrs from Koresh's flock and future martyrs. The white robes confirm that all the dead have been judged at the time of this seal.

Between the fourth and the fifth trumpet is Rev. 8:13: "And I beheld, and heard an angel flying through the midst of heaven, saying with a loud voice, Woe, woe, woe to the inhabitors of the earth by reason of the other voices of the trumpet of the three angels, which are yet to sound."

The last three seals are each to be accompanied by the execution of a judgment; for example, some who reviled Lois Roden died in the fire at Mount Carmel.

The fifth trumpet is Rev. 9:1–11: "And the fifth angel sounded, and I saw a star fall from heaven unto the earth; and to him was given the key of the bottomless pit, as the smoke of a great furnace; and the sun and the air were darkened by reason of the smoke of the pit. And there came out of the smoke locusts on the earth, and unto them was given a power, as the scorpions of the earth have power. And it was commanded that they should not hurt the grass of the earth, neither any green thing, but only those men which have not the seal of God on their *foreheads. And to them it was given that they should not kill them, but that they should be tormented five months: and their torment was the torment of a scorpion, when he striketh a man." The rest of the passage describes the locusts and their leader, Christ in his guise as destroyer of the wicked.*

V.T. Houteff describes these locusts (as Christian soldiers) and their leader, Christ in robes of vengeance, in his excellent tract, "Final Warning." Actually, this is the gist of Lois Roden's message: that a woman representative of the Holy Spirit will have an integral part in the harvest and the judgment. The bottomless pit is Satan's domain; the woman helps God's people to escape. The message of the fifth seal is that martyrdom of God's people will take place in founding the Kingdom of God.[36] The seal is the name of the star, New Jerusalem, the Kingdom of God.[37]

His "letters from the field" leave little doubt: already by 1955, Ben Roden had come to believe himself blessed with the spirit of "living prophecy," privileged to possess the "present truth," and so divinely appointed to shepherd the Davidian church further toward its destiny. Not least because Victor Houteff had understood himself to be the seventh and last angel of Revelation, Ms. Houteff and her council foresaw no successor. Mr. Roden, however, discerned an intervening step between Houteff's message and the cleansing of the earth. Appealing especially to the Book of Zechariah (3:8 and 6:12), he argued that the true church of the coming Christ would be an offshoot of the Davidian church, that its leader's name would be the Branch, and that its mission consisted in the "investigation" of the elect — the identification, conscription, and spiritual training of the Christly army.[38] Well into the 1960s, Mr. Roden continued to assert that the army would have to find its way with him to historical Jerusalem in order to be ready for the annihilation of the wicked at Armageddon. Lois Roden and he began proceedings to purchase the remaining acres of New Mount Carmel in 1965 and took up residence there shortly thereafter.[39] Far fewer conscripts joined them than they had hoped. They visited Israel several times but did not emigrate — or at least, not in this life. Mr. Roden died on 22 October 1978. With the aid of the friends she had made in Israel, before and after his death, Lois was able in 1982 to arrange for the transfer of his remains for burial on the Mount of Olives (Tabor and Gallagher 1995: 40).

Late in 1977, sometime between two and three o'clock in the morning, Lois herself was given a vision: "a silver angel, shimmering in the night."[40] From it, she would come to acquire her own present truth: that the Holy Spirit was a feminine aspect of the Godhead, and that She had returned to help hasten the spread of the message of the church to the world at large. Charles Pace, a former Catholic and even today among her most devoted admirers, would gradually persuade her of yet another truth: that the Godhead was not triune but quaternary, and that its fourth aspect was feminine, a Holy Spirit Daughter. Well before she was persuaded, Lois rechristened the church the "Living Waters Branch."[41] She established the dove as its cardinal emblem. In 1980, she retitled its principal publication "Shekinah" — a Hebrew noun of feminine gender denoting the divine pneuma. If not altogether original to Christian thought, her truth was indeed timely. She was not in her own eyes a feminist. She did, however, advocate the clerical ordination of women. At least occasionally, she seems to have been prepared to assert that the heavenly equality of the Father and the Holy Spirit was a model for the earthly status of the sexes.[42] She favored emendations of the King James Bible that would more accurately convey the genders of its personages.[43] By 1981, she was declaring to reporters that the coming Messiah "would appear in female form."[44] She consequently attracted the interested and often sympathetic ear of a far from negligible audience in Texas but also nationally. Mr. Pace organized her delivery of a series of lectures in the easterly provinces of his native Canada. She was honored in the Philippines. With Lois Roden, the church had acquired its first — though hardly its last — public personality.

Under her mantle, the church would also begin to manifest symptomatically the potential incompatibility of the double principles of ecclesiastic succession that Ben Roden had first put into place. That the proper Davidian president was a living prophet, a professor of a truth more fully present, more fully complete than what his or her predecessors were able to tell, was already a source of schismogenetic antagonism.[45] Typology could sometimes feed such antagonism, as it did in Ben's debate with Ms. Houteff and council. It could just as easily serve to dampen it. A regressive-progressive method in its way, typology would permit Victor Houteff to preserve Ellen White's authority at the same time that it would permit him to render it past; it would permit Ben to do the same with Mr. Houteff and Ms. White alike. In the hands of an inspired rhetor, typology could thus be an instrument of both rebuttal and revision. As an instrument of revision, it could facilitate the transformation of an apparent failure of prophecy into a partial success. The anthropologist might thus speak of the routinization of charisma through a technology of interpretation, of a "discursive" routinization of charisma.

As early as 1965, Ben was opening the way for a different mode of routinization. With Victor Houteff, he reckoned the number of the Christly army to be precisely 144,000. Departing from Mr. Houteff, he further reckoned all its members to be of common blood:

... note that John [the author of Revelation] says that the 144,000 are lineal descendants of the twelve tribes of Israel. Read Rev. 7–8. They have accepted Jesus as the Messiah, joining the Christian church. . . . [T]hey are found in God's true church (the one teaching the Sabbath and Sanctuary truth) when they are sealed as first-fruits, not being contaminated with spiritual Babylon and her false doctrines.

The first 12,000 sealed are from the tribe of Judah (Rev. 7:5), and we conclude that some are descendants of the early Christian Jews who have lost their Jewish identity and who are now not known as Jews, but Christians. However, some may yet be known as Jews.[46]

Religious affiliation aside, surnames remain a crucial clue to lineal membership. For example:

"Roden" means "ruler" in Hebrew. Rod, referring to the King of Israel, Isa. 11:1 states, would come from the stem of Jesse, the father of King David. See Matt. 1:6; Acts 13:22. The Shepherd's Rod believers who were from the SDA church (antitypical Jesse) were providentially called Davidians. Hence the message about the Branch (Christ) prophetically followed the SDA and [Davidian] SDA messages in fulfillment of this type.[47]

Lois would for her part come to recast the number of the army as tropic, not literal.[48] She would not, however, reject her husband's conviction that the elect bore their anointment in their blood. She would instead supplement it with an onomastic argument of her own. In 1985, she observed that "it was the tribe of Dan, one of the ten taken captive by Assyria, who had the peculiar commission to name each place they conquered after their family name 'Dan' (Jud. 18)."[49] Hence, the River Jordan, but also Danzig; also Denmark; also Roden.

Blood perhaps prevailed over Ben's deathbed assignation of a specific ecclesiatic task to four of his sons. Hence, George was "given the responsibility of building the temple like Solomon who followed David, even the responsibility of the new King of the Branch."[50] A problem, however, soon came to the fore: the new king, author of an eyebrow-raising tract that he titled "Rough Wind," did not appear to be a living prophet in his own right; to many of the Branch Davidian flock, in any case, he seemed to have no present truth of his own. Lois had been acting as the president of the church as early as 1977. An epistle seeking the congregation's affirmation that she was their sole executive was distributed at the turn of spring in 1979.[51] Relations between mother and son were tense, even acrimonious; one investigative journalist reports that Lois filed an injunction in court to prevent him from ever claiming the presidency of the church as his own.[52] They would deteriorate even further when a certain Vernon Howell decided to join the Living Waters Branch some two years later.

Mr. Howell was born in Houston on 17 August 1959. A sometime resident of Tyler, Texas, dyslexic, aspiring rock guitarist and songwriter, spiritual seeker, gifted improvisational preacher, he had first made his way to New Mount Carmel in the summer of 1981. Lois had captivated him, and only a few months later he became one of her permanent boarders. She grew increasingly impressed with his command of the Bible and increasingly inclined to treat him as her protégé. Nor, by all accounts, was their involvement with one another merely spiritual.[53] George was horrified but hesitant to intervene before 1984, when Mr. Howell broke off his affair with then seventy-year-old Lois to marry fourteen-year-old Rachel Perry, daughter of a longtime Branch Davidian. In 1985, he traveled to Israel with Rachel and, while there, claimed to have received a revelation of his distinctive spiritual mission (Tabor and Gallagher 1995: 42). Even before he left, he had already convinced a majority of the residents of New Mount Carmel of his spiritual virtuosity. Not long after he returned, George succeeded in evicting him from his "Rodenville" and in sending his supporters off with him. The exiles set up a temporary and bedraggled camp nearby, at the edges of the town of Palestine. In November 1986, Lois Roden died; she, too, would be put to rest, beside Ben, on the Mount of Olives. In the early autumn of 1987, George and Amo married.[54] In November of the same year, Mr. Howell and he would at last come to blows. From a reliable source, who refers to Mr. Howell as "Koresh":

> George Roden dug up the body of Anna Hughes, a Davidian who had died at eighty-four and had been buried for twenty years on the Mount Carmel property. He put the casket in the [community's] chapel and challenged Koresh to a contest to see who could raise her from the dead. Koresh asked the McLennan County sheriff to arrest Roden for corpse violation but was told he would need to bring proof. Koresh and seven of his loyal followers tried to sneak onto the property to take a photo of the corpse. They were dressed in camouflage fatigues and heavily armed. A forty-five-minute gun battle ensued, each side blaming the other for firing first. Roden was wounded slightly in the hand. Koresh and his men were charged with attempted murder, and surely one of the strangest trials in Waco history was held in 1988. The jurors found the others not guilty but were split over the question of Koresh's guilt. The judge declared a mistrial. Six months later George Roden was charged with the murder of a fifty-six-year-

old man in an unrelated incident. He was found not guilty by reason of insanity and was sentenced to an indeterminate stay in the state hospital in Vernon, Texas. In the meantime Koresh came up with the money to pay the back taxes on the Mount Carmel property, and his group returned triumphantly and began to rebuild.[55]

Not until 1990 did Howell legally change his name. He replaced "Vernon" with "David." His new surname, "Koresh," is the Hebrew form of the more familiar Greek "Cyrus" — the Persian monarch whom the prophet Isaiah designated a messiah and the ordained conqueror of an imperious and infidel "Babylon."

By 1991, David Koresh was (it would seem) in his own eyes and (more certainly) in the eyes of those who lived with him at Mount Carmel a "messiah," a "christ," a man divinely chosen and divinely touched. He was, more precisely, among Weber's "emissary prophets," the voice and instrument of "news," of a revealed truth.[56] The boy Howell had the example of the emissary Nazarene. But he had also been tutored in the more immediate, perhaps less exotic examples of William Miller and Ellen White, for he, too, had been a member of the SDA Church.[57] The man Koresh was no longer welcome in its mainstream.[58] Like Victor Houteff and the Rodens before him, he nevertheless continued to regard Miller and White as his own precursors. He agreed with Mr. Houteff that the church of the elect was the church of the house of David. He agreed with Ben Roden that the present was a period of investigation.

Initially at least, he seems to have shared with both Ben and Lois Roden the presumption that Revelation's reference to Armageddon (16:16) was a literal reference to the plain enclosed since 1948 within the borders of the modern state of Israel.[59] By 1991, he would add a qualification. By 1991, Mr. Koresh was in his own eyes and in the eyes of those who lived with him at Mount Carmel the seventh and final angel of the Book of Revelation, that emissary through whom the present truth would be made eternal (cf. Rev. 10:7). His flock and he were that assembly of testimonialists whom Revelation (6:9) destined to be slain "for the word of God." Their moment was the moment of the breaking open of the seal of the fifth of those seven vials in which the elixirs of both epistemic and historical plenitude had been stored. Their enemy: the "beast" (Rev. 13:1) who presided at "Babylon" (17:5) and from Babylon ruled over the whole world (13:7). By 1991, Mr. Koresh may not yet have fixed the identity of the beast. The identity of the beast's political apparatus was, however, patent enough.[60] The final Babylon could only be the United States and its instrument of global hegemony, the United Nations. Before 1991, Mr. Koresh seems to have envisioned that his flock and he would be among the first to fall at the literal Armageddon, defending the state of Israel against the onslaught of an international invasion. Not an advocate of aggression, but no advocate, either, of the uncompromising temporal pacifism of the Nazarene, he had accordingly begun to collect a sizable arsenal. Not, however, until reflecting on the locus and the agencies of the Gulf War does he seem determinately to have envisioned the possibility that the battle for which he was preparing, that battle which would culminate on the Israeli plain, could begin almost anywhere; that it could indeed begin at the Mount Carmel compound itself; that his arsenal could thus have its first deployment before it ever left home.

Mr. Koresh is reported not to have been unduly surprised — is even reported to have expected — to discover that in early 1992[61] the compound had been infiltrated by one Robert Rodriguez, an undercover agent of the Bureau of Alcohol, Tobacco, and Firearms (BATF) appointed to gather evidence of the violation of law — at least of that law governing the possession, buying, and selling of weapons.[62] Before Mr. Koresh had arrived, the Branch Davidians had lived peaceably enough on their seventy-seven prairie acres, beneficiaries of the entrenched conservative tolerance that had attracted so many other Christian sectarians to the environs of Waco. If not widely admired for their commitments, they were often simply ignored. The strife that led to George Roden's deposition may, however, have been pivotal. In any event, in response to rumors that began to circulate not long after Mr. Koresh settled in as leader, the local Bureau of Child Protective Services subjected the community to a somewhat perfunctory and ultimately inconsequential investigation.[63] By late February 1993, the *Waco Tribune-Herald* was set to publish a seven-part exposé of both leader and community tellingly titled "The Sinful Messiah."[64] Could all the instruments, all the signs have pointed more definitively to special trials, special troubles? Sometime during the morning of 28 February 1993, shortly before the fact, Mr. Koresh in any event is reported not to have been unduly surprised to learn that a substantial and heavily armed brigade of agents of the BATF was set to move on the Mount Carmel compound to deliver a search warrant. Opinion is still divided over whether he was at all surprised by what transpired in the aftermath of the brigade's arrival: an exchange of gunfire, still of uncertain provenance; a standoff, unresolved for some fifty-one days and concluding — though we can hardly even yet speak of conclusion — with its now iconic fire; and the death of four BATF agents and what official tallies reckon at eighty Branch Davidians, Mr. Koresh prominent among them.[65]

For Amo, *the next few days were a blur. I found myself crying several times, and felt it was for the Branch Davidian children. A lot of good Christians died in that fire.*[66] Yet, she has subsequently delineated the shadows of this and other tragedies she has had to endure.

Jud. 17:1–2: "And there was a man of Mount Ephraim, whose name was Micah. And he said unto his mother, the eleven hundred shekels of silver that were taken from thee, about which thou cursedest, and spakest of also in mine ears, behold, the silver is with me; I took it. And his mother said, Blessed be thou of the Lord, my son."[67]

George Roden is Micah. His father was of the tribe of Judah, his mother of Ephraim. He is the literal joining of the two sticks, Judah and Ephraim. The eleven hundred shekels of silver represents the eleventh-hour church of V.T. Houteff and Ben Roden. Micah's mother is Lois Roden, who had the spiritual message of the church after Ben Roden died.

Jud. 17:3–4: "And when he had restored the eleven hundred shekels of silver to his mother, his mother said, I had wholly dedicated the silver unto the Lord from my hand for my son, to make a graven image and a molten image: now therefore I will restore it unto thee. Yet he restored the money unto his mother; and his mother took two hundred shekels of silver, and gave them to the founder, who made thereof a graven image and a molten image; and they were in the house of Micah."

On Ben Roden's death, George took control of the church from his mother, who had the spiritual message and therefore should have led the church. As a result of the struggles over the church, Lois leaves the church with two leaders, both of whom are idols to themselves and their supporters. George Roden is the graven image, and David Koresh is the molten image. The two hundred shekels is the part of the church that accepted one or the other of them. Most of the church would have neither.

Hab. 2:9–11: "Woe to him that covet an evil covetousness to his house, that he may set his nest on high, that he may be delivered from the power of evil! Thou hast consulted shame to thy house by cutting off many people, and hast sinned against thy soul."[68]

George Roden coveted the leadership of the end-time church which founds the Kingdom of God without rendering obedience to God's law. In doing so, he set himself both above God and above God's law. He cut off many righteous people from the church, and shamed his parents' memory, and placed his soul in jeopardy. The structural members of God's temple, the stones and the beams, are symbolic of those who found the Kingdom of God. The stone, the woman God chooses to

61

hold the door of the newborn Kingdom open, shall utter the loud cry. The righteous are called lively stones. The beam of the timbers is a great man or woman; this is the other witness who stands up in judgment. The establishment of the witnesses is God's judgment on George Roden.

Hab. 2:12–14: "Woe to him that buildeth a town with blood, and stablisheth a city by iniquity. Behold, is it not of the Lord of hosts that the people shall labour in the very fire, and the people shall weary themself for very vanity? For the earth shall be filled with the knowledge of the glory of the Lord, as the waters cover the sea."

David Koresh built Jerusalem, the city that stands for the Kingdom of God, by theft and lies and bloodshed. God's judgment burns all of the work of the Koreshites, and after, causes them to weary themselves proclaiming a silly thing, that David Koresh was the second coming of Christ. All this so God can show his power once again in fulfilling prophecy, and restore His Bible to an exalted place as a revelation of Himself. All the earth is to come to worship God (Isa. 66:23).

Jud. 17:5–6: "And the man Micah had an house of gods, and made an ephos, and teraphim, and consecrated one of his sons, who became his priest. In those days there was no king in Israel, but every man did that which was right in his own eyes."[69]

After Lois' death, the church remained George's. He chose his son, Joshua, as his successor. Although George behaved as a king, the Kingdom was yet to be established.

Jud. 17:7–13: "And there was a young man out of Bethlehemjudah of the family of Judah, who was a Levite, and he sojourned there. And the man departed out of the city from Bethlehemjudah to sojourn where he could find a place: and he came to Mount Ephraim to the house of Micah, as he journeyed. And Micah said unto him, Whence camest thou? And he said unto him, I am a Levite of Bethlehemjudah and I go to sojourn where I may find a place. And Micah said unto him, Dwell with me, and be unto me a father and a priest, and I will give thee ten shekels of silver by the year, and a suit of apparel, and thy victuals. So the Levite went in. And the Levite was content to dwell with the man; and the young man was unto him as one of his sons. And Micah consecrated the Levite; and the young man became his priest, and was in the house of Micah. Then said Micah, Now know I that the Lord will do me good, seeing I have a Levite to my priest."

Here we see a person of the tribe of Judah, who joins the church to become a priest and so subsequently makes his living. At least initially, he was acceptable to George Roden. This is Charles Pace, the third prince of Israel to be overturned before idolatry is taken from the church.

Isa. 27:7: "Hath he smitten him, as he smote those that smote him? or is he slain according to the slaughter of them that are slain by him?"

Referring to the death of Dale Adair at George Roden's hands in Odessa in 1989, the first question asks: Was it self-defense, as George states? The second refers to David Koresh. Note that bones were bull-dozed from under the foundation of the compound on May 12, 1993.

Isa. 27:8: "In measure, when it shooteth forth, thou wilt debate with it: he stayeth his rough wind in the day of the east wind."

George Roden's "Rough Wind" promoted great controversy among Branch Davidians, and caused many to fall away. The publication was stayed by George's imprisonment. The day of the east wind is when the fruit of the church's message is dried up (see Eze. 19:10).

Isa. 27:9: "By this therefore shall the iniquity of Jacob be purged; and this is all the fruit to take away his sin; when he maketh all the stones of the altar as chalkstones that are beaten in sunder, the groves and the images shall not stand up."

God's rebuke to George Roden is that since, in his pride and arrogancy, he caused many of the faithful (altar stones) of the church to sin, he is no more a priest; altars are a sin to him (see Hos. 8:11).

Isa. 27:10: "Yet the defenced city shall be desolate and the habitation forsaken, and left like a wilderness: there shall the calf feed, and there shall he lie down, and consume the branches thereof."

The destruction of the compound at Mount Carmel is prophesied here. Koresh, the molten image, is a golden calf to his followers, who are led to forsake God's law by him. He lies down at Mount Carmel in peace, and there he consumes his followers with iniquity.[70]

Isa. 28:7–8: "But they also have erred through wine, and through strong drink are out of the way; the priest and the prophet have erred through strong drink, they are swallowed up of wine, they are out of the way through strong drink; they err in vision, they stumble in judgment. For all the tables are full of vomit and filthiness, so that there is no place clean."[71]

David Koresh has deluded his followers, preaching that there is salvation for the wicked, and leading them into abominations.

Isa. 29:9–13: "Whom shall he teach knowledge? And whom shall he make to understand doctrine? them that are weaned from the milk, and drawn from the breasts. For precept must be upon precept; line upon line, line upon line; here a little, and there a little: For with stammering lips and another tongue will he speak to this people. To whom he said, This is the rest wherewith ye may cause the weary to rest; and this is the refreshing: yet they would not hear."

Charles Pace comes to the Solemn Assembly in 1984 and tries to make Koresh's followers heed the law and the prophets. It is as if he *spoke a foreign language and mumbled; they cannot understand him. This is a snare to them, because they knew the Branch Davidian message; they are damned for following Koresh.*

Isa. 30:8–11: "Now go, write it before them in a table and note it in a book, that it may be for the time to come for ever and ever: That this is a rebellious people, lying children, children that will not hear the law of the Lord: Which say to the seers, See not: and to the prophets, Prophesy unto us the right things, speak unto us smooth things, prophecy deceits: Get you out of the way, turn aside out of the path, cause the Holy One of Israel to cease from before us."[72]

In 1984, about the time Satan was cast to earth, he directed his attention to the Branch Davidian church. At that time, the church at a distance chose George Roden by ballot. The church at the assembly split into two factions, the larger choosing David Koresh, the smaller choosing Lois Roden and Charles Pace. In doing so, the majority of the church turned their back on the prophetic voice of the church, exactly as Satan planned they would.

Isa. 30:12–14: "Wherefore thus saith the Holy One of Israel, Because ye despise this word, and trust in oppression and perverseness, and stay thereon: Therefore shall this iniquity be unto you as a breach ready to fall, swelling out in a high wall, whose breaking cometh suddenly at an instant. And he shall break it as the breaking of the potter's vessel that is broken in pieces; he shall not spare: so that there shall not be found in the bursting of it a sherd to take fire from the hearth, or to take water withal out of the pit."

This message is specifically for the portion of the church that chose David Koresh to lead them into perverseness. It foretells the destruction of his movement, leaving no one capable of carrying a Holy Spirit (fire) or living water message out of their damnation. All that can be found are unclean.

Isa. 30:15–17: "For thus saith the Lord God, the Holy One of Israel: In returning and rest shall ye be saved; in quietness and in confidence shall be your strength: and ye would not. But ye said, No; for we will flee upon horses; therefore shall ye flee: and, We will ride upon the swift; therefore shall they that pursue you be swift. One thousand shall flee at the rebuke of one; at the rebuke of five shall ye flee: till ye be left as a beacon at the top of a mountain, and as an ensign on a hill."[73]

If those who chose David Koresh had simply remained within the church, following Lois Roden (returning) and accepting a gradual change of leadership to Charles Pace, who had the prophetic message of the Holy Daughter, they trusting in God would never have been without a prophet. Instead, God forced them to flee, and many perished in that flight. The whole church (one thousand) fled at the rebuke of

George Roden's "rough winds"; David Koresh's followers fled at the rebuke of five—the men with the slaughter weapons of Eze. 9. The beacon fire of April 19, 1993 has called the world to Mount Carmel, and despite the best efforts of the oppressors, the ensign is still there.

Hab. 2:15–17: "Woe unto him that giveth his neighbour drink, that puttest thy bottle to him, and makest him drunken also, that thou mayest look on their nakedness! Thou art filled with shame for glory: drink thou also, and let thy foreskin be uncovered: the cup of the Lord's right hand shall be turned unto thee, and shameful spewing shall be on thy glory."[74]

Charles Pace is also judged.[75] God leads His Kingdom in the end-time by the sure word of prophecy (Isa. 33:22). Charles Pace has chosen to delude his followers into choosing his leadership instead of God's for motives which do him no credit. God tells him to drink also and delude himself. God will show him to be uncircumcised—not a member of God's congregation—hand him the cup of God's wrath, and make his religious message appear as vomit in men's eyes. Charles Pace is the government's choice of leader for the Branch Davidians because his chronic inactivity aids the cover-up.

Isa. 27:1–3: "In that day the Lord with his sore and great and strong sword shall punish leviathan the piercing serpent, even leviathan the crooked serpent; and he shall slay the dragon that is in the sea. In that day sing ye unto her, A vineyard of red wine."[76]

Three manifestations of Satan are mentioned here. The first is Koresh, who pierced George Roden with a bullet; the second is George Roden, who is perverse (crooked) in his religious message. The third is Charles Pace, a representative of the great men who make idols of themselves in the church (source of all waters, living water, spiritual message, sea).[77]

Hab. 2:18–19: "What profiteth the graven image that the maker thereof hath graven it; the molten image, and a teacher of lies, that the maker of his work trusteth therein, to make dumb idols? Woe unto him that saith unto the wood, Awake; the dumb stone, Arise, it shall teach! Behold, it is laid over with gold and silver, and there is no breath at all in the midst of it."[78]

George Roden, the graven image, never profited a single person who accepted him as leader. Neither did David Koresh, the molten image. Nor will Charles Pace, a teacher of lies, who perverts the message of the church to proclaim himself leader.

Isa. 5:15: "And the mean man shall be brought down, and the mighty man shall be humbled, and the eyes of the lofty shall be humbled."[79]

As charming as David Koresh was, he was mean enough to send persecutors after an undefended woman and child. As mean-spirited as George Roden was, he was mighty enough to hold off an army of Ko-

reshites. As learned as Charles Pace is, he has looked on a crown that is not his.

Those are fighting words, of course. They amply underscore — if further underscoring is needed — that there is no love lost between Ms. Roden and the surviving (and later converted) Koreshites, who have the host of a radio talk show to thank for sponsoring the recent construction of a church building for them at Mount Carmel. Nor is there any love lost between Ms. Roden and Charles Pace, who completed the construction of his own church building at Mount Carmel several years ago. Rival claimants to Lois Roden's spiritual legacy, the two diverge over a great many doctrinal details and, by no means least, over the details of the identity of the Holy Daughter. Ms. Roden adheres to the genealogical literalism of her in-laws. She consequently argues that, for all his failings, George Roden himself must be the literal sire of the Holy Daughter (who is her own daughter as well). Concerning the proscriptive and prescriptive details of marriage, she advocates a "feminist" position that invokes Lois's precedent but also goes beyond it.

> *Under the Mosaic law (Remember ye the law of Moses my servant, which I commanded unto him in Horeb for all Israel, with the statutes and judgments [Mal. 4:4]), a man could have many wives (If he take him another wife, her food, her raiment, and her duty of marriage, shall he not diminish [Exo. 21:10]), but a woman could have only one husband. Lois Roden . . . described herself as Vernon Howell's polygamous wife. In describing herself thus, Lois Roden was returning polygamy to the Branch because she knew the Mosaic law. David Koresh accepted polygamy, as did George Roden, based on her message.*[80]
>
> *It is obvious from Ezekiel 4 that the restoration of the Bible law is a slow but steady process, with each reformer, starting with Luther, bringing more truth.*[81] *However, some papist error continues until the dawn of the millennium.*[82] *Ellen White can scarcely be blamed for her stand against polygamy. Nevertheless, there is no more Biblical evidence for the end of polygamy than for the change in the Sabbath. And the Bible is our lawbook. Even more controversial is the thought that if a man take another wife, his first wife might take another husband. This, of course, is lifting the curse on Eve that she have only one husband, and that her husband rule over her (Gen. 3:16). Under Mosaic law, if a woman has sex with any man but her one husband, she commits fornication. For a married woman, fornication is adultery. But the idolatry of our day is regarded by God as spiritual fornication or whoredom.*

Hos. 4:12: "*My people ask counsel at their stocks, and their staff declareth unto them: for the spirit of whoredom has caused them to err, and they have gone a whoring from under their God.*"

A stock (tree trunk) is the raw material for creating an idol; the staff is a symbol of a shepherd. God's people allow their leaders and their pastors to think for them, and they uplift them in place of the word of the Bible. Because of the idolatry of men, God has set women free, extending the perfect law of liberty to them.[83]

Mr. Pace is not a genealogical literalist; he is very much a committed monogamist and so must dismiss Ms. Roden's reasoning virtually in its entirety. For that matter, he dismisses much of what the Koreshites avow as well. So the schismogenesis that emerged in the early 1980s now stands.

More is at odds, however, than doctrine alone. The legal title to the Mount Carmel property is also unresolved. A civil trial, several times postponed, is at this writing still pending. The McLennan County court-house in Waco is the repository of the scores of briefs, depositions, and injunctions to which it has already led. Nor is it the only issue that has brought the Branch Davidians squarely into the inner sancta of the temporal order. Several of the surviving Koreshites were joined by the relatives of those who died in the 1993 conflagration in pursuing a suit against the federal government. They alleged that certain agents surrounding the Mount Carmel compound were responsible for igniting the fire, an accusation that gained renewed attention after the discovery in the summer of 1999 that the FBI had neglected to report that it had made use of potentially flammable tear-gas canisters in its effort to force surrender. Pointing to the peculiar flashes recorded on a videotape that has long been in public circulation, they alleged further that at least a few of the agents shot at their intended prisoners after the fire had erupted. The tape was formerly deemed irrelevant, but it, too, came under the scrutiny of the third congressional commission convened to review the evidence that remained. On 20 March 2000 the commission oversaw a "simulation" of the closing moments of the siege to determine whether the video's images were indeed those of exploding gunpowder. The results did not convince the advisory panel assembled to assess the plaintiffs' allegation; its first judgment was squarely in favor of the government's denial of liability. The trial judge ultimately agreed. The plaintiffs appealed his decision, but their case was dismissed for lack of merit.

The trial (in the strict sense of the term) has thus reached its conclusion. Ms. Roden was not a party to it but had some sympathy for it. She could certainly agree that the government should be taken to task for its improprieties. Indeed, she has always suspected various of its agents and agencies of improprieties far more elaborate and extensive than those that any of the investigative commissions entertained. She suspects that a cover-up was underway long before the morning when David Koresh was to have been confronted with a search warrant. She shares many of her views with her friend, activist attorney Linda Thompson, whose American Justice Foundation produced the earliest (and among the most controversial) documentary retrospectives of the Mount Carmel episode. Titled *Waco: The Big Lie*, the documentary never found a national distributor and was immediately attacked in the local press for its putative distortions and fallacies. It was nevertheless the first to dwell on the smoke that a camera revealed to be drifting up from out of an underground "bunker" slightly before 6:00 A.M. on 19 April some fifteen minutes before the government's final actions officially began. None of the media bothered to attend to the appearance of the smoke at the time, which turns out to have been the product of the pyrotechnic canister that would belatedly arouse so much controversy. Nor did the media attend to a tank that simultaneously moved against the compound itself, effecting the collapse of that end of the building where a "trap door" was located, which might have allowed anyone taking refuge in the bunker to escape. As if this were not enough, the narrator offers "further evidence that the Branch Davidians were murdered." The screen shows what appears to be a bright orange jet of fire twice spouting from another of the tanks that punctured the compound walls. Shortly after flames begin roiling out of a second-story window, it shows an agent riding atop yet another tank, apparently removing a "fireproof-type hood." It shows other agents, walking casually about the burning compound, apparently unconcerned about the risk of further assault. Over their heads, helicopters circle, the passengers within them brandishing rifles. The narrator reminds the viewer that "in any ordinary crime scene, great pains are taken to preserve the evidence." On the screen, tanks busily push and press debris into the center of the fallen, smoldering compound, where it, too, would gradually disintegrate into ashes.

Even more controversial is the documentary's treatment of the inauguration of the standoff fifty-one days earlier. The narrator of the video instructs the viewer to "watch closely" as eight BATF agents move on the compound, using ladders to climb to its roof. She draws attention to government helicopters that appear as three inky spots low on the horizon; to the sound of the automatic fire of BATF guns. Even having achieved the roof, the team of eight for its part seems to have met with no hostile response. Two of its members break open an upper-story window. They toss what appear to be "smoke grenades" into the room they have breached. They follow the grenades into the room, accompanied by a third agent. A fourth agent appears briefly on the screen; then the tape jumps with a "badly edited cut." Its next image captures the same agent tossing yet another grenade into the breached room. The narrator wonders whether he can have had any intention other than that of injuring his own men. It makes no sense for him to be throwing anything at all into a room where the three BATF agents have just gone, unless he intends to injure his own men. She remarks that he also fires his automatic weapon into the room "twice, without looking." The video shifts to slow motion and offers a reprise. The agent fires his weapon into the room. From inside, someone returns fire. The agent on the screen fires again. Another return of fire. On the roof, the agent falls. A bullet has struck his helmet but has not penetrated it. He manages an awkward retreat down the nearest available ladder. For the three agents who had entered the room, a different fate: all were killed.

Was it merely coincidental that all had happened to serve as Bill Clinton's bodyguards during the course of his campaign for president? Had they perhaps seen something that they should not have seen? Did they know something that they should not have known? Could the raid possibly have served at once as the cloak and the technology of their elimination? The narrator does not say but insinuates a complex collusion in which the BATF was far less player than pawn. By the fourth day of the standoff, the latter agency had ceded control of all police operations to the FBI. Henceforth, the media would be restricted to a site some three miles from the Mount Carmel property. FBI agent Rob Ricks would offer them an official version of each subsequent day's events. Nearby Fort Hood would provide tanks and other material with which the compound was soon surrounded. The narrator of Thompson's video informs the viewer that "it is illegal to use military troops against United States citizens under the Posse Comitatus Act, 18 United States Code 13855" but adds a qualification.[84] The National Guard and military materiel might be deployed legally against citizens involved in the manufacture or sale of illicit drugs. The narrator dismisses the possibility that the Koreshite community might have had any such involvement. Yet what of the rumor that Mount Carmel hid a methamphetamine laboratory? Could the BATF have promulgated the rumor in order to secure then Texas governor Ann Richards' authorization of the use of tanks? And why, even long after it had become clear that the rumor was ill-founded, did the governor not retract the authorization she initially granted? Did she find the course of events wrested from her hands? Or was her inaction by her own design?[85]

If densely conspiratorial, the idiom of Ms. Thompson's documentary is resolutely secular, an idiom in which the human exercise of power reveals its excess in illegality, in the transgression of the laws of the land. It is a political idiom, the critical standards of which derive from the familiar model of checks and balances; more specifically, it is juridico-political in its subjection of the executive to the scrutiny of the legislator and the judge. It might strike the more mainstream of sensibilities as reactionary. But it is liberal (or libertarian) in two respects. It reiterates an enduring liberal reprimand of the pretensions of State Reason. It speaks on behalf of the disenfranchised but from a franchise, a platform, of its own — liberal constitutionalism.

Ms. Roden is a promoter of Ms. Thompson's documentary and is far from politically neutral. The idiom in which she prefers to articulate and to give context to her politics is not, however, a secular one. It might thus seem to violate the directives even of the Nazarene himself, who took pains to stress the disjunction between Caesar's realm and his (or God's) own. It can only seem a logically mixed bag for anyone who presumes that political and religious thought, or political and religious values, are essentially or in principle distinct, and so for the great majority of Western social and cultural theorists from the later eighteenth century to today. Even though partial, the meeting here of so many fractious minds is unusual; among social and cultural theorists, it is perhaps unique. It brings evolutionary positivists into broad accord with Marxists and neo-Marxists. It brings the Enlightened assassination of superstition into broad accord with the existentialist displacement or misplacement of God. It brings the early Emile Durkheim into very broad accord with the later Max Weber, and Hannah Arendt into very broad accord with Jürgen Habermas.[86] Intellectual (and other) historians must determine whether such near consensus owes more to late medieval and early modern crises of political legitimation, to the Enlightenment glorification of a monological reason, to the Romantic redefinition of the Cartesian construal of the relation between the subjective and the objective, or to some combination of all, or to some but not others, or to none at all. In any event, call it the principle of the separateness of estates.

In its more abstract and model-theoretic modalities, the principle can stand the assault of the many empirical counterexamples that might be brought against it. In practice, the religious and the political are often of a piece, but in practice, the human way is after all frequently the way of the mixed bag. One might still wonder whether it mistakes the odd for the representative, a civilizational peculiarity for what — in practice, at least — is far from being the anthropological rule. At the cusp of the third millennium, one might wonder further whether the separation of the religious from the political is as obvious even in the West as, a century earlier, it might have seemed to be. Whether such a separation is desirable is another matter. Even if it is desirable — and this professional infidel thinks it is — it may or may not be logically or sociologically compelling. Later in his career, Durkheim seems to have come to the conclusion that such a separation was little short of sociologically catastrophic. The anthropologist need not embrace his argument that the real referent of religious ideation is society itself in order to take seriously what the compendious ethnographic chapters of *The Elementary Forms of the Religious Life* more definitively illustrate: that religious discourse is a master discourse, consistently and coherently generative of ideas of both ultimate and proximate order, of the ontological and the merely ontic. Nor are its illustrations altogether sociologically original. They have a close (if surprising) companion in those historical chapters of Weber's *Protestant Ethic and the Spirit of Capitalism* that focus on the "inner-worldly asceticism" of the Calvinist and Puritan reformers. Weber was less interested in Calvinist politics than in Calvinist mercantilism. He was well aware, however, that the former was as much religiously derived as the latter, whether in Geneva or in those other cities on the hill that immigrant colonists would later establish on the North American east coast. In *The Protestant Ethic*, he noted nothing either logically or sociologically lax in such theocratic unity. Some two decades after its publication, he proposed that the separation of religious from both political and economic "spheres of value," their mutual drift into a tense but "lawful autonomy," was one vector of "rationalization" among many others (1946: 328). In his first monograph, he identified the mutation of the Calvinist conduct into a more godless "utilitarianism" as itself an irruption of the irrational, as an absurd gap or rupture that finally allowed the forces of technical rationalism to break free of the spiritual constraints that had formerly kept it in check.[87]

Perhaps Weber was right to correct himself. But after Foucault's analyses and all the further analyses they have inspired, Weber's model of rationalization seems at best a partial model of discursive dynamics, religious or secular. It seems even more partial as an interpretive schematic of the scriptural scene of instruction in which the principle of the separateness of estates was originally delivered. Read to imply the logical autonomy of political and religious values, the Nazarene's disjunction between Caesar and God would both anticipate and consecrate the modern, Western, and liberal expectation that the twain in question should never meet. Yet, neither the authors nor the canonists of the New Testament give any indication that they understood it to imply any such thing. In this respect, they were of one mind with those early Christians who preferred to martyr themselves instead of declaring their allegiance to Rome. For that matter, they were of one mind with the pagan Romans. "Our" apolitical Christ is not the Christ who had vowed to return to sit at the head of an eternal kingdom (as he does, for example, in the twentieth book of Matthew). If he urged a policy of accommodation, he was far from urging a policy of permanent resignation. No modern cynic, this Christ: his principle of the separateness of estates was not philosophical; it was "pneumo-strategic," and what it suggested as much to those who adhered to it as to those who distrusted it was not a religious rejection of the world but a religious critique of its prevailing powers, at once human and divine. Caesar, after all, did not stand merely for a political empire. He stood also for an imperial pantheon. Rome did not merely enforce the payment of taxes. It also enforced the confession and the worship of its gods. The pagans were thus no fools: this Christ was no more otherworldly than they were; he really was a subversive.

Weber himself demurred from Nietzsche's diagnosis of Christ's appeal as residing in nothing more than a certain pedagogy of *ressentiment* (1946: 270). Most religious historians would now demur from diagnosing it further as residing in a pedagogy of the oppressed. The Nazarene appealed to the semiotically and politically alienated, many of whom were oppressed, but also to many others, perhaps most of whom were without the narrative means to make sense of themselves as mere commoners who were nevertheless enjoying good fortunes. So his appeal endures. His pneumo-strategics was occasionally populist, occasionally proto-socialist. His broader discourse was not, however, a politically dependent discourse. It was instead subsumptive, incorporating what one might now distinguish as a political idiom but subordinating its apparatus of legitimation to another, a "higher court."[88] In the latter, the legitimacy of human interests is always relative to the good. The legitimacy of human beliefs is always relative to the truth. The legitimacy of the exercise of power is always relative to that limit at which goodness, truth, and potency coincide.

Discursively, the Narazene's absolute point of reference is merely one substantive version of what might be called the "transcendental operator" that perhaps distinguishes anything we might be able to recognize or interpret as distinctively religious from institutional talk of other kinds. This anthropologist at least can see no other point of reference, no other operator, from which anything remotely resembling an anthropologically adequate heuristic criterion of what distinguishes religious talk (or, correlatively, religious practice) might proceed. It is a register of holiness or, rather, holiness-as-limit, which from a typical human distance can only appear in Janus-face, which is the poetic face of the sublime: at once dreadful and alluring, polluting and cathartic, grotesque and beautiful, violent and serene. Call it "the sacred," after Durkheim, or "the ultimate," or less plausibly, the "supernatural": the transcendental operator is the register of a discourse that is capable of functioning not merely as a master discourse, a "total" discourse in a sense approximating that which Durkheim mistakenly ascribed to the religious only at its "primitive origins" (1995 [1912]: 423).[89] Hence, perhaps, its appeal to two different, though not mutually exclusive, cadres of the powerful: those (Louis IX, for example, that great Crusader) as confident of their own holiness as of others' corruption; and those (former president Ronald Reagan, that great anti-communist) lacking confidence in the rectitude or constancy of human opinion itself.[90] Their differences aside, both cadres have regularly inclined toward that particular pneumo-strategics that might be called a "spiritual politics," or as Alessandro Pizzorno would have it, an "absolute politics," a politics distinctive for its ritualism, its direct intervention in the definition and production of knowledge, and its energetic assault on "the enemy," internal or external as the case may be (1987: 31–49).

The spiritual objectivism of such a pneumo-strategics resonates in the response that Ms. Roden (who thus proves to be no theological nominalist, and no deconstructionist either) gave to me when I asked her on one occasion how she had managed to sustain her "faith." She said: *for me, it isn't a question of faith; God is present with me*. It resonates further in the absolutism of the counter-politics with which she would confront the liberal (and conservative) constitutionalists of the McLennan County Court:

> *Gentlemen (and judges), the law belongs to God (Lev.).*[91] *You may no longer use it to deceive and oppress the righteous. You may no longer use it to enrich the wicked (Isa. 5:22–24; Isa. 59:9–15). What is the difference between kings and tyrants? Kings of old had no bounds. You were bound by a profoundly religious law, the United States Constitution. You have burst your bounds and, laughing, cast aside God's yoke (Jer. 5:5). You have turned a God-fearing Christian nation into a habitation of devils (Rev. 18:2; Jer. 5:28), a mold of foul spirits (Rev. 18:2; Jer. 5:26), and a cage of unclean and hateful birds (Rev. 18:2; Jer. 5:27).*
>
> *Thomas Jefferson wrote the Declaration of Independence for every American. And for their churches. God caused the Bill of Rights to be written for the same beneficiaries. You have made the First Amendment of no effect by persecuting unto death those who have spoken against you, and by persecuting the Branch Davidian Seventh-day Adventist Church in your courts for over thirty years. You have besmirched the Second Amendment by infringing the right to bear arms. You have quartered a federal agent at my farm and encouraged him to steal and vandalize my property, in violation of the Third Amendment.*
>
> *You have repeatedly stolen documents from the Branch Davidian*

73

Seventh-day Adventist files, in violation of the Fourth Amendment. You have denied hearing, that bedrock of due process, to Branch Davidian Seventh-day Adventist defendants, in violation of the Fifth Amendment. You have delayed trials, tampered with juries, and suborned attorneys to their clients' detriment in prosecutions of Branch Davidian Seventh-day Adventists, in violation of the Sixth Amendment. You have refused jury trial to Branch Davidian Seventh-day Adventists where the law as well as the Seventh Amendment guaranteed jury trial. You have made bail a punishment to Branch Davidian Seventh-day Adventists where you could not bring charges, despite the Eighth Amendment. You have never empowered the Ninth Amendment. As tyrants, the state and federal judiciaries have restricted life, liberty, and the pursuit of happiness by enforcing as law numerous classes of crimes where there are no victims, in defiance of the Tenth Amendment. You have added provisions to the Eleventh Amendment by judicial fiat to protect yourselves from the lawsuits of an outraged citizenry; despite the provisions in the Constitution itself that any amendment of the Constitution may only be made by the combined legislatures of the federal government and the states. How long can they lie to them of their doings (Jer. 9:1–8)?

To the people of Babylon (the United States), I can only say, if you will not read your Bibles, read your Constitution and the Declaration of Independence. Are not these tyrants worse than the kings of old? Let the righteous among you now understand the parable of the bridegroom and the bride (Isa. 61:10–11), for shall not God unite the Jews who walk in His law and the Jews who walk in His Holy Spirit, the descendants of Abraham among the Christians? Shall not God marry His testaments, the Song of Moses and the Song of the Lamb? And shall not this union produce his church? And the one hundred forty-four thousand on Mount Zion, singing with the Lamb? And shall it not bring forth the Kingdom of the Righteous?

The wicked have hid the time from the righteous since the resurrection of Christ was hidden by liars (Matt. 28:1–14), since Peter testified to the Jews and Paul testified to the Gentiles. Was not Peter overcome in Israel, and was not Israel as Egypt for sins after they crucified Christ (Yashua)? Was not Paul overcome in Rome, and was not Rome as Sodom for oppressions (Rev. 11:8)? Having sent living witnesses to Judah (the two tribes), shall not God send living witnesses to Israel (the ten tribes)? Is not Israel still more sinful than Egypt and Babylon (the United States) more oppressive than Sodom? Shall not God judge the nations for the murder of children in a church (Matt. 18:1–14)? And plead with His people that they open their eyes?

*And now to the judges, the scornful men who say in their hearts,
"It is not of God, He shall not bring evil upon us" (Jer. 5:12): Have
you not been judged? Behold, God has sent serpents and cockatrices
among you (Jer. 8:17; Isa. 14:29; Isa. 59:3–5). Babylon is snared and
caught (Jer. 50:24), and her great men are caged as unclean and hate-
ful birds. Babylon is fallen, is fallen and her idols broken unto the
ground (Isa. 21:9; Jer. 5:28).*

*Now hear the verdict of God, you scornful men. Shall not the fifty
days you tormented the righteous children be as a jubilee (Lev. 25:8–
17) to the righteous, and shall not the tyranny of unjust law unjustly
applied be lifted from their backs?*[92] *Shall not the judges of Babylon,
who have sought to destroy civil and religious liberty for over two
hundred years, stand judged? He that is unjust, let him be unjust still:
he that is filthy, let him be filthy still: he that is righteous, let him be
righteous still: he that is holy, let him be holy still (Rev. 22:11).*

*As for me and my church, we will stand as an ensign unto the
righteous (Isa. 11), for we will no longer bear allegiance to those who
serve themselves of us with persecutions, oppressions, and murder.
From henceforth ever, we will serve only God (Yahweh) (Josh.
24:14–15).*

If absolute politics is the politics of the (potential and often actual)
oppressor, and absolute counter-politics typically the politics of the oppressed, both remain politics of alienation in a precise sense. Both have
their threshold at that line in the sand at which interests or platforms no
longer permit adjudication or compromise. Beyond that line, both the
oppressor and the oppressed see the enemy: the "evil empire" and its
minions, external or internal as the case may be. Beyond it, politics can
only take the form of war, or of covert operations, or of mutual con-
tainment. Beyond it, political sensibilities turn toward distrust. Couple
them with the semiotics of suspicion, and the machinics of distinctively
political theories of conspiracy is securely in place. "We" liberal (or
conservative) constitutionalists worry about the "unreasonableness" of
absolute politics, about its ethical abandonment of "responsibility" in
favor of "commitment," its "anti-humanism," its "special" penchant
for coercion, for corporal violence. We are not altogether wrong to do
so. But we should not forget that liberal regimes also need their Others.
They, too, need their "deviants" to remind them of the substantive
values (liberty among them) on which — beyond the empty formalism of
fair procedure — they rest. That deviance is now as frequently deemed
"sick" as it is deemed either "criminal" or "evil" should not lead us to
overlook that it is still the enemy and thus subject to the hyperbolic
demonization that the enemy regularly inspires. Nor should it obscure

that deviance continues, now as ever, to incite, to invite violence, however subtle the mechanisms of the liberal perpetration of it might be. At the very least, it continues — rightly or wrongly — to be subject to the violence of disenfranchisement. Any constitutionalist regime that is generative even of that violence — which is to say, every constitutionalist regime that has ever existed, past or present — is thus productive of the conditions that nourish absolutism. The existential (and other) insecurities of modernity are real enough, but they should not be the waters in which the constitutionalist Pilate seeks to wash his hands of the "fanatic."

Not to deny it: we, who survive, can be deeply relieved not to have been among the riders when certain of the adherents of the sect formerly known as Aum Shinrikyo began with what must be labeled malice aforethought to break open canisters of the nerve gas sarin within the cars and tunnels of the Tokyo subway. We can be just as relieved not to have been among the hundreds who were apparently executed for demanding the return of their fortunes and possessions when the world did not end as a defrocked Ugandan priest had promised. We can profess our horror even at imagining the reluctance of perhaps many of the adults and children assembled at Jonestown to drink the cyanide-laced Kool-Aid that had been brewed for them. We can insist on the horror of adults and children being burned alive at Mount Carmel. Perhaps David Koresh really was a criminal — petty, if his only infraction consisted in his failure to pay taxes, and considerably more than petty (though hardly different from millions of other men, past and present) if he regularly invited pubescent girls to his bed. We have the right to our pieties.

The anthropologist must nevertheless oppose those pieties that allow human (or inhuman) nature — the normal or the pathological — to enter by way of the back door without even so much as a security check. Without necessarily embracing Maurice Halbwachs' argument that suicide is of the same genus as sacrifice, he must wonder whether the suicides of at least some twenty-eight members of the Heaven's Gate community might better be understood as the manifestation not of depression or brainwashing but ritual devotion.[93] And if not those suicides, then perhaps many of the others, more or less witting, that martyrs the world over have found preferable to adopting the gods of an alien empire, to enduring rape or enslavement, to resigning passively in the face of murder or war. As the violation of normatively constituted boundaries, sacrifice and suicide are certainly violent in their own right and no less violent when, as with Buddhist self-immolation, they are committed as a protestation of violence (Faubion 1998b). And is the act of self-immolation any less a ritual protestation when its agent is, in some suitably clinical definition of the term, "depressed"? Should we not heed it, even so? Violence perpetrated against others is perhaps another matter. Yet the religious — even the most politically absolutist of them — hardly have a premium on it, and their penchant for it may be far less systematic than we often demonologically presume. Among the religious, millennialists present a challenge to the census taker. Estimates of the number of millennialist communities merely within the present-day United States vary greatly. Perhaps there are a thousand; perhaps three thousand; perhaps more.[94] The vast majority of such communities actually known to scholars of the past and the present have never perpetrated violence against external others so long as they have been left to their own devices. The cases that we savor with such demonological relish are exceptional cases, the case of an Aum Shinrikyo the most exceptional of all. This stops few of us from regarding them nevertheless as the monstrous rule. And is that just (our) human nature?

At the very least, we, who survive, should also add that we are greatly glad not to have been within the fetid trenches of the Maginot Line; or among the unsuspecting residents of Pearl Harbor, or Dresden, or Hiroshima, or Nagasaki, or Mai Lei; or to have been included in the body counts from Vietnam; or to have been included in the rosters of other bodies, identifiable or beyond identification, that came earlier from the concentration camps at Auschwitz or Dachau; or included in those that have recently come or continue to come from Kosovo, or Chechnya, or Rwanda, or Sri Lanka, or Kashmir, or Cambodia, or Columbia. There, too, but for the grace of some god.

The sixth message is brought forth by Amo Paul Bishop Roden. The message is given in Rev. 14:18: "And another angel came out from the altar, which had power over fire; and cried with a loud cry to him that had the sharp sickle, saying, Thrust in thy sharp sickle, and gather the cluster of the vine of the earth; for her grapes are fully ripe."

Coming from the altar and having power over fire both mark this messenger as a representative of the Holy Spirit. As this is the only place in the Bible where the words "loud cry" occur, it is safe to conclude that this is the loud cry. The grapes being fully ripe indicates that everyone in the Branch Davidian church has enough of an understanding of the message of the church to make an informed decision as to whether they will serve God or Satan. This is true of the Branch now, and will be true of the world at the time of the final judgment.

The sixth messenger is described in Rev. 3:7–13: "And to the angel of the church in Philadelphia write; These things saith he that is holy, he that is true, he that hath the key of David, he that openeth, and no man shutteth; and shutteth, and no man openeth. I know thy works: behold,

77

I have set before thee an open door, and no man can shut it: for thou hast a little strength, and hast kept my word, and hast not denied my name. Behold, I will make them of the synagog of Satan, which say they are Jews, and are not, but do lie; behold, I will make them to come and worship before thy feet, and to know that I have loved thee. Because thou hast kept the word of my patience, I also will keep thee from the hour of temptation, which shall come upon all the world, to try them that dwell upon the earth. Behold, I come quickly: hold that fast which thou hast, that no man take thy crown. Him that overcometh will I make a pillar in the temple of my God, and he shall go no more out: and I will write upon him the name of my God, and the name of the city of my God, which is New Jerusalem, which cometh down out of heaven from my God: and I will write upon him my new name. He that hath an ear, let him hear what the Spirit saith unto the churches."

I am a hard worker, but God opened the door at the Branch Davidian property known as Mount Carmel and God has beaten back every attempt to close this place to the public since August 24, 1993. For my part, I have kept God's law, and given credit to Him for the miracles He has accomplished here. The members of the synagog of Satan are those who lie about me. Rev. 21:8 clearly indicates that ALL *liars have no inheritance in the Kingdom of God.*[95]

Contrary to my critics, I do not lie, steal, or teach abominations.[96] *God could not use someone who did. I have waited on God for three long years, and soon He will let others fight the battle. Those who serve God faithfully (overcome) will be marked by Him for glory.*

Those, too, are fighting words (written in 1997). Beyond their polemics (and, yes, beyond what "we" must see as their overweening arrogance), however, they signal the transformation — yet another Branch Davidian transformation — of the iconic imagery of apocalypse into the determinately indexical imagery of a gnosis, a knowledge of things spiritual, that is also a knowledge of the self, of its spiritual identity and spiritual presence (or in any event, its presence in 1997). Whatever else might be said about them, they are not tantamount to a claim to divinity. Asserting herself to be the "sixth angel," Ms. Roden is reiterating both her election and her inspiration, and perhaps her future salvation, her future immortality. She is not asserting her divinity; "angel" as she understands it is the derivative of the Greek *angelos*, "messenger," a mouthpiece, if of God, not itself a god. She will later clarify that she understands her "cry" to be an "amplification" of the third angel's message — specifically, of Victor Houteff's message that the prophecies recorded in the Bible would be fulfilled first in the church and as a prelude

78

to their fulfillment in the world at large.[97] Her amplification is twofold: literally louder but also antitypically more complete, more consummate.

As O'Leary appropriately observes, authority is yet another of the commonplaces of apocalypse and frequently one of its most troubled. Were Ms. Roden to have rested the authority of her self-identification as the sixth angel solely on her reading of a few of the verses of Revelation, she would surely admit not even to having persuaded — much less convinced — herself. The Millerite (and pre-Millerite) presumption of the unity of Scripture implies, however, that none of the verses or books of the Bible speaks or stands alone. What can thus be said of its verses and its books can be said of its dramatis personae as well. Ms. Roden goes further; in her interpretive practice, she proceeds from the presumption that the fulfillment of the promise of salvation is a unitary and all-encompassing process, a condensation and compression of all the disparate types of the biblical past — its persons, places, events — into an increasingly dense and imbricated whole. Only at the telos of the process does the imbrication, the overlap, assume the character of an identity that is also an essence and an essential presence. Only there is God the plenitude of the Word, and the Word the plenitude of God. The sixth angel has her way to go. Still, she is near and her overlaps accordingly many.

At this interpretive juncture as elsewhere, Ms. Roden remains broadly consistent with the methodology of the Millerites. A literalist at the limit, an ardent analogist, she remains broadly consistent with the typological methodologies that such contemporary theologians as Elliott Johnson (1992) have advocated as well. As she advances in her *lecture de soi*, her interpretive indexicalization of self, she nevertheless gives more free reign to allegorical extrapolation than the more stringent of typologists past or present would easily tolerate. Like Victor Houteff and Ben and Lois Roden before her, she draws often, if selectively, on the descriptive meaning of proper names. She sometimes permits herself to accord an episode a significance — literal or allegorical — at least partially independent of the plot that includes it. A practical interest in self-emplacement governs such a shift of emphasis. So, too — and here, many of the theologians would balk — does the increasing degree to which the extra-textual world, here and now, weighs on the determination of the meaning of the text itself:

Ruth 1:2: "And the name of the man was Elimelech, and the name of his wife Naomi, and the name of his two sons Mahlon and Chilion, Ephrathites of Bethlehemjudah. And they came into the country of Moab, and continued there."[98]

79

Elimelech (My God is King), Naomi (Pleasantness of the Lord), Mahlon (Great Infirmity) and Chilion (Pining, Consuming) are a family with ties to the tribes of both Judah and Ephraim. These are messages rather than messengers, and Elimelech (My God is King) is Ben Roden's message of the restoration of the ceremonial law and judgment of the living. Ben told you he was of the tribe of Judah. Naomi (Pleasantness of the Lord) is Lois Roden's message of the femininity of the Holy Spirit, the Comforter. The Bible tells you that Lois is of the tribe of Ephraim.[99] As the names makes obvious, Mahlon (Great Infirmity) is George Roden's abominable message. None of his siblings Chilion (Pining, Consuming) have [sic] messages at all.

Historically, the somewhat forced marriage between the tribes of Judah in southern Caanan and that of Ephraim and the other "Israelites" in the north was King Saul's original achievement, but it reached its heights with his successor, David. The "United Kingdom," as it is usually known, would endure only a century, but the Davidic theology that Victor Houteff invoked had long guaranteed its restoration. With Ben and Lois Roden, it regains its principles and its house of worship, if not yet its fuller territories. Hence, a *hieros gamos*, a "sacred marriage," fertile in its way, but still short of fecundity.

Restoration would require another marriage, further fruits:

Ruth 1:3–5: "And Elimelech Naomi's husband died; and she was left, and her two sons. And they took them wives of the women of Moab; the name of one was Orpah, and the name of the other Ruth. And Mahlon and Chilion died also both of them; and the woman was left of her two sons and her husband."

Ben's Roden message passes, and so do those of his children.

Ruth 1:6–18: "Then she arose with her daughters in law, that she might return from the country of Moab: for she had heard in the country of Moab how that the Lord had visited his people in giving them bread. Wherefore she went forth out of the place where she was, and her two daughters in law with her; and they went on the way to return to the land of Judah. And Naomi said unto her two daughters in law, Go return each to her mother's house: the Lord deal kindly with you, as ye have dealt with the dead, and with me. The Lord grant that ye may find rest, each of you in the house of her husband. Then she kissed them; and they lifted up their voice and wept. And they said unto her, Surely we will return with thee unto thy people. And Naomi said, Turn again, my daughters: why will ye go with me? are there yet any more sons in my womb, that they may be your husbands? Turn again, my daughters, go your way, for I am too old to have an husband. If I should say, I have hope, if I should have an husband also to night, and should also bear sons; would you tarry for them till they were grown? would ye stay for them from having husbands? nay, my daughters, for it grieveth me much for your sakes that the hand of the Lord is gone out against me. And they lifted up their voice, and wept again: and Orpah kissed her mother in law; but Ruth clave unto her. And she said, Behold, thy sister in law is gone back unto her people, and unto her gods: return thou after thy sister in law. And Ruth said, Intreat me not to leave thee, or to return from following after thee: for whither thou goest, I will go; and where thou lodgest, I will lodge: thy people shall be my people, and thy God my God: Where thou diest, will I die, and there will I be buried: the Lord do so to me, and more also, if ought but death part thee and me. When she saw that she was steadfastly minded to go with her, then she left speaking unto her."[100]

Of the family, one daughter-in-law remains absolutely faithful to the message.[101] *She is parted from her family to follow it. This is Ruth, the earthly woman who represents the Holy Spirit.*

Ruth 1:19–22: "So they two went until they came to Bethlehem. And it came to pass, when they were come to Bethlehem, that all the city was moved about them, and they said, Is this Naomi? And she said unto them, Call me not Naomi, call me Mara: for the Almighty hath dealt very bitterly with me. I went out full, and the Lord hath brought me home empty: why then ye call me Naomi, seeing the Lord hath testified against me, and the Almighty hath afflicted me? So Naomi returned, and Ruth the Moabitess, her daughter in law, with her, which returned out of the country of Moab: and they came to Bethlehem in the beginning of the barley harvest."

Sadly enough, no Roden is left in the message; Lois Roden's entire family has been lost. This is bitterness. Ruth comes to the Kingdom at the beginning of the barley harvest, Passover 1993. The executive phase of the judgment of the living and the gathering of the righteous has begun.

The biblical Ruth is the grandmother of King David, and the book bearing her name thus a documentation of David's "cosmopolitan" heritage; the Moabites were not Jews. Ruth is also a person of the most uncommon loyalties: she is a Moabite devoted to an Ephrathite, a Jewess; she is a Gentile devoted to the god of the Jews; she is a daughter-in-law devoted to her mother-in-law (Hayes 1971: 106, 273). Lois Roden, the antitypical Naomi, died in 1988. Only her message could thus return to its antitypical kingdom in the spring of 1993. Nor was its return merely spiritual. Among the many items that her daughter-in-law maintained on the tables and boards she initially set up at Mount Carmel were several of Lois Roden's tracts. Among the far fewer items that she has continued to display since the destruction of her exhibits in 1997 are several hundred pages of Lois Roden's collected letters and lessons.

So, then, Amo is aware of her virtues. She is also aware of her failings and of their consequences. This, too, is an aspect of her gnosis, and her confession of it is a humbling of the self that is at once an atonement and a catharsis. Employing a secular idiom, she finds the means to satirize herself. Recalling her life in 1989: *I always knew that I was too horny to be a saint. Back in those days, I parted my hair in the middle and washed it every day for a round-faced brillo-pad look.*[102] Resorting to a secular idiom, she turns the obligation to witness upon herself. She "martyrs" herself—but never in the interest of her own salvation alone. In this idiom, when speaking of herself she always also speaks as a martyr of, and for, her church:

> *Jer. 2:20–25: "For of old time I have broken thy yoke, and burst thy bonds; and thou saidst, I will not transgress; when upon every high hill and under every green vine thou wanderest, playing the harlot. Yet I had planted thee a noble vine, wholly a right seed: how then art thou turned into the degenerate plant of a strange vine unto me? For though thou wash thee with nitre, and take thee much sope, yet thine iniquity is marked before me, saith the Lord God. How canst thou say, I am not polluted, I have not gone after Baalim? See thy way in the valley, know what thou hast done: thou art a swift dromedary traversing her ways; A wild ass used to the wilderness that snuffeth up the wind at her pleasure; in her occasion who can turn her away? all that seek her shall not weary themselves, in her month they shall find her. Withold thy foot from being unshod, and thy throat from thirst: but thou saidst, There is no hope: no, for I have loved strangers, and after them will I go."*[103]
>
> *This is a harsh rebuke to me for sexual promiscuity and lack of faith in God.*[104] *In my time of trouble in 1984, I married* [my second husband] *after living with him for three weeks.* [He] *was anti-Christian and a wicked man. The full rebuke is Jer. 13:15–27. This is the reason that the church refused even to hear me at the Solemn Assembly in October, 1994.*

In the late summer of 1994, during the course of my third conversation with Ms. Roden, I learned of the plan for the autumn convocation of a "Solemn Assembly" at Mount Carmel that was expected to draw some two hundred Branch Davidians from as far away as South Carolina and Pennsylvania. I asked if I might attend as an observer. Ms. Roden paused for a moment, then said that I might, that there would likely "be enough room." I did not leave her hesitation unremarked but did not let it inhibit me from traveling to Mount Carmel for the event. I was simply pleased that I could pay it during a mid-semester university vacation and would not have to rearrange my schedule of classes. Mount Carmel was golden and sunlit when I arrived. On a knoll at some distance from the ruins of the compound stood a large open-air tent, which sheltered several rows of folding chairs and a small pulpit. Scattered around it were several smaller tents, portable residences of the more temporary congregants. Not until I had made my way to the informational exhibit did I notice a large sign that had been posted at the roadside announcing that holy observances were in progress and that the public would again be welcome the following week. I shrugged off my gaffe as one of those typical missteps of fieldwork and began to seek out Ms. Roden. The crowd in whose midst I found myself did not approach two hundred, but it was unusually diverse: several of its members were African-American and a few evidently foreign; women slightly outnumbered men; the middle class appeared to be the dominant class. I was not the object of undue attention and certainly not of unfriendliness — for awhile. I was having little luck locating Ms. Roden and so tried to make myself as unobtrusive as possible while the tent was readied to house a liturgical service. The rabbinical-looking man whom I would learn only a few months later to be Charles Pace summoned an audience. I decided to take advantage of the minutes preceding the commencement of the service to approach a woman who had quickly taken her place in the rearmost row of shaded seats. I asked her if she knew where Ms. Roden might be. She graciously directed me to the tiny office that sat at the perimeter of the exhibition. Peering through its screen door, I did indeed see Ms. Roden — lying on a cot in a posture so obviously distraught that I could not bring myself to disturb her. I subsequently conceived of writing her a brief note apologizing for the inappropriateness of my having imposed myself at a private affair and proposing that I return another day. I enclosed a small monetary donation with it and asked the woman whom I had previously approached if she would mind delivering it when Ms. Roden arose and was feeling better. She said that she would be happy to do so. Mr. Pace happened to observe our exchange. He asked the woman what I had given her. When she answered, he asked her why I was not delivering the note myself. She told him that I did not want to disturb Ms. Roden while she was resting. Then he asked to see the note. He read it. Without looking at me directly, speaking to the messenger instead, he said, "Oh, a reporter. Go ahead, let him pay for what he wants to know from her." I would not learn until sometime later that Mr. Pace had been instrumental in debarring Ms. Roden from the pulpit that very day; the two were having a decided falling-out. He was far from interested in arranging for her to be interviewed. At the time, I was simply taken aback by such sudden hostility. I suppressed an unseemly urge to flee, lingering beyond the margins of the tent for several minutes after Mr. Pace began his sermon. I have no memory of what he said. From that day—that Day of Atonement—forward, I would learn what I could of Branch Davidian lives other than Ms. Roden's own largely from indirect and secondary sources.

The bearing of witness now transpires within many scenes of instruction—juridical, aesthetic, even anthropological. As an articulation and objectification of the experience of the world, or of the world itself, as a speaking of the truth, it might simply be cathartic. It need not even be that. Its regulative morality might be purely deontological; one might cogently bear witness simply because one must. Witnessing thus requires a certain liberty but only the barest modicum of it—the liberty to say what one believes to be true, even if only to oneself. It might remain a cogent practice even in the absence of any use, any reformist or remedial effect. Its wit might be tragic; its burden is the burden of every Cassandra. For all her sense of the tragic, however, Ms. Roden is not a witness merely for its own sake. Much less does she fashion herself a Cassandra. The limits of her predestinarianism are already implicit in Pauline typology itself. For Paul as for Ms. Roden, biblical types point to a future, but as "ensamples" they point also to our responsibility at least to try to live up to it, actively to become the part that we would play in a script we have been given in advance. If the Pauline witness is thus a dutiful witness, he or she is also a critic, counselor, and practical advisor:

> Jer. 2:26–30: "As the thief is ashamed when he is found, so is the house of Israel ashamed; they, their kings, their princes, and their priests and their prophets. Saying to a stock, Thou art my father; and to a stone, Thou hast brought me forth: for they have turned their back unto me, and not their face: but in the time of their trouble they will say, Arise and save us. But where are the gods that thou hast made thee? Let them arise, if they can save thee in the time of thy trouble: for according to the number of thy cities are thy gods, O Judah. Wherefore will ye plead with me? Ye all have transgressed against me, saith the Lord. In vain have I smitten your children; they received no correction: your own sword hath devoured your prophets, like a destroying lion."
>
> The whole church is held guilty of idolatry and transgression against God. He used me as a sword against you; through the entire moral lesson God is teaching, he has pitted one member of the church

against another. They are even accused of complicity in the death of their leaders.

Jer. 2:31–37: "O generation, see ye the word of the Lord. Have I been a wilderness unto Israel? A land of darkness? Wherefore say my people, We are lords, we will come no more unto thee? Can a maid forget her ornaments, or a bride her attire? Yet my people have forgotten me days without number. Why trimmest thou thy way to seek love? Therefore hast thou also taught the wicked ones thy ways. Also in thy skirts is found the blood of the souls of poor innocents: I have not found it by secret search but upon all these. Yet thou sayest, Because I am innocent, surely his anger shall turn from me. Behold, I will plead with thee, because thou sayest, I have not sinned. Why gaddest thou about so much to change thy way? Thou also shall be ashamed of Egypt, as thou wast ashamed of Assyria. Yea, thou shalt go forth from him, and thine hands upon thine head: for the Lord hath rejected thy confidences, and thou shalt not prosper in them."

Here God finds us all guilty of relying on ourselves rather than upon him; and of forgetting him. Also, most of us are guilty of unchastity and abortion. He pleads with the whole generation of the church because they claim innocence. He predicts that you who depend on the powerful to sustain you now will be ashamed as you were of your former ties with the government. He reminds you that you were formerly arrested at Mount Carmel.

There is, moreover, hardly a more colorfully brutal biblical mode of critique, of counsel, of practical advice than the mode of the jeremiad, which makes up for what it lacks of apocalyptic Wisdom with an unrivaled imagistic arsenal of accusation and reprimand. The historical Jeremiah was active between the seventh and the sixth centuries B.C.E., a recognized sermonist from an established priestly family and an adamant defender of Yahwism against the syncretic and "oriental" devotionalism of the Judah and Jerusalem of which he was such a virtuoso witness (Hayes 1971: 204–8). He was not always the friend of the Israelite kings. Indeed, he was a concerted contrarian and frequently suffered punishment and ridicule. Like the other Israelite prophets, however, he occupied a role that was at once socially approved and sacrally protected. His ancient counterparts could be found among several of the other societies bordering the eastern Mediterranean; anthropologists have met (and still might often meet) his more recent counterparts among the peoples of sub-Saharan Africa, among the indigenous peoples of the American Southwest, in Taiwan, and elsewhere. We permit only secular prophets within the walls of our regnant regime of truth. However, Jeremiah's denunciations retain some of their ancient force. As for going forth with one's hands upon his or her head, as for arrests — yes, there have been more than a few at the Texan Mount Carmel. In the months following the conflagration, five of the nine Koreshites who had survived were held on charges ranging from conspiracy to commit murder to the use of a gun in the commission of a crime; seven other Koreshites, who had not been inside the compound when the fire erupted, were taken into custody on similar charges.[105] Ms. Roden would once again find herself being taken briefly into custody as well, once for breaching the fence that surrounded the ruins of the compound, which had been put under quarantine due to lead contamination, another time for firing a gun during a hostile encounter with several adversary Branch Davidians. Her first transgression cost her a fine of $85 for disorderly conduct.[106] The second led to an arraignment, but the case was soon dismissed.[107]

Not that Ms. Roden thinks herself undeserving of any punishment whatever. The critic, the counselor, the advisor has the voice of the text as her own critic, her own counselor, her own advisor:

> *Jer. 3:6–11: "And the Lord said also unto me in the days of Josiah the king, Hast thou seen that which backsliding Israel hath done? She is gone upon every high mountain and under every green tree, and there hath played the harlot. And I said after she had done all these things, Turn thou unto me. But she returned not. And her treacherous sister Judah saw it. And I saw, when for all the causes whereby backsliding Israel committed adultery I had put her away, and given her a bill of divorce; yet her treacherous sister Judah feared not, but went and played the harlot also. And it came to pass through the lightness of her whoredom, that she defiled the land, and committed adultery with stones and with stocks. And yet for all this her treacherous sister Judah hath not turned unto me with her whole heart, but feignedly, saith the Lord. And the Lord said unto me, The backsliding Israel hath justified herself more than the treacherous Judah."*[108]
>
> *Israel (Amo Paul Bishop Roden) loses God's protection for harlotry.*[109] *Judah (the followers of David Koresh) loses God's protection for idolatry because they make an idol of David even as they continue to claim that they follow God. God chooses between sinners on the basis of willingness to obey his voice.*
>
> *Jer. 3:12–13: "Go and proclaim these words toward the north, and say, Return thou backsliding Israel, saith the Lord, and I will not keep mine anger forever. Only acknowledge thine iniquity, that thou hast transgressed against the Lord thy God, and has scattered thy ways to the stranger under every green tree, and ye have not obeyed my voice, saith the Lord."*

All this I have done.

Jer. 4: 1–2: "If thou wilt return, O Israel, saith the Lord, return unto me: and if thou wilt put away thine abominations out of my sight, then thou shalt not remove. And thou shalt swear, the Lord liveth, in truth, in judgment, and in righteousness; and the nations shall bless themselves in him, and in him shall they glory."[110]

I have returned and sworn to do nothing except on orders from God. The reformation of the church is seen here.

In the Hebraic tradition, prophecy precedes apocalypse by several centuries. The prophet is less world-historical in his purview than the writer of apocalypse. His division between the elect and the damned is far less pronounced because he primarily speaks to the elect alone. His is thus an endogenous critique, a warning to the wayward blessed. As text, biblical prophecy might thus seem ambiguous in its register, or at least larger than its mark. Its accusations are general; its figures are pluralities. Historically, however, prophecy was delivered as an oral sermon or posted proclamation. Its first dimension is performative, and as performative, its prevailing figure is the figure of hyperbole, a sublime figure, and most often in Jeremiah, a representation of its grotesque side. It reminds its audience of their collective responsibility for the sin among them while it reminds each member of the audience of the impact of his or her sins on the condition of the collectivity as a whole. It is thus an individualizing and a totalizing figure and as such provides the primary avenue for Ms. Roden's witnessing of the church in the self and the self in a church conceived as the house of the elect, even if a house whose residents do not all have equal right to dwell in it.

In her witnessing, the Book of Jeremiah has a special importance for at least two reasons. The first is that it serves largely as an auxiliary in the writings of the elder Rodens: both cite it frequently, but neither seems to have thought it in need of an exegesis as systematic as that of the books of Daniel and Revelation, or of such prophetic books as those of Ezekiel, Zechariah, and Isaiah; it is thus left without full light. The second is that it is the most systematically and volubly "judgmental" of any of the books of the major prophets: Ms. Roden has also undertaken exegeses of the books of such minor prophets as Joel, Micah, Haggai, and Amos, but in Jeremiah she sees the most complete typification of a judgment of the church that her predecessors had foreseen only in a darker glass. For Ms. Roden, the light of Jeremiah is a light much closer to the end of the ultimate tunnel:

Jer. 4:3–4: "For thus saith the Lord to the men of Judah and Jerusalem, Break up your fallow ground, and sow not among thorns. Circumcise yourselves to the Lord, and take away the foreskins of your heart, ye men of Judah and inhabitants of Jerusalem: lest my fury come forth like fire, and burn that none can quench it, because of the evil of your doings."

You who followed David are advised to become husbandmen rather than scatterers of the message. You make a decision that shows no pity, and send the government to persecute me so that I can't raise the church that refused David against you.

Jer. 4:5–10: "Declare ye in Judah, and publish in Jerusalem; and say, Blow ye the trumpet in the land: cry, gather together, and say, Assemble yourselves, and let us go into the defenced cities. Set up the standard toward Zion: retire, stay not: for I will bring evil from the north, and a great destruction. The lion has come up from his thicket, and the destroyer of the Gentiles is on his way; he has gone forth from his place to make thy land desolate; and thy cities shall be laid waste, without an inhabitant. For this gird you with sackcloth, lament and howl: for the fierce anger of the Lord is not turned back from us. And it shall come to pass at that day, saith the Lord, that the heart of the king shall perish, and the heart of the princes; and the priests shall be astonished, and the prophets shall wonder. Then said I, Ah, Lord God! Surely thou hast greatly deceived this people and Jerusalem, saying, Ye shall have peace, whereas the sword reacheth unto the soul."

I begin to circulate the Sixth Angel's message in the spring of 1992. I am so poor that I only send ten copies. You who follow David Koresh realize that you have offended the government, and begin to fear them.

Jer. 4:11–12: "At that time it will be said to this people and to Jerusalem, A dry wind of the high places in the wilderness toward the daughter of my people, not to fan, nor to cleanse, Even a full wind from those places shall come unto me; now also will I give sentence against them."

Day after day, the government releases gas upwind of my house; for this God sentences you. As a result of this persecution, George Roden's daughter is taken away from me.

Or the darkness at the end of the tunnel, as the case may be. Ms. Roden has frequently speculated that the Koreshites were in collusion with the government — specifically with the CIA — before running afoul of it.[111] She has long suspected that both were actively harassing her. The anthropologist cannot confirm that the miasmata she senses in the prairie air have the source she ascribes to them. He can at least confirm that, if only as a spectral and "key" symbol, such miasmata have had their effect on her body and well-being. Taken in, negatively internalized, they have become the stuff of genuine poison.

Ms. Roden did indeed lose custody of her daughter, who was removed from her after the second of two hearings convened to review allegations of neglect. Ms. Roden vehemently denies that she was a poor caretaker. She has, however, also told the anthropologist that her solitude is ordained, that it would have been impossible at once to be a good mother and to carry out the mission to which she has been appointed. She tells him further that it was in fact her daughter who pronounced the ordination—a report of the first of the divine messages that she would receive. Since then, the child has lived under the guardianship of one of her maternal aunts.

However ordained, Ms. Roden's loss would not be without its consequences for those who forced her to suffer it. Her determinations speak largely for themselves:

Jer. 4:13: "Behold, he shall come up as clouds, and his chariots shall be as a whirlwind: his horses are swifter than eagles. Woe unto us! For we are spoiled."

The assault on the Branch Davidian compound begins.

Jer. 4:14: "O Jerusalem, wash thine heart from wickedness that thou mayest be saved. How long shall thy vain thoughts lodge within thee?"

I turn to man's courts for justice in the theft of my daughter, only to find myself driving them to greater corruption to cover up what they have done.

Jer. 4:15–16: "For a voice declareth from Dan, and publisheth from Mount Ephraim. Make ye mention to the nations; behold, publish against Jerusalem, that watchers come from a far country, and give out their voice against the cities of Judah."[112]

George Roden and I meet the press over the standoff. I am trying to expose how David took over the church, and the theft of my daughter . . . George is saying that the followers of David Koresh are getting what they deserve. The media take the story of the standoff to the world.

Jer. 4:17–18: "As keepers of the field, are they against her round about; because she hath been rebellious against me, saith the Lord. Thy ways and thy doings have procured these things unto thee, this is thy wickedness, because it is bitter, because it reacheth unto thine heart."

Jer. 12:7–12: "I have forsaken mine house, I have left behind mine heritage; I have given the dearly beloved of my soul into the hands of her enemies.[113] *Mine heritage is unto me as a lion in the forest; it crieth out against me: therefore have I hated it. Mine heritage is unto me as a speckled bird, the birds round about are against her; come ye, assemble all the beasts of the field, come to devour. Many pastors* have destroyed my vineyard, they have trodden my portion under foot, they have made my pleasant portion a desolate wilderness: for the sword of the Lord shall devour from one end of the land even to the other end of the land: no flesh shall have peace."

I have gone from my house because I could not keep the persecutors out at night, become estranged from my family because I couldn't tell them about the persecution, and lost my beloved because I would not acknowledge the lies used to take her; the Lord forbade me to do so. The second hearing saw all the hypocrites and perjurers fighting against me. The church is trampled underfoot for false interpreters, and so the spoilers (FBI) have come to devour her. Our ways have brought these punishments upon us.

Jer. 4:31: "For I have heard a voice of a woman in travail, and the anguish as of her that bringeth forth her first child, the voice of the daughter of Zion, that bewaileth herself, that spreadeth her hands, saying, Woe is me now! For my soul is wearied because of murderers."

This, the persecution that sought to take my life, is the reason for God's judgment on the followers of David Koresh.

Jer. 5:25–29: "Your iniquities have turned away these things, and your sins have withholden good things from you. For among my people are found wicked men: they lay wait, as he that setteth snares; they set a trap, they catch men. As a cage is full of birds, so are their houses full of deceit: therefore they are become great, and waxen rich. They are waxen fat, they shine: yea, they overpass the deeds of the wicked: they judge not the cause, the cause of the fatherless, yet they prosper; and the right of the needy they do not judge. Shall I not visit for these things? saith the Lord: Shall not my soul be avenged on a nation such as this?"[114]

Here is the worst of your sins, that you accepted wicked men among you. Because you did, the fatherless child of George Roden was poisoned in her yard by the people whom you sent to kill her destitute mother.

Jer. 5:30–31: "A wonderful and horrible thing is committed in the land; the prophets prophesy falsely, and the priests bear rule by their means; and my people love to have it so: and what will ye do in the end thereof?"

David Koresh led his followers astray, and they loved him. How else could it end?

Jer. 6:1: "O ye children of Benjamin, gather yourselves to flee out of the midst of Jerusalem, and blow the trumpet in Tekoa, and set up a sign of fire in Bethhaccerem: for evil appeareth out of the north, and great destruction."

The federal agents are told to gather together to flee the fire with *the hostages; their tents are aroused for the assault; the hospital in Dallas is warned to expect burn victims.*[115]

Jer. 6:22–25: "Thus saith the Lord, Behold, a people cometh from the north country, and a great nation shall be raised from the sides of the earth. They shall lay hold on bow and spear; they are cruel and have no mercy; their voice roareth like the sea; and they ride upon horses, set in array as men for war against thee, O daughter of Zion. We have heard the fame thereof: our hands wax feeble: anguish hath taken hold of us, and pain, as of a woman in travail. Go not forth into the field, nor walk by the way; for the sword of the enemy and fear is on every side."[116]

The siege is here described in its fearfulness.

Jer. 6:26: "O daughter of my people, gird thee in sackcloth, and wallow thyself in ashes: make thee mourning, as for an only son, most bitter lamentation: for the spoiler shall suddenly come upon us."

Who could help crying over the loss of righteous children?

Jer. 6:27: "I have set thee for a tower and a fortress among my people, that thou mayest know and try their way."

Micah 4:8: "And thou, O tower of the flock, the strong hold of the daughter of Zion, unto thee shall it come, even the first dominion; the kingdom shall come to the daughter of Jerusalem."

The first dominion is the Garden of Eden. My farm, even though choked with briars and thorn trees, is like unto the Garden of Eden in its thirty fruit trees and twenty nut trees, grapes, and berries. The fortress is my stronghold on Mount Carmel, where God has founded Zion, the Kingdom of God.

Jer. 8:6–7: "I hearkened and heard, but they spake not aright: no man repented him of his wickedness, saying, What have I done? Every one turned to his course, as the horse rusheth into battle. Yea, the stork in the heaven knoweth her appointed times; and the turtle and the swallow and the crane observe the time of their coming; but my people know not the judgment of the Lord."[117]

In the Mount Carmel tragedy, God founded Zion. Should his church be blind to it?

Jer. 8:8–9: "How do ye say, We are wise, and the law of the Lord is with us? Lo, certainly in vain made he it; the pen of the scribes is in vain. The wise men are ashamed, they are dismayed and taken: lo, they have rejected the word of the Lord; and what wisdom is in them?"

The whole church has rejected Bible truth; all their work is in vain.

Jer. 8:10–12: "Therefore will I give their wives unto others, and their fields to them that shall inherit them: for every one from the least even unto the greatest is given unto covetousness, from the prophet even unto the priest every one dealeth falsely. For they have healed the hurt of the daughter of my people slightly, saying, Peace, peace; when there was no peace. Were they ashamed when they had committed abomination? Nay, they were not at all ashamed, neither could they blush: therefore shall they fall down among them that fall; in the time of their visitation they shall be cast down, saith the Lord."

God threatens the lives of the whole apostate church; everyone would take a blessing that is not his. The death decree has fallen on the prominent women of the church because Lois Roden's work strongly suggests that a woman Holy Spirit messenger will follow her. This woman has been persecuted by the government since November, 1991. Meanwhile, the men of the church, who claim to represent the Holy Spirit, publish peace because only the women are persecuted. This is an abomination in God's eyes.

Jer. 8:13: "I will surely consume them, saith the Lord: there shall be no grapes on the vine, nor figs on the fig tree, and the leaf shall fade; and the things that I have given them shall pass away from them."[118]

The end-time church will be stripped clean of members because they refused the Kingdom of God.

Jer. 8:14–15: "Why do we sit still? Assemble yourselves and let us enter the defenced cities, and let us be silent there: for the Lord God hath put us to silence, and given us water of gall to drink, because we have sinned against the Lord. We looked for peace, but no good came; and for a time of health, and behold trouble."

God has rebuked you: How can you expect peace and health in the time of Jacob's trouble?

Jer. 8:16: "The snorting of his horses was heard from Dan; the whole land trembled at the sound of the neighing of his strong ones; for they are come, and have devoured the land, and all that is in it; the city and those that dwell therein."

The viper from Dan has frightened the horses to unseat the riders.[119]

Gen. 49:16–18: "Dan shall judge his people as one of the tribes of Israel. Dan shall be a serpent by the way, an adder in the path, that biteth the horses' heels, so that his rider shall fall backward. I have waited for thy salvation, O Lord."

These horsemen are they that devoured David Koresh's church.

Jer. 8:17: "For behold, I will send serpents, cockatrices, among you, which will not be charmed,"

Lois Roden was the serpent's root; Amo Paul Bishop Roden is the serpent's branch; [her daughter], the fruit of the cockatrice George Roden, is also the serpent's fruit.

"and they shall bite you, saith the Lord."
And we did.

Though not an unremitting predestinarian, not a fatalist, Ms. Roden is
a cosmological essentialist. She believes that what is yet to happen cannot in every respect be predicted in advance, that it depends among
many other things on whether human beings choose or refuse to obey
the dictates of God. She believes as much that what has already happened had to have happened, that what has actually occurred must necessarily have occurred. She expresses her position narratively, not axi-
omatically, and is thus able to avoid the inevitable air of paradox
that has lingered in the work of those more axiomatic essentialists, neo-
Aristotelian or Augustinean or Kantian, who have explicitly attempted
to reconcile their determinism with the apparent freedom of the will.
Yet — as many readers will surely already have noticed — even she labors
with a certain double vision. She sees a past that is written in stone, that
had to be what it came to be. She sees the present and the future, however, as still somewhat open, though less and less open as they approach
their telos. She is thus an interpretive heir of both the ancient Hellenes
and the Jews. Homeric epic and its oracular and tragic companions are
as "biopic" as Judaic prophecy and apocalyptic. For Hellenes and Jews
alike, biopic narrative is a cardinal pedagogical vehicle for emphasizing
not only the gap between the human and the divine vantage but also the
hubris of conflating the two. For both, it teaches the virtue of epistemological humility. Especially in its Judaic realizations, it further
teaches the virtue of epistemological attentiveness to the divine, to those
of its dictates and truths that might be known, the neglect of which fills
the larger catalog of sins. Far more clearly in its Judaic than Hellenic
realizations, biopic narrative owes its coherence not to any mechanistic
determinism but, once again, to the performative logic of the promise,
of the divine willing that establishes necessity without being subject to
it. It thus rests in the metaphysics of a promise that will and must be
fulfilled, but the fulfillment of which is fraught with any number of
provisos and delays. It establishes a future as the object not of perfect
prediction but instead as the far less certain, far more enigmatic object
of expectation.

Writing in 1997, with an eye toward her own future, Ms. Roden
would find an index in the pious Zerubbabel:

*Zech. 4:1–3: "And the angel that talked with me came again, and
waked me, as a man that is wakened out of his sleep, and said unto
me, What seest thou? And I said, I have looked, and behold a candlestick all of gold, with a bowl upon the top of it, and his seven lamps*

93

thereon, and seven pipes to the seven lamps, which are on the top thereof: and two olive trees by it, one upon the right side of the bowl, and the other on the left side thereof."

V.T. Houteff has drawn a picture of this vision, in which he identifies the main candlestick as the purified church, the bowl as the spirit of prophecy, the olive trees as the Old and New Testament, the seven pipes as the ministry, and the seven lamps as the laity. His work shows how truth will come to the congregation of the churches that establish the Kingdom.

Zech. 4:4–6: "So I answered and spake to the angel that talked with me, saying, What are these, my Lord? And the angel that talked with me answered and said unto me, Knowest thou not what these be? And I said, No, my Lord. Then he answered and spake unto me, saying, This is the word of the Lord unto Zerubbabel, saying, Not by might, nor by power, but by my spirit, saith the Lord of hosts."

The bowl, the spirit of prophecy, is the word of the Lord to Zerubbabel; a stream of Bible truth is the means that the Lord has chosen, rather than might or power, to accomplish his work. Zerubbabel is chosen also to be a sign to God's people of the time of the end.[120] Zerubbabel is a person, a personification of the Holy Spirit, and one of the seven spirits of God.

Zech. 4:7: "Who art thou, O great mountain? Before Zerubbabel thou shalt become a plain: and he shall bring forth the headstone thereof with shouting, crying, Grace, grace unto it."

The mountain is the church, which has been an insurmountable obstacle to Zerubbabel; now they shall lie down in her place.

Isa. 51:22–23: "Behold, I have taken out of thine hand the cup of trembling, even the dregs of the cup of my fury; thou shalt no more drink it again: but I will put it in the hand of them that afflict thee; which have said to thy soul, Bow down, that we may go over: and thou hast laid thy body as the ground, and as the street, to them that went over."[121]

Zerubbabel has done everything that humility could do to try to restore the church to a proper attention to the end-time harvest; now God helps her. That God is pacified toward her before she drinks the dregs of the cup of his wrath possibly explains why the death decree which she has endured for over three years has not succeeded in killing her. The return of Christ, the headstone of the corner of God's temple of lively stones, is to be announced by Zerubbabel.[122]

Zech. 4:8–10: "Moreover the word of the Lord came unto me, saying, The hands of Zerubbabel have laid the foundation of this house; his hands shall also finish it; and thou shalt know that the Lord of hosts has sent me unto you. For who hath despised the day *of small things? for they shall rejoice, and shall see the plummet in the hand of Zerubbabel with those seven; they are the eyes of the Lord, which run to and fro through the whole earth."*

The foundation of the Kingdom is the sixth angel's message.[123]

Isa. 51:16: "And I have put my words in thy mouth, and I have covered thee in the shadow of mine hand [messenger unrecognized], that I may plant the heavens, and lay the foundations of the earth, and say unto Zion, thou art my people."

The implication is that Zerubbabel will write not only the sixth message, but also the seventh. The judgment that Zerubbabel be slain with the sword (Eze. 23:10) has apparently been removed. Those who are willing to take the work from a small beginning shall rejoice. They will see the plummet, the white stone, the Holy Daughter, in Zerubbabel's hand; they will see the seven spirits of God.

As descendant of David and governor of Jerusalem in the later sixth century B.C.E., the historical Zerubbabel joined the priest Joshua in overseeing the rebuilding of the Temple that had been destroyed during the Babylonian conquest some half century before (Hayes 1971: 268–69). Zechariah was the most bold of his prophetic contemporaries in proclaiming both the messianic duumvirate of the restored, eternal kingdom of Davidic theology (Hayes 1971: 269). For Ms. Roden, who here as at many other junctures has abandoned the constraints of gender in her quest for types and antitypes, the Zerubbabel whom she has become must thus be expected to fulfill not simply her penultimate but also her more exhaustive messianic, or angelic, task. She must remain to "write" the seventh message. The crier, the governor, must, however, finally be an amanuensis — for another. Ms. Roden has herself never claimed the identity of the seventh angel. She claims instead to have succeeded in identifying him — or her. After several years of resistance, the woman whom Ms. Roden has accordingly hailed has recently acknowledged the call. Yet another Branch Davidian index — if only one of several competing versions — is thus nearly complete. And gnosis with it.

But then again, not quite.

Sabbath, April 24, 1999

Dear Dr. James,

I hope you will forgive me for taking the liberty of addressing you as I think of you.

As you know (I think I told you), the message God sends through me just keeps flowing. You did ask me to send the continuance along. I am therefore enclosing "Messiah and Elijah, The Second Coming," the scriptural promise of the announcement of the Second Coming (as a Thief) and the seven Spirits of God. I also have rewritten "Unsealing the Thunders" because I thought the last page was pretty limp. After I wrote it, God showed me that the unsealing of the Book of Daniel was the type and put me in a position to show from both the thunders and the seals that the revelation was to be the meaning of the prophecy of the Bible.

I have also understood myself to be antitypical Elijah on Mount Carmel confronted with the prophets of Baal (professional liars about God).

Well, I knew that already; I wrote about it in the tract "The Elijah Message." But now God has given me light on the twelve dousings with water poured on the altar before God sets it aflame. I am to relate them to the attempts to stop me:

1. My arrest in July 1993.
2. My first arrest in July 1994.
3. My second arrest in July 1994.
4. My arrest in November 1994.
5. Locking up the display and robbing the office of typewriter, pictures, tapes and cash in November 1994.
6. Looting the religious literature and artifacts from the locked museum in December 1994. Clinton re-elected.
7. Arson of the museum complex in January 1997.
8. My arrest in August 1997.
9. Tearing down the information pavilion in March 1998.
10. Death threats and breaking of displays by [a man I can identify by name] in April 1998.
11. Tearing apart the display structure in August (?) 1998.
12. Tearing apart rebuilt display structure and theft of displays, November (?) 1998.

As you see, God might light this anytime. Tell V. and W. to hurry.
                                                          Love, Amo

Ms. Roden's letter came about six months after William Dull and Victoria Mukerji visited Mount Carmel in order to explore the possibility of producing a documentary on what had become of the Branch Davidians and of Branch Davidianism in the aftermath of the conflagration. The anthropologist provided them with an introduction but could not accompany them. They returned to Houston with several of Ms. Roden's latest writings; occupied with teaching and the usual array of "urgent" projects, the anthropologist was at last prompted to read them at the letter's direction.

The prophet Malachi (4:5–6) foretold that Elijah, his distant predecessor, would return to proclaim the coming of the Messiah and the gathering of the Kingdom. The authors of the Gospels of the New Testament understood him to have been reincarnated as, or antitypically fulfilled in, the person of John the Baptist (Hayes 1971: 342). In her earlier writings, Ms. Roden had never ventured to cast herself as John's successor and consummation. What she has written from the spring of 1998 forward is consistent in its assertions of what is thus a recent self-discovery, a recent self-identification. Previously, she never claimed knowledge of the identity of the second Christ. As Elijah, as John, this knowledge, too, has come to be her gnosis. Nor is it merely an extention of what she had already taken to be true. It constitutes a revision of the proclamations of her prophetic predecessors, a revision of proclamations that she had long adopted as her own. The elder Rodens saw Victor Houteff as an antitypical Moses, a law-giver who would lead his flock to the doorstep of a promised land that he could not himself enter. Ms. Roden herself now sees him quite differently:

[Whether] V. T. Houteff [was] the second coming of Christ is not a question many have asked. Christians should. Houteff was the founder and prophet of the Shepherd Rod church, the Davidian Seventh-day Adventists, a small man with no beauty that made him desirable, a Bible interpreter who created a solid foundation for Bible students, an immigrant to America from Bulgaria.

Did he come as a thief as Christ said he would? (Rev. 3:3) Yes, indeed, Houteff came in the footsteps of Christ. Christ stole the righteous of the flock from the duly-appointed but corrupt priesthood (Num. 18:1–7) and justified himself because he was the true shepherd (John 10:1–11). So Houteff stole the righteous flock from the duly-appointed but corrupt priesthood of the Seventh-day Adventist Church.

. . . prophecy says: "And he (Christ) shall be for a sanctuary; but for a stone of stumbling and for a rock of offense to both the houses of Israel, for a gin and for a snare to the inhabitants of Jerusalem" (Isa. 8:14). Both the houses of Israel refers to the whole twelve tribes, the two tribes known as Judah and the scattered ten tribes known as Ephraim. . . . Did Houteff come to finally fulfill the downfall of the hypocrites among the ten tribes?

The answer is in Revelation, where Houteff clearly fulfilled two prophecies of the Lamb. The seven seals (Rev. 6–8:1) are on the seven thunders. "And when the seven thunders had uttered their voices, I was about to write: and I heard a voice from heaven saying unto me, Seal up those things which the seven thunders uttered and write them *not" (Rev. 10:4). Those seven thunders are the revelation of the complete mystery of the Bible. "But in the days of the seventh angel (after the seven thunders), when he shall begin to sound, the mystery of God should be finished, as he hath declared to his servants and prophets" (Rev. 10:7). The first seal is opened by the Lamb, and this is the seal that reveals the prophecies of the Kingdom of God (Rev. 6:1–2). Houteff's writing specifically reveals these prophecies, explained and illuminated. Building on the work of Miller and White, he also explained all of the prophecies of the Book of Daniel. And that is important, because it proves that what I said about the seals being on the thunders is true. . . .*

Not only was Houteff the Lamb that opened the seals, he was also the Lamb in the third angel's message of Rev. 14 [a forewarning of the punishment of unrighteous, the "smoke" of whose torment will ascend "up for ever and ever"]. *Houteff announced the beginning of Ezekiel 9* [a forewarning of the slaughter of the unrighteous among the residents of Jerusalem] *in 1930: . . . "The prophecy of Ezekiel gives the information in detail from the beginning of Luther's reformation to Ezekiel 9."*

That the Holocaust fulfilled this prophecy went unnoticed in Houteff's time. God closed Houteff's eyes to it just as he hid the seven thunders from him so that Houteff might fulfill the suffering servant of Judah, Christ come as a thief, rather than Christ come in glory. . . .

The application of Ezekiel 9 foretold by Houteff actually took place [in accord with the prophetic chronology of Ezekiel] *four hundred and thirty years after Luther's personal reformation. Luther was ordained a priest in 1507 and posted the Ninety-five Theses on the church door in 1517. That corresponds to the ten-year period from 1937 to 1947, the years of Holocaust that preceded the formation of Israel in 1948. . . .*

. . . Houteff's sealed flock, which included Ben and Lois Roden of the Branch, stood as the holy angels that they will rise up to be, and Houteff stood as the Lamb he was during the Holocaust, and the smoke of the crematoriums arose in a sorrow and a horror that will never be forgotten. And because Houteff was the Lamb that took the Bible from God's hands, and also the Lamb on the earth during the Holocaust, he can be none other than Christ come as a thief, the second coming of Christ.[124]

That the final Elijah, the final John, should not precede but instead follow the Christ does not surprise her: *Let's consider a good thief. A good thief comes unheralded and leaves unnoticed. It is obvious that the Elijah for a Messiah who comes as a thief must herald him after he is gone.*[125] Elijah's construction of an altar of twelve stones in the midst of the "prophets of Baal" is recorded in the first Book of Kings. Enclosed within a water-filled trench, the altar is consecrated as "Israel." On its table, Elijah lays out a series of offerings, each burned, then extinguished, save the last:

> . . . it came to pass at the time of the offering of the evening sacrifice that Elijah the prophet came near, and said, Lord God of Abraham, Isaac, and Israel, let it be known this day that thou art God in Israel, and that I am thy servant, and that I have done all these things at thy word. Hear me, O Lord, hear me, that this people may know that thou art the Lord God, and that thou hast turned their heart back again. Then the fire of the Lord fell, and consumed the burnt sacrifice, and the wood, and the stones, and the dust, and licked up the water that was in the trench. And when all the people saw it, they fell on their faces: and they said, The Lord, he is the God; the Lord, he is the God. (1 Kings 18: 36–39)

Whether with Ms. Roden or with competing interpreters, the indexical transformation of apocalyptic eschatology into a gnosis of presence does not merely forge a bond between the Text of the World and the here and now of the world itself. It further forges a bond among text, world, and the climactic heights and depths of history, its narrative denouement. This is what every millennialist — as millennialist — knows, or believes that he or she knows. This is the common thread of millennialist Wisdom. Call it "millenarianism" proper.[126]

Millenarianism thus understood is episodic; it comes and goes, winning greater or fewer adherents from one place and time to the next. It seems not to be culturally universal. It is rare or absent when and where cyclical or infinitistic cosmologies remain in force. Anthropologists have accordingly met no millenarians among the (non-Christian) Balinese. They have met no millenarians among the non-Christian aboriginal peoples of Australia. Taoism has occasionally nourished millenarian visions; Confucianism has not. Inveterate cosmological pessimism, the positing of the historical process as increasingly and irreversibly entropic or decadent, would appear to serve millenarianism no better but has rarely if ever acquired an institutional imprimatur imposing enough to thwart it. The myth of the decline of the ages (or races), for example, circulated throughout the ancient Near East and around the Mediterranean, but it did not prevent the burgeoning of messianic theology and apocalyptic eschatology among the Israelites. In a version of at best ambiguous implications, it found its way into Hesiod's *Cosmogony* and lingered as an occasional Hesiodic echo in later pagan thought. The esteem in which Hesiod was held among the citizens of the polises is, however, less a correlate than a cause of the near (perhaps even complete) absence of anything that might clearly be identified as pagan millenarianism, not only in unconquered Greece or republican Rome but also in imperial Egypt. Granted, the observation may amount to an *argumentio ex silencia*. The evidence that survives is nevertheless suggestive. From a comparative vantage, what is initially striking about it is less its pointing to a common Mediterranean shore than to its pointing to the relatively transparent and relatively inclusive exercise of civic power — whether strictly sacerdotal, strictly secular, or (as was often the case) an indiscriminate blend of the two, even when it was imperialistic and imperialistically oppressive. Or perhaps especially when it was imperialistic, and oppressive: in this millenarian void, democratic Athens seems to have been the greater hotbed of the conspiratorial (if not the salvationist) imagination than either of its venerable counterparts. In this respect at least, none of the ancients was greatly subtle and democratic Athens no more subtle in its treatment of those external populations that would become its subjects than the Spartans with their Helots. No millenarian uprisings among any of them: some of the subject would straightforwardly submit and others straightforwardly resist, not infrequently at the cost of their lives. Not until the vastness of scale of Alexandrian Greece (which included much of Egypt) was combined with the increasingly inward turn of the postrepublican Roman political elite did a spiritual apocalypticism find a wide audience. Only then would the exercise of power itself take on the aura of a mystery and so invite spiritual and esoteric counter-imagination, counter-theorization, counterstrategics.

What is equally striking from a comparative vantage is that the societies in question — if Greece more resolutely than Rome, and Rome more resolutely than Egypt — tended to relegate their prophets and sages to territories far beyond their city walls. All had room for diviners. For all of them, however, the civic cultus, with its typically aristocratic array and aristocratic command of ritual, was institutionally (and geographically) distinct from the extra-civic "mystery cult" or oracular preserve that it might tolerate, and in which its religious and civic elite (when these were separate) might unashamedly (and in their quietly, aristocratically antipopulist way) take part. In the later Roman empire, the boundary between civic and spiritual mystery seems to have become much more fluid, for two reasons. One has already been mentioned: power itself was becoming more mysterious — more secret and more private — in its execution. The other must be equally stressed: a wealthy and well-traveled stratum of commoner merchants had gradually emerged among the leading material powers of an empire that, like its Greek predecessor, had long taken the mutual implication of wealth and aristocratic status for granted.[127] Theirs was not the fate of the straightforwardly oppressed; they were instead the ancient predecesors of the contemporary disenfranchised, for whom disenfranchisement is never merely a political fact, a matter of oppression or bodily exclusion, but just as much a cultural fact — a matter of the deprivation of the power to voice an opinion, of the power of the political voice and the voice of possible truth.

Peter Brown has argued that the urban adherents to Christianity were a different lot from the saintly (and often millenarian) visionaries around whose potent relics they tended to gather (1989 [1971]: 66–67, 82–83; cf. also Brown 1980). He is entirely convincing in emphasizing that the Good Tidings had as great an ear among the merchant stratum as among their poorer brethren. He is far less convincing in his insistence that the urban merchant class was largely communitarian in its spiritual focus. It was indeed communitarian, but there is every reason to believe that it was also infused with, if not entirely made up of, millenarians and that it would remain so until (and — an *argumentio ex silencia* would have it — long after) the early fathers of the church pronounced and enforced their skepticism of any too "imminent" readings of the Scriptures and their condemnation of any too carnal dreams of paradise. An institutional divide thus came to be established between the Christian "assembly" and its spiritual virtuosi, and it would suffer no great disruption, in Europe or elsewhere, until the Reformation. In contrast, when and where everyday religious life incorporates or invites the periodic participation of the prophet or the oracle — as it did in ancient Israel and again during the Reformation — there millenarianism finds more fertile ground. Well beyond the ancient world, the millenarian Israelites (whether old or new) are not alone, and the list of their fellow travelers is of epic proportions. It includes the Native American participants in the Ghost Dance; the followers of the Shawnee prophet Tenskwatawa; the followers of the Xhosa prophet Makanna; the cargoists of New Guinea and the Polynesian archipelago; the Shi'ite Mahdiya of Sudan and the Ahmadiyah of India; the early Quakers; the Rastafarians; the Tupinamba migrants to the "land of immortality"; and many others.[128] Many millenarians are indebted to one or another of the sacred texts of the Abrahamic tradition, whether Jewish, Christian, or Islamic — but not all, and not all equally. If there are thus millenarian traditions, more or less venerable, millenarianism is itself not traditional. It is trans-traditional.

Just what is trans-traditional about it, however, requires careful specification. Millenarianism does not consist in a doctrine, a common creed. If trans-traditional, its expressions always come in the colors of a tradition, or of a mixture of traditions, and they vary further with the methods and the imaginations of their charismatic and prophetic propounders. Both premillennialists and postmillenialists are, moreover, millenarians, but they by no means have a common estimation of the past, the present, or the world imminently to come. Though of similarly climactic sensibilities, they diverge over the matter of the climax they await. Indeed, any substantive definition of millenarianism is likely to fail in the face of the indefinite diversity of its inevitably historically specific expressions. To raise only the best known example, Norman Cohn's: "[A]ny religious movement inspired by the phantasy [sic] of a salvation which is to be a. collective, in the sense that it is to be enjoyed by the faithful as a group, b. terrestrial, in the sense that it is to be realized on this earth and not in some otherworldly heaven, c. imminent, in the sense that it is to come both soon and suddenly, d. total, in the sense that it utterly transforms life on earth, so that the new dispensation will be no mere improvement on the present but perfection itself, and e. accomplished by agencies which are consciously regarded as supernatural" may well be a millenarian movement (1970: 15). The issue of "phantasy" aside, Cohn's checklist suffices to distinguish millenarians from other "heresies" in the Christian Europe that was the focus of his first research. It suffices to distinguish most cargoists from their more conventional fellows. It is, however, too theocentric to be able to embrace most of the millenarians of Taoist cosmocentric persuasions, who often have only themselves through whom to bring about their salvation. Nor does it succeed in encompassing those more gnostic or more Manichean millenarians who, in what would seem to be a common league with the recently departed adherents of Heaven's Gate or The Solar Temple, have undertaken to liberate themselves from their mortal bodies in order to prepare for the imminent salvation of their immortal souls.[129]

If Cohn's definition is thus too narrow, the sort of definition that might be derived from a topological analysis such as O'Leary's runs the risk of being too broad. That time is finite, authority an issue of appointment or anointment, and election the diacritical of salvation may well be the commonplaces of every millenarian discourse. But they are also the commonplaces of many eschatologies, finitistic but of indefinite historical scope. Nor is it enough to supplement such commonplaces with the additional requirement that they function indexically and "presentistically," that they pick out the here and now. Millenarian discourse does indeed function indexically — but just what constitutes the here and now, just what constitutes the climactic horizons of the present itself varies from one millenarian to another. Millenarians may all be telling stories of "revolution," even if, as Bryan Wilson has rightly emphasized, they cannot all be classified as "revolutionaries."[130] They do not, however, all agree about how far the revolution has proceeded, nor about how far it has left to go. The distinction between premillennialism and postmillenialism is the register only of the largest of such disagreements. As Timothy Weber has shown, many further, many more refined fractures are inscribed on the millenarian terrain (1979: 9–12). One can consequently hear the reproach of the resolute nominalist: "There is no such thing as millenarianism; there are only millenarianisms, each one what it is and not another thing."

True enough, but it is not a violation of nominalism to posit that — for all of what is, again, their inevitable historical specificity — millenarianisms have a certain family resemblance, a crudely common physiognomy, that invites comparing them. Tentatively (the inevitable manner of any such comparison), one might first of all return to temporality itself. Every human language has the tools to differentiate among before, now, and not yet. Beyond this bland universal, the cosmogonic and cosmological reckonings of the historical process of which anthropologists and historians have so far made note are much more variable. Yet, their variations tend to conform to or be constructed from the syncretic combination of a limited array of schemas or templates. The latter tend in turn to fall into an even more limited array of experientially available types. Analytically at least, one might thus deem "naturalistic" those cosmogonies and cosmologies that echo or elaborate on the schemas afforded by one or another meteorological or astronomical process: the oscillation of the seasons, with its typically annual repetition of the pregnant fact of decline and renewal; the cyclicality of the phases of the moon and the position of the sun, with their regular ecliptic interludes; the grand procession of the planets and constellations (Trompf 1979; D. Brown 1988: 304–30; Koselleck 1985: 3–54).

One might in contrast deem "sociological" those cosmic or calendrical reckonings that derive the processual order of things from the norms of collective organization or those events that have assumed the status of normative watersheds in the collective memory. To be sure, the relative sway of natural and social schemas is next to impossible to determine in any number of cases. The Durkheimian might insist that the cyclicality of the cosmos of the aboriginals of Australia is a symbolic representation of the cyclicality of their kinship and marriage systems. The phenomenologist or even the structuralist might insist that the cyclicality of the seasons provides the common aesthetic for both cosmos and kinship. The less theoretical ethnographer must rest simply with noting the homologies between the two. Unmoored from the circularity and infinitude of the logic of gift exchange, however, the norms of descent and succession often appear to dominate the cosmic imagination, even where countervailing schemas have widespread practical currency. Subordinating the lunar to the lineal (and the linear), the Davidic imagination accords the succession of generations both cosmogonic and cosmological priority, from the books of Kings to the gospel of Matthew. Imperial Egypt counted its days, indiscriminately secular and sacred, with reference to the terms of its pharaohs, though it had and made use of many of the other numerologies at its disposal. The entropic cosmogony that Hesiod only slightly revised would also appear to have lineal succession as its schematic ground, but succession saturated sentimentally with that particular pathos that, in another context, Michael Herzfeld has called "structural nostalgia" (1991: 75).

The temporality that unfolds from a "great event," from a monumentalized moment or period, a collective crisis, also permits entropic developments and derivations but is anthropologically more familiar as the temporality of "persistent peoples," a minor (or minority) temporality that locates in the past—often a past of suffering or catastophe—the stigmata of a difference that confers identity in the present and in perpetuity. The Babylonian captivity left such stigmata on the Jews of antiquity just as the Holocaust has left it on their contemporary descendants. Many African-Americans similarly recall the Middle Passage (cf. Carpenter 2001). The Guyanese Saramanca recall their flight from slavery into the wilderness of the rainforest (see Price 1983), the Philippine Ilongot the Japanese invasion (see Rosaldo 1980), the Southwestern Yaqui their defeat and dislocation in the face of invading and colonizing armies (see Spicer 1971). Though typically in more triumphal guise, the monumentalized event can also do majority service, and does so in the more or less official histories of nations and states and empires and the more or less official historiographies of great women and men, great discoveries, great conquests, great steps forward. Here, the serialization of crisis—in its ancient sense, as that which demands decision or judgment, as a rupture of the ordinary—constitutes an irregular but momentous time line and a selective memory of collective distinction. If, as Reinhart Koselleck and others have suggested, the collective experience of the French and American Revolutions gave birth to the idea that human beings could indeed take the world into their own hands, then modern temporality is in its origins also a temporality of crisis, however soon it would be detached from its social context and transformed into the fetish of the infinitude of progress (see Koselleck 1985: 39–54; cf. Blumenberg 1983: 77–87).[131]

Millienarian temporality is also a temporality of crisis, its time line a record of eruptions and disruptions of genuinely world-historical proportions. As the indexical resolution of apocalypse, it might be thought to acquire its finitude from the narrative closure characteristic of apocalypse itself. Yet, as the temporality of climactic crisis, millenarian temporality still leaves history sufficient length for events to unfold along their fateful and final course. Its here and now are not immediacies; they are not vanishing points. If the template that at once establishes and limits their range is easily overlooked, this is perhaps because it is so obvious. The millenarian Christ of the gospel of Matthew is entirely explicit in his foretelling of "the end of the world" (Matt. 24:3). After recounting all its signs and portents, he tells his disciples: "When the branch is yet tender, and putteth forth leaves, ye know that summer is nigh: So likewise ye, when ye shall see all these things, know that it is near, even at the doors. Verily I say unto you, This generation shall not pass, till all these things be fulfilled" (Matt. 24: 32–34). Here at least, the voice of the Christ is the voice of every millenarian prophet. Millenarian temporality is the temporality of the present — of "this" — generation. Its template is the template of the (almost inevitably) finite human life course.

Lacking the supplemental provision of a fateful day and hour, then, millenarian historicity is still an indeterminate historicity. Its here and now are diffuse, their latitude of sufficiently approximate degree to permit a hundred visions and revisions of apocalyptic truth. Even for the millenarian, the failure of prophecy of which Festinger and his colleagues have written (1964) thus allows for deferral. Boyer has in this regard gleefully pointed out the self-corrections of the many televangelists who initially determined that the biblical Armageddon would see an anti-Christly Soviet Union at war with the United States and Europe. The subsequent shift of geopolitical fortunes deprived their conclusion of its former resonance. As Boyer points out, however, most of the same evangelists had presumed that the Islamic Middle East would at least ally itself with the Soviets, if not lead the anti-Christly forces (1992: 326–27). Hence (and in contrast to Boyer himself), they found nothing hermeneutically untoward in reassigning the Islamic enemy to center stage with the Iraqi invasion of Kuwait and the subsequent outbreak of the Gulf War (Boyer 1992: 327–31). But of course they are not the first oracles whose pronouncements and predictions reveal a tendency to go with the flow of the geopolitical tide. The Pythians are their ancestors, as is Jeremiah, among others. Nor are they the first millenarians to reevaluate those of their decryptions to which the times have failed to bear witness. Like other millenarians, however, they remain convinced (or at least appear to remain convinced) that the world will indeed have its end, its denouement, in their own lifetime.

Like other millenarians, moreover, they foresee a denouement that has its own internal complexity. The climax they await will not transpire in the space of a moment. It will require time to coalesce, for its

forces to identify themselves and pass muster, for its driving antagonisms to grow sharp and implacable, and above all for the elect to suffer the full passion of their election, to know themselves, to atone and
renew themselves, to die and be reborn. Not all millenarians construct
the world's final act as they would construct it, to be sure, and not all
would construct it as elaborately as either they or the Bible before them
would. Yet the historical and anthropological records uniformly attest
that millenarians recognize that the end of time takes time, if still only
the time of a human generation.[132] It has multiple episodes. It has distinct phases that have a distinct structure. Adopting the vantage of theodicy, Kenelm Burridge has summarized that structure as tripartite and
evolutionary: from old rules, to no rules, to new rules (1969: 105–16).
The summary is apt for the theodicies of millenarian movements, past
and present, well beyond the bounds of Burridge's Melanesian cases.

Burridge nevertheless adopts a specific vantage, perhaps a somewhat
misleading one to the extent that it diverts attention to the millenarian
perception of the juridico-political order at the expense of its typical
preoccupation with the passion and the salvation of the elect. At the
very least, he does not pose the question of whether the phase structure
of millenarian theodicy is isomorphic with the phase structure of millenarian soteriology and eschatology, of whether millenarian discourse, in
Melanesia or elsewhere, might have a uniform rule of formation, a single syntax or logic. Posing just such a question not of the Melanesian
cargoists but instead of the New England divines of the First Great
Awakening in the young United States, James West Davidson identifies
what he calls an "afflictive model of process," the logic of which is the
logic of "conversion":

> New Englanders were no strangers to soul troubles, and their Puritan
> predecessors had long before provided detailed guides to the appro-
> priate paths a soul traveled from darkness to light. Authorities dif-
> fered on details (some broke the process into as many as ten steps)
> but everyone agreed about the basic points. The traditional state of a
> "civil," unconverted man was a numb sleepiness. No matter how reg-
> ularly he attended church or how superficially pious he appeared,
> underneath lay a spiritual pride, a secret conviction that his good
> works were acceptable to God. Thus, a man's first step toward salva-
> tion was an awareness of his total sinfulness. He had to realize that
> the moral law which demanded perfection convicted him in the eyes
> of the divine Judge. . . . Finally, from out of this ultimate despair
> came the new birth: the faith that God, through his love and mercy,
> had granted salvation. This grace acted as a new "inward principle,"
> first reordering a man's relation to God, and then transforming his
> relations with others in the world. (1977: 130–31).

Davidson emphasizes that "for New Englanders" (and, one might add, for many other millenarians as well), the process of conversion "was perhaps more important than the theology" (1977: 131). Among the several implications he proceeds to develop, two are particularly striking. The first is that premillennialists and postmillennialists are of a common rationality. All of them understand the phase structure of the end-time to be conversional. All agree that like the individual believer, so too the world must pass from a condition of hubristic complaisancy into a catastrophic fallenness, and from fallenness at last into the uplift of an eternal redemption. Their disagreement is instead substantive: premillennialists anticipate the plunge; postmillennialists think an uplift in the near offing.[133] The second implication is already implicit in the first: the model of conversion — the process of individual awakening, catharsis, and the acquisition of grace — is the microcosm of millenarian temporality itself. Individualized, writ small, conversion is always a personal history. Totalized, writ at its largest, it is not merely ecclesiastic but planetary. For the millenarian, individualization and totalization are the warp and woof of a single loom. The personal is world-historical (and vice versa: see Davidson 1977: 136–63).

As a practical matter, conversion is more complex (and more social) in eighteenth-century New England and elsewhere than the skeletal model Davidson discerns in it would suggest. As a skeleton, as the bare bones of the rationality of millenarian climacticism, it is nevertheless sufficient and more than sufficiently suggestive as it stands. Confirming Burridge's intuitions, it is in fact a tripartite model, the model of a progression from the banality of evil through the darkness of purgative suffering to the bright beatitude of grace. More explicitly than Burridge, Davidson underscores its simultaneous personality and collectivity; and more explicitly than Burridge again, he underscores its progressivism, its projection not simply of change but of betterment, of increase, of the enhancement of both self and world. All this seems obvious enough. What is apparently less obvious to the many anthropologists and historians of millenarianism who have failed to note it (Burridge and Davidson included) is that the finitistic phase structure of world climax in question conforms precisely to another model (or in any case to a differently named model) with which anthropologists at least should be familiar. Victor Turner is a rare, though partial, exception: before and beyond him, remarkably few scholars have dwelt at any length, if at all, on the structure of millenarian historicity and the structure of that decidedly trans-traditional (indeed, culturally universal) trinitarian unity I have already mentioned — the rite of passage.

Arnold Van Gennep's analysis endures (1960 [1909]). From graduations to funerals, from marriages to initiations, whether sacralized or secular, the ceremonials through which human beings tend almost im-

107

pulsively to recognize and legitimate transformations in social status are themselves phasic, and though liable to much secondary elaboration and many temporal modulations, their phase structure is a succession of three basic steps. The first is the step into separateness, the symbolic (and usually literal) removal of the ritual subject from the world at large. The second is the step into liminality, into a pedagogical "threshold" in which the subject is stripped of his or her former status, his or her former identity, and prepared to assume a new one. The third is the step back into collectivity. Van Gennep characterizes its ritualism as a ritualism of "reaggregation," but the subject does not always return to the world whence he or she came. Initiation may culminate in admission to secret societies or to private cloisters of peers and superiors. The more familiar rites of passage tend toward the progressive, toward the increasing of status, but not all. Some initiates may, at the end of their passage, find themselves united with the company of their fellow convicts, their fellow lepers, their fellow fools. For better and for worse, rites of passage in any event remain one of the elementary forms of social life in transit.

In *The Ritual Process*, Turner rediscovers Van Gennep only to reduce his tripartite categories to a more fundamental two (1969: 94–113). His rationale stems in part from Lévi-Strauss's then authoritative conviction in the fundamentally binary and digital nature of human thought (Turner 1969: 106–7; cf. Lévi-Strauss 1966: 268–69). It stems in another part from his seeking to apply an avuncular anthropological wisdom to the events of his day. From Van Gennep's formalism, Turner extracts a foundational opposition between *societas* and *communitas*. The former groups together the before and after of rites of passage with the many other modalities of social life that are saturated with stratification, functional differentiation, norms, rules, and conventional proprieties, whatever they may be. The latter is the human heart of liminality, a modality of being and of being together that celebrates democracy, intimacy, and creativity and rejects *societas* as inimical to them all (Turner 1969: 95–130). At his most speculative, Turner suggests that the inevitable pressures and frustrations of *societas* demand a regular outlet in the undiscriminating and unburdened commensalism of *communitas*. Having had their outlet, they leave the commensalist all the better prepared to return to *societas* with renewed vigor. Hence, the socially positive function of occasionally letting go. Turner draws his most compelling examples from such rites of inversion (and otherwise forbidden revelry) as Carnival. His intellectual centerpiece, however, is the Generation of Love, whose flower children were only just beginning to fade when *The Ritual Process* was published (Turner 1969: 112–13, 164–65). His message is constructive, at least for the troubled parent whose dropout son or daughter could indeed be seen as going through a phase, and even a somewhat virtuous one at that. In retrospect, it also seems too rapidly dismissive of the political (and social-structural) precipitants of a remarkable generational upheaval. History has nevertheless vindicated him — though perhaps not proven him correct.

However vindicated, Turner's analysis is strained at several junctures. It illuminates less than it obscures rites of passage, which are not dualistic oscillations between the structured and the antistructured but instead linear trajectories from one status to another. The liminality that is most typical of them is, moreover, only rarely the liminality of free play and unfettered communion. As Turner was in fact well aware, it is far more commonly an interim of degradation, of physical hardship, of terror, of the hand of authority at its most heavy. The liminal initiate may receive the same treatment as his or her co-initiates. All who are liminal may find themselves in a common condition. Rarely if ever do they find themselves the beneficiaries of democratic egalitarianism or the sweet humanism of an Erasmus. As an approach to millenarian movements, the analysis fares only slightly better. Turner is certainly correct in observing that such movements tend toward liminality. Once again, however, neither democracy nor humanism is the source of their turn (quite the contrary, as it is perhaps needless to say). As "antistructure," liminality is a feature of any movement, any community or group whose leadership is charismatic. Roving warlords and mystic dervishes join millenarians in their liminal hostility to routine. On the other hand, none of them are typically hostile to stratification. Charismatic hierarchies may be less stable than their more routinized counterparts, but the distinction between leader and follower is typically no less palpable. Turner's intuition of the link between liminality and millenarianism is far more compelling as the intuition of a gnosis, of yet another bit of indexed apocalyptic Wisdom. Millenarians might not agree precisely where they stand, but they know that they stand on and at a threshold, personal and world-historical alike. They know that they are passing and that the world is passing with them.

The Bible might seem a text of so many secondary, tertiary, and even further elaborations that any trace of an elementary logic, whether that of the conversional rite of passage or of any other, would be irrecoverably buried. The climactic (and ostensibly some of the most narratively peculiar) verses of the Book of Revelation nevertheless remain surprisingly transparent in their way.

The author of the historical Revelation, who was apparently the first explicitly to refer to his visions as an *apokalupsis* (literally, a "discovery"), identifies himself as John. Exiled during the reign of the Emperor

Domitian to the island of Patmos, where his enshrined cave dwelling is still a significant site of pilgrimage, he was not John, son of Zebedee, apostle of Jesus, and author of the fourth gospel. That the canonists may have mistaken him for the latter is sometimes proposed as an explanation for the inclusion of Revelation in the Bible at the expense of several contemporary contenders. For all its patent resemblance to Old Testament prophecy, especially to the Book of Daniel, it stands distinctly apart from the gospels themselves, for which eschatology is far less central than moral and ethical didactics. John claims to have received his Wisdom from an "angel," actually several angels, who ordered him to write epistles to seven Christian churches and blessed him with foreknowledge of the imminence of Christ's return. The attribution of intentions is always perilous, but biblical historians largely agree that what John cryptically foretold was the downfall of the Roman Empire and that his most excoriating caricatures are those reserved for Rome and her emperors.

> Rome . . . is described as the "the great whore," "the woman sitting upon the scarlet beast" who had seven heads and ten horns. The seven heads represented the seven hills (of Rome) and the seven emperors. These seven emperors are designated as follows: "five of whom have fallen" (Augustus, Tiberius, Caligula, Claudius, and Nero), "one is" (Vespasian), the other has not yet come, and when he comes, he must remain only "a little while" (Titus, who ruled only two years). The last reference denotes that the writer produced his work under the eighth king (Domitian) but pretended to be writing during the time of the sixth (Vespasian). His description of the eighth as one of the seven implies that he considered Domitian in his persecution of the Christians to be "Nero returned." The idea that Nero had not died (he had committed suicide during a period of revolt and anarchy) but would return to Rome at the head of a Parthian army was current in the Empire and actual pretenders ("pseudo Neros") did put in appearances. The writer of Revelation took up this and interpreted Domitian as the returned Nero. In Rev. 13:18, the number of the beast is said to be six hundred, sixty-six. Nero Caesar spelled in Hebrew has this numerical value. . . . The eighth emperor was to appear with the ten horns (the ten Parthian provincial kings) and wage war upon the Lamb (Christ) but would be defeated. After this, Babylon (Rome) would fall and the New Jerusalem would be established on earth and the apocalyptic scheme played out. (Hayes 1971: 459)

So, in broad strokes, the new criticism would generally have it.

At the beginning of the fourteenth chapter of Revelation, John proclaims to have seen "a Lamb" who "stood on the Mount Sion, and with him an hundred and forty-four thousand, having his Father's name written in their foreheads." He continues:

> And I heard a voice from heaven, as the voice of many waters, and as the voice of great thunder: and I heard the voice of harpers harping with their harps: And they sung as it were a new song before the throne, and before the four beasts, and the elders: and no man could learn that song but the hundred and forty and four thousand, which were redeemed from the earth. These are they which were not defiled with women; for they are virgins. These are they who followeth the Lamb whithersoever he goes. These were redeemed from among men, being the firstfruits unto God and unto the Lamb. (Rev. 14:2–4)

So the faithful, dressed in robes washed white "in the blood of the Lamb" (Rev. 7:14), of the crucifixion, have been separated from the masses.

The denouement of the book comes most explicitly some two chapters later, in all the colors of grand and catastrophic violence, replete with fire and brimstone, plagues, thunder and lightning, a great earthquake, and hailstones the weight of a talent (Rev. 16:18–21). These are the presages of the great battle, Armageddon, at the end of which the forces of the recently returned Christ defeat both Babylon and Satan himself (Rev. 17:14–19:21). Satan's fate would at first seem to be straightforward, but soon takes a curious twist:

> And I saw an angel come down from heaven, having the key of the bottomless pit and a great chain in his hand. And he laid hold on the dragon, that old serpent, which is the Devil, and Satan, and bound him a thousand years, and cast him into the bottomless pit, and shut him up, and set a seal upon him, that he should deceive the nations no more, till the thousand years be fulfilled: and after that he must be loosed a little season. (Rev. 20:1–3)

The millennium, the thousand years of Christ's initial reign, is a time of the "first resurrection," during which all the fallen martyrs are called back to join the saintly army. At its end, Satan is indeed unleashed to deceive the nations once again and bid them to make yet another war on "the camp of saints." Here, John dispenses with any lurid details. In the course of a verse, unholy adversaries are devoured in God's fire; in the next, Satan is cast again into "the lake of fire and brimstone," to be tormented there "for ever and ever" (Rev. 20:9–10). The Final Judgment follows. In its aftermath, John is witness to the new Jerusalem "coming down from God out of heaven" (Rev. 21:2) and hears "a great voice out of heaven saying, Behold, the tabernacle of God is with men, and he will dwell with them, and they shall be his people, and God himself shall be with them, and be their God" (Rev. 21:3).

Every abstraction must do violence to particularity, and the abstraction of the model of the rite of passage from so dense a narrative within a narrative is no different. Yet, just such an abstraction seems called for in order to account for the trans-traditional near ubiquity of both apocalypse and millenarianism themselves. Moreover, for all the historical specificity of its generic, numerological, and (covertly) referential substance, the pattern of that condensed apocalypse which is the denouement of Revelation is not merely that of a rite of passage, but of a rite coded in what one might dare call the most blatant possible of signals. Its initiates are the elect, the people of God themselves. John mentions their stigmata — their white robes, their inscribed foreheads — not once but several times. Were their distinction, their remove from the common run of mankind not already sufficiently clear, their military role at Armageddon would render it a certainty.

The narrative rationale of Satan's return is for its part obscure at best. Though the text does not definitively state the omnipotence of either Christ or God, it hardly encourages any other interpretation. What is thus odd is that Satan should be allowed or be begrudged to return at all. An omnipotent Godhead would seem capable of rendering his banishment permanent at the first blow. However narratively odd, the episode is of the highest ritual propriety. The first world-historical battle, the first and most dire catastrophe, Armageddon itself, marks the ritual crossing of the initates beyond the threshold into liminality proper. The thousand years of Christ's initial reign is thus the time of liminality itself, a time of preparation and consolidation that proves also to be well within the life course of the initiates, who are not destined for death but immortality. The second battle marks the ritual close of liminality and is the commencement of the rapid transition to the aggregation and reaggregation of all of God's people — this legion of immortal peers — in the new and eternal City of God. The rite, the passage, is thus complete and a dramatic change of status complete along with it.

Millenarian finitude is thus finitude with a qualification. Bounded by the temporal limits of the (ordinary) human life course, its time is the time of crisis but more precisely of the crisis of the threshold. For the premillenialist, the crisis is one of the threshold into liminality, of first battle, of trial by fire. For the postmillenialist, the crisis is instead one of the threshold out of liminality, of the rupture that must precede the founding of the Kingdom to come. The premillennialist and the postmillenialist are frequently of different outlooks, different casts of mind, to be sure. Postmillennialists, moreover, have the greater tendency to drift beyond millenarianism into one or another version of the historicity of the *longue durée*. As millenarians, however, both remain true to a far more truncated historicity, the historicity of their own mortality and its more intimate *événementialité*. Both are "afflictive progressivists." That the model to which they ultimately cleave is the model of the rite of passage does not imply that they understand either their own lives or the historical process itself actually to be a rite of passage. It implies only that, here as in so many other instances, the social itself is the source of the imagination of both self and cosmos. That such a Durkheimian conclusion runs counter to the theoretical psychology to which Turner was attracted seems appropriate. Millenarianism is not, after all, a psychic fact, neither humanly universal nor exclusively particular. It falls in between; it is a social (and cultural) fact. But what, then, of the apparent "trick" through which the life course of the elect loses the limitations of mortality to become never-ending? Surely this has no social or cultural source? On the contrary. The passage to immortalization is itself a finite passage and its millenarian finitude still that of the bounded life course. In John's envisioning, it has two moments: those of the first resurrection and of the Final Judgment (Rev. 21:5–15). Its finitude is further that of the promise itself, the promise that to some there will be given a gift that they cannot possibly repay, a moment of reception beyond which nothing will ever be needed or sought again. For the millenarian, the moment is near at hand, within the hand of "this" generation; this as well is his, or her, gnosis.

PART THREE

An Ethics

SAINT PAUL was a millenarian and, more specifically, a premillennial-ist who understood himself to be living in the days in which the "son of perdition," the Antichrist, would be revealed and whom Christ would return to destroy (2 Thess. 2:2–15; cf. 1 Thess. 4:12–5:6).[1] Many of the congregations he addressed in his epistles plainly shared his expectation, some more fervently than others. Though controversy lingers over whether it is indeed of Paul's hand, the second epistle to the congregation at Thessalonike is the most explicit in addressing yet another organiza-tional problem to which charismatic millenarian communities are sim-ilarly vulnerable: the problem of maintenance, of temporal continuity. Certain of the Thessalonians to whom the epistle is addressed seem to have been awaiting Christ's return not simply within the space and time of their own generation but in a very near future. They seem further to have arrived at the conclusion that with so radical a change of fortune so closely in the offing, they had little reason to pursue the drudgeries of merely mundane life. Anthropologists have more recently met others of like minds, especially among the Melanesian cargoists.[2] The Thessalon-ians, for their part, are doubly admonished: for losing sight of the time that would necessarily be required for the signs and portents of the return to be fulfilled (2 Thess. 2:1–12); and for neglecting their duties in the interim. The writer offers his own comportment during a previous sojourn among them as an "ensample":

> And we have confidence in the Lord touching you, that ye both do and will do the things which we command you. And the Lord direct your hearts into the love of God, and into the patient waiting for

117

Christ. Now we command you, brethren, in the name of our Lord Jesus Christ, that ye withdraw yourselves from every brother that walketh disorderly, and not after the tradition which he hath received of us. For yourselves know how ye ought to follow us: for we behaved not ourselves; Neither did we eat any man's bread for nought; but wrought with labour and travail night and day, that we might not be chargeable to any of you: Not because we have not power, but to make ourselves an ensample unto you to follow us. For even when we were with you, this we commanded you, that if any would not work, neither should he eat. (2 Thess. 4–10)

For Paul, this chronotopic interim, this interstice lying between the present and the Parousia, is the space and time of neither passive waiting nor anticipatory self-indulgence. It is the space and time instead of adherence to Jewish tradition, of the restoration of traditions that have lapsed, and of the cultivation within the bounds of tradition of those special and diverse gifts that God had seen fit to bestow upon one or another of his elect. Hence, Paul would cultivate his celibacy and an evangelical mission that he did not demand of others less or differently blessed. Hence the millenarian would also become the communitarian, the greatest of the early Christian moralists, and the most explicit pedagogue of the duties and diverse possibilities of a Christian ethics.

In that antitypical interstice which is our present, the space and time of our generation, Ms. Roden maintains a Pauline sensibility, even though she has never recognized herself as the antitypical fulfillment of Paul himself. She is not idle. She has her work to do. She is a moralist but recognizes with Paul the distinction between the duties and liberties common to all true Christians and the more particular duties and liberties suited to a person of her special gifts, her special burdens and blessings. No more than Paul's is her religiosity confined only to the cultivation of gnosis. It includes the extension of gnosis into practice. It includes further the testing, the trial, the potential correction of gnosis in practice and as practice. It demands a constant monitoring, a vigilant examination of the self. It also demands a *historia*, an "inquiry" that reaches in more than one sense to the ends of the world itself.

Scholars are not beyond sneering at the (would-be) morals of religious movements and the ethics of their activist members, especially those morals and activists that strike them either as too mutable, dogmatic, or self-serving. So, for example, John Lofland's well-known study of several members of the Unification Church lingers frequently on the secretive and calculating strategies the converted deploy to recruit others to their flock (1966: 120–89). David Van Zandt's more recent study of the Children of God is more neutral than Lofland's in characterizing its subjects as "deviant" from a strictly label-theoretical point of view. Its tone is more reserved, yet remains ironical, bemused by the ostensibly odd mélange of absolutist spirituality and hardheaded, "pragmatic" realism it records (Van Zandt 1991; cf. Wallis 1982). And to each his own ethical and religious position, of course. The peril for anything deserving of the name of an "anthropology of ethics" (which is ultimately related to but still different from an ethics of anthropology) lies, however, precisely in imposing on its subjects the standards of an ethics not their own, at least before investigating in what such standards might actually consist. That peril is all the greater when its subjects (by their own account) and their ethics (similarly) are "religious" and thus vulnerable to the further imposition of criteria of religiosity (or irreligiosity) that might once again be foreign to them. The anthropologist cannot begin to do any more justice to Pauline ethics than to Ms. Roden's own if he or she calls on the dualism of the sacred and the secular (or the otherworldly and the this-worldly, or spirit and flesh, or body and soul) to evaluate the religious authenticity of ethical practices that do not have any such dualism as their point of departure. Weber's precedent (especially in *The Protestant Ethic and the Spirit of Capitalism*) is of more analytical service than the contemporary mainstream of the sociology of religion and religious studies alike.

It is, however, a precedent in need of certain adjustments. Weber's broad preoccupation with the greater or lesser fit or affinity between particular designs of practical conduct ("ethics" as he understood it) and the functional demands of particular institutional orders remains as crucial now as it was a century ago. His analysis of the affinity between Calvinist ethics and industrial capitalism remains compelling, even if our postindustrial economy of consumption has rendered it of more historical than contemporary relevance. Though he made it only implicitly in *The Protestant Ethic*, his distinction between an ethics of commitment (a "value-rational" ethics) and an ethics of responsibility (a value-rational ethics tempered, or diluted, by a metaethics of value-pluralism and the virute of expediency) remains useful—so long as one keeps in mind that it is an ideal-typical distinction and perhaps not so much a matter of contradictories as Weber himself often seems to have assumed. More on this later. For now, it is enough to note that all of the ethical portraits with which Weber has left us—those of the Calvinist and his more "pragmatic" epigones, of course, but also those of the Chinese mandarin, the Hebraic prophet, the Hindu yogi, the scientist, the politician, the aesthete—are all wrought as contributions to the sociology of rationalisms and rationalization.[3] Whether synchronic or diachronic, his axes of comparison are predominantly logical axes. They

are often fruitful (no more fruitful than when they illuminate the intellectual's life as belonging to an "unbrotherly aristocracy" [1946: 355])
but have two shortcomings. First, precisely because they are ideal-typical
axes, they operate at a remove from the fuzzier logic of practice and the
contextual boundedness of actual conduct. Second, if they do not ex-
clude, they do not encourage the highlighting of other axes, the making
of other comparisons, the taking of other analytical directions than the
"ethological." Granted, Weber has much to say—much of it boldly psychological rather than logical—about the human urge to value. It is
curious that he has little to say about what might be called the ethical
imagination—beyond its (alleged) intolerance of contradiction, at least
in its more modernized realizations.

Anthropologists have as yet done little to improve upon him. They
may worry at present over the stance they should take toward the Islamic veil, pharaonic circumcision, the Occidentalist trappings of the
notion of universal human rights, or Alfred Kroeber's ostensibly pater-
nalistic regard of his Yahi informant Ishi (and of Ishi's remains), but
they have yet systematically to put the ethical itself into anthropological
question, systematically to inquire into the social and cultural themes
and variations of ethical discourse and ethical practice, into the social
and cultural lineaments of what, for lack of any better terminological
placeholder, one might simply call the "ethical field."

Perhaps they have thought such questioning unnecessary, or if not
that, then at least largely exhausted. After all, the ethnographic corpus
is well stocked with sustained case studies of ethics—conceived as explicit codes of conduct—from Ruth Benedict's *Patterns of Culture*
(1934), Richard Brandt's *Hopi Ethics* (1954), and Gregory Bateson's
Naven (1958) to Clifford Geertz's *Religion of Java* (1960). Such studies
do indeed reveal something of the range and the systematicity of the
ethical imagination. The great majority of them, however, suffer from
shortcomings of their own that preclude their full recuperation in the
present. It is not uncommon, in what Bourdieu has appropriately labeled an "objectivist fallacy," for them to manifest a tendency (not quite
Weber's) to dissolve value into obligation, the desirable into the normative, of which the very definition of ethics as "codes of conduct" is
already guilty (Bourdieu 1977: 126–27). It is even more common, and
much more anachronistic, for them to manifest a tendency—relativist if
not precisely subjectivist—to confine the scope of ethical validity within
the tidy and closed boundaries of one or another "culture" or "tradition." As an increasing number of anthropologists have become aware,
we must now face a much less tidy, less insular sociocultural landscape
in which the boundaries of neither cultures nor traditions can be taken
either analytically or methodologically for granted, and in which the

cultural relativism of Boas and his heirs must consequently always fall short.[4]

Even if Ms. Roden were not its occasion, then, a return to the ethical field would seem anthropologically timely, if not patently overdue.[5] It has a farther-reaching urgency as well. Virtually all the behavioral sciences and many of their humanistic cousins have long been laboring with an understanding of action that continues to leave them wavering between two mutually repellent extremes. One has its purest expression as decisionism, whether economistic or Sartrean. The other appears as determinism in any number of guises. Both are recognizable in the familiar oppositions between agency and structure, between choice and compulsion. Ostensibly falling somewhere in the middle, "social constructionism" has garnered increasing popularity since the 1980s. Yet social constructionism, which comes in its own multitude of guises, often turns out to repeat one or the other of the alternatives it is designed to transcend. In Ian Hacking's persuasive judgment (1999), it is often more analytically impoverished than at first sight it seems; what it all too often lacks is a full regard of the ethical field itself. In clearer focus, the latter certainly includes choice but also reveals an array of human activities that are neither deliberative nor "driven." It is also the privileged setting for a distinctive sort of cultural events. Or so, if in what can only be a digression at once extended and schematic, I shall argue.

Putting the ethical field into clearer focus is no easy matter, and modern philosophy is less an aid than a further hindrance. On the one hand, Kant and his diverse successors have insisted on the subordination of the "good" to the "right," of the consequential to the deontological (cf. Rawls 1971). On the other hand, utilitarians and the majority of their conventionalist and subjectivist confreres have objectified the good, but only at the cost of reducing it to what one or another person (or community, society, or civilization) believes it to be.[6] Each of these positions executes at least a partial erasure of the ethical, whether in reducing it to a moral residuum or a moral radical. The erasure has been carried so far by now that the "ethical" and the "moral" are in many discursive quarters — including the quarters of ordinary English usage — virtual synonyms. The analytical distinction between character and precept is thus all but lost.

Aristotle offers a more felicitous starting point. In his view, ethics concerns the promotion and procurement of *eudaimonia*, of "thriving" or "happiness" — which for human beings is good in itself. It thus concerns *aretē*, "virtue," and virtuous conduct, which is "proper" in promoting or procuring happiness most effectively and securely. Virtuosity allows for general formulation, for a catalog of rules. Yet however instructive it might be, such a moral catalog could never serve as an exhaustive ethical guidebook. Precisely because of its abstraction, it would always remain substantively indeterminate. Even the sheer applicability of any one of its entries would always remain to be assessed in light of the irrevocably particular situation in which any instance of conduct, proper or improper, must unfold. Genuine ethical virtuosity consists for Aristotle always in something more, or something else, than what we now think of as "moral imperatives." It demands the active exercise of *fronēsis*, that "practical wisdom" which enables us to come to terms with what is best for each of us to do in the particular here and now of our always somewhat singular lives.

One need not embrace either Aristotle's eudaemonism or his psychology to give due credit to his recognition of the gaps between even the most categorical of imperatives and the vexing contingencies that impinge on our doing the right thing from one ethically sensitive occasion to the next. His person of practical wisdom might indeed even be categorically ignorant — or at least largely so (6.7.7). Beyond *empeiria* (experience), he or she is most in need of that special sort of *aisthēsis* (perception or intuition), which discerns the particularities of things (6.8.8).[7] Or call it what one will: the heuristic value of Aristotle's focus on practical *aisthēsis* lies in its inviting us to attend to all that distinguishes the ethical field beyond mere obedience (or mere transgression). Virtually alone in the latter half of this century, Michel Foucault had begun systematically to take up that invitation and, with it, to effect an anthropological renovation of the Aristotelian enterprise well beyond Weber's own. The renovation was still incomplete at the time of Foucault's death. It merits further development.

Foucault distills the ethical into that *rapport à soi* or "relation of the self to itself" that manifests itself as the "considered [*réfléchie*] practice of freedom" (1997 [1984]b: 284), a practice always analytically distinct from the moral principles and codes to which it has reference. His later genealogical investigations do not, however, merely recover and repeat a previously forged divide. They also cast into novel relief certain ethical parameters that the ancient authors — Aristotle among others — left relatively obscure. The heuristic (or methodological) potential of those parameters is signal, but I am impelled to enter my evaluation of them through something of a back door. The analytics of the ethical field that might be extracted from Foucault's investigations have, at present, far fewer admirers than detractors. Even some who do admire it fail to do justice to its genuine complexity. Three theses in particular demand immediate attention. Least surprising, one is that Foucualt's analytics is subjectivist, even radically subjectivist. Another is that his analytics is aestheticist, perhaps radically aestheticist. Somewhat paradoxically in light of the other two, yet a third is that his analytics reveals the ethical field to be nothing more than yet another field of "subjugation."

In "On the Genealogy of Ethics," Foucault asserts that "from the idea that the self is not given to us, there is only one practical consequence: we have to create ourselves as a work of art" (1997 [1984]a: 262). Championing the cause of Jürgen Habermas and many other latter-day Enlighteners, Walter Privitera would have us read the assertion as "a kind of philosophical confession" (1995: 123), a late admission of the moralism cryptically embedded in the labyrinths of so many earlier works. He would further have us infer from it a certain "romantic positivism," an extension of Gaston "Bachelard's critique of substantialist epistemology . . . into a critique of morality that more or less unites all the motifs of [Foucault's] thought into one extreme, synthetic form" (1995: 123). Privitera's Foucault calls for the "reappropriation of pre-Christian ethics" and for an activism that concentrates no longer "on the political level of social confrontations" but instead on "individual life plans, the political relevance of which must be understood indirectly, via gradual cultural processes" (1995: 124). Privitera's Foucault may be "a sensitive measure for changes in the Zeitgeist of Western countries, where the retreat from politics is accompanied by an increase in 'private' and aesthetic efforts at self-cultivation" (1995: 124–25), but a measure which precisely demarcates the shortsightedness to which those changes have led: "the reduction of the individual to the mere ability to creatively plan a new lifestyle without taking into account the individual's interactive dimension as a socialized being" (1995: 125). Or to put it somewhat differently: "after a sincere and lifelong process of revising his views, the thinker of the 'end of the individual' . . . turns to a form of extreme subjectivism that obscures the socialization problematic" (1995: 125).

I cannot address all of the presumptions that guide Privitera's portrait, in which Foucault the subjectivist and Foucault the aestheticist merge into one. I might at least point out that Foucault never poses himself as a thinker of the "end of the individual" but rather of the end of Man—a different creature indeed. Further, the interview of which Privitera makes most regular use in constructing his portrait is the same interview in which Foucault explicitly rejects both the possibility and the worth of transporting the past into the present (1997 [1984]a: esp. 259, 261). Finally, Foucault fashions his analytics of ethics only as part of a much broader analytics of governmentality. If "the concept of governmentality makes it possible to bring out the freedom of the subject *and its relationship to others*—the very stuff of ethics" (1997 [1984]b: 300; my emphasis), it is further concerned with "the whole range of

123

practices that constitute, define, organize, and instrumentalize the strategies that individuals in their freedom can use in dealing *with each
other*" (1997 [1984]b: 300; my emphasis). Perhaps Privitera would read
such remarks as mere lip service. As we shall see, however, they are
entirely programmatic.

Whether any or all of the same remarks further serve as an adequate
rebuttal to allegations of romantic positivism is unclear largely because
"romantic positivism" is a virtually hollow and primarily polemical category. In any event, Foucault is no nostalgist. Does he nevertheless grant
aesthetics an ethical pride of place? Does he, as Privitera would have it,
elevate an "art of living in which the pleasures and exigencies of life
attain the perfection of a successful balance, as in the case of a work of
art," to the status of a cardinal ethical ideal? (1995: 124). Is Foucault a
"romantic" at least in this respect? Whatever else might be said, there is
simply nothing in Foucault's thought, early or late, that would justify
attributing to him a valorization of so classical, or so static, a conception of art as Privitera does. Throughout, his interest in aesthetics is not
an interest in classical standards of beauty but in avant-gardist explorations of the formal limits of signification. His exemplar is certainly not
Racine.

In "What Is Enlightenment?" Foucault remarks with evident approval
on Baudelaire's decisively anti-nostalgist dictum that the genuine modern must not despise but instead heroize the present (1997 [1984]d:
310). He follows Baudelaire in applauding that modern attitude for
which the hyperbolization of the value of the present would be "indis-
sociable from a desperate eagerness to imagine it, to imagine it otherwise than it is, and to transform it not by destroying it but by grasping
in it what it is" (1997 [1984]d: 311). He follows him further in emphasizing that such an attitude implies not simply an exaggerated relation
to the present but also an ascetic relation to the self: "to be modern is
not to accept oneself as one is in the flux of passing moments; it is to
take oneself as the object of a complex and difficult elaboration" (1997
[1984]d: 311). This is Baudelaire's dandy. This is the man who "makes
of his body, his behavior, his feelings and passions, his very existence a
work of art" (1997 [1984]d: 312).

It is, however, just this man from whom Foucault proceeds immediately to distance at once himself and the philosophical ethics he goes
on to outline. The Baudelairean dandy subsists only within art, as a sort
of institutional consummation. He is — or at least strives to be — "all
style." For precisely this reason he is not yet an avant-gardist.
Foucault's more determinate precedent lies accordingly not even with
Baudelaire but instead with Maurice Blanchot. Blanchot is Foucault's
more genuine thinker of the "outside," who willfully transgresses the

stylistic criteria that distinguish one genre from another, who conflates fiction with philosophical reflection, critique with narration (1998 [1966]). It is far less Baudelaire than Blanchot who resonates in Foucault's characterization of the modern philosophical ethic as grounded in a "limit-attitude" for which style is simply one of many limiting categories susceptible to a "practical critique which takes the form of a possible crossing-over [*franchissement*]" (1997 [1984]d: 315). Aestheticist? Or anti-aestheticist? Let us put it this way: Baudelaire's dandy may function as a reference point for the modern philosophical ethic, but only because the dandy and the modern philosopher both labor under the obligation to stylize — to give form — to themselves (Rabinow 1997: xxx–xxxi). But the philosopher, alas, cannot stop there. He, or she, has a broader and more restless obligation to resist all complacency, to put both the world and the self to continual test. The ethics of Foucault's philosopher has as its telos not formal perfection but instead "the release of oneself from oneself" [*se déprendre de soi-même*], an ostensibly mystical activity that Paul Rabinow has rightly suggested might far better be understood as "a form of continual self-bricolage" (1997: xxxix).

Foucault's own ethical stance — even, or perhaps particularly, as a modern philosopher — does not imply that his analytics is itself normatively biased. It certainly does not imply that everyone should aspire to be a modern philosopher. Yet the fact that such a stance is one — if one of indefinitely many others — that his analytics is designed to resolve and encompass is enough to render chimerical that third Foucault, for whom ethics could merely be reduced to subjection. This last Foucault nevertheless seems to be too bewitchingly disenchanted a presence to bid good-bye. So, for example, he is revived in Judith Butler's *Psychic Life of Power* (1997), wearing a guise uncomplicated by even a single reference to any of his work beyond the first volume of *The History of Sexuality* (1978 [1976]). He appears again in Giorgio Agamben's recent and ostensibly more comprehensive summary:

> One of the most persistent features of Foucault's work is its decisive abandonment of the traditional approach to the problem of power, which is based on juridico-institutional models . . . in favor of an unprejudiced analysis of the concrete ways in which power penetrates subjects' very bodies and forms of life. . . . [I]n his final years Foucault seemed to orient this analysis according to two distinct directives for research: on the one hand, the study of the *political techniques* (such as the science of the police) with which the State assumes and integrates the care of the natural life of individuals into its very center; on the other hand, the examination of the *technologies of the self* by which processes of subjectivation bring the individual to bind

125

himself to his own identity and consciousness and, at the same time, to an external power. (1998: 5)

Were Agamben's terminology accepted as an entirely general, unexceptionable construal of Foucault's analytics of governmentality, ethics would once again effectively be under erasure; the considered practice of freedom would effectively disappear into an oddly Hegelian void in which self-formation would consist only in surrender to the transcendent. Not that such an outcome should be regarded as a historical impossibility: one of the most incisive aspects of Foucault's treatment of political techniques and technologies of the self is that it never takes the ethical for granted. It acknowledges the considered practice of freedom as a human possibility. It does not, however, perpetrate the error of presuming that the actualization of such a possibility is always historically given. For Foucault, ethical practice requires not simply a repertoire of technologies but also an "open territory," a social terrain in which a considered freedom might be exercised. In ancient Greece, that terrain was largely the province of citizen males; women and slaves had little if any access to it. In the panoptic apparatus, it is (by design) nowhere to be found. Within such an apparatus, within any perfectly functional disciplinary apparatus, one might observe only the dynamics of subjugation, a dynamics at the ethical zero degree.

Even through the writing of the first volume of *The History of Sexuality*, Foucault often seems of the opinion that our modern "liberal" polities diminish ethical possibilities nearly to a zero degree. During the course of the long interruption between the first and second volumes of the *History*, he undergoes a change of mind (see Faubion 1998a: xxxiii–xxxix). He never comes to presume that liberalism had led to anything approaching a true ethical commons but does come to acknowledge in the present a greater array of ethical interstices than he had previously recognized. Such interstices are not removed from power. They are not, however, spaces or places of the political micromanagement or psychosocial bondage that Agamben would mistakenly have them be.

Political domination, economic exploitation, and psychosocial subjugation are the Foucauldean limits of the ethical. Power relations, those mobile, malleable, and fluid asymmetries of force and influence that charge even the most egalitarian of interactions, are its proper social and governmental matrix (Foucault 1997 [1984]b: 296). Nor should we misconstrue even what Foucault names *assujetissement* — "subjectivation" — as the final, much less the efficient cause of any ethical project. Foucault's parameters of the ethical field define not causes but a constellation of points of reference. On the one hand, no ethical project is altogether free. Or as Foucault puts it:

if I am . . . interested in how the subject actively constitutes itself in
an active fashion through practices of the self, these practices are nevertheless not something invented by the individual himself. They are
models which he finds in his culture and which are proposed, suggested, imposed upon him by his culture, his society, and his social
group. (1997 [1984]b: 291; translation slightly modified)

On the other hand, here as elsewhere, Foucault himself alludes to multiple gaps between proposal and commitment, between suggestion and
intention. Neither culture nor society nor the social group thus stands,
always and everywhere, as an insuperable boundary, either to the ethical imagination or to ethical practice. Here, I think, is where not simply
the anthropological promise but also the analytical provocation of Foucault's analytics of ethics lie. It forsakes subjectivism but also straddles
those supra-individual enclosures within which cultural relativism and
social conventionalism have long been confined. It is perhaps a sort of
historical relativism in its own right; but as we shall see, it is so with
several important and surprising qualifications.

The alternative it offers begins to emerge clearly in the preface to *The
Use of Pleasure*, under the regulative idea of "problematization," a process that Foucault characterizes in a subsequent interview as one through
which and in which thought reveals its specific difference:

What distinguishes thought is that it is something quite different from
the set of representations that underlies a certain behavior; it is also
something quite different from the domain of attitudes that can determine this behavior. Thought is not what inhabits a certain conduct
and gives it its meaning; rather, it is what allows one to step back
from this way of acting or reacting, to present it to oneself as an
object of thought and to question it as to its meaning, its conditions,
and its goals. Thought is freedom in relation to what does, the motion by which one detaches oneself from it, establishes it as an object,
and reflects on it as a problem. (1997 [1984]c: 117)

Problematization is not only an ethical process, not a possibility for
ethical thought alone. Yet it is problematization that provides the thematic bridge between a historically specific genealogy of ethics and
what, borrowing from the vocabulary of contemporary systems theory,
I venture to call a comparative anthropology of the pedagogies of autopoiesis. It is problematization that aids Foucault (and might also aid the
anthropologist) in clarifying the dynamics not simply of ethical homeostasis but also of ethical change, within as well as across cultural and
social boundaries.

Foucault directs us to ask four primary questions of any given ethical

127

project, the answers to which must be derived from the discourses and practices of a given sociocultural environment. First, what is the substance of the project, the *prima materia* of ethical concern? In ancient Greece, the project of cultivating self-mastery had as one of its substances *ta afrōdisia* "carnal pleasures." With later Stoicism, such pleasures were only one part of the broader substance of the passions. Nor must an ethical substance always be "bodily." Among such spiritual virtuosi as Saint Augustine, as among his many followers, the project of cultivating worthiness before God had as its substance not the body — which was mere dross at best — but the soul. Among the Hageners of highland New Guinea, the *prima materia* of subject–formation would appear to be the social relations that any particular individual establishes and maintains with others (Strathern 1991). Such variations are surely not endless, but they are just as surely more plural than the moral high ground would have them be.

Foucault's second question: What mode of subjectivation accompanies the project? What manner or manners of coming to be an ethical subject does the actor embrace or appeal to in orienting his or her conduct? A fine question, even though Foucault's gloss of it is somewhat misleading. In introducing the mode of subjectivation as the way "in which an individual establishes his relation to [a] rule and recognizes himself as obligated to put it into practice" (1985 [1984]: 27), Foucault plainly seeks to direct our attention to the historical, cultural, and social diversity of the avenues through which actors might assess or be directed to assess the personal applicability of any given moral standard. But if so, the concept of the rule (if not too vague) is too narrow; it at least seems to run the risk of excluding other sorts of moral standards besides norms and other sorts of moral directives besides that of obligation. The general point must be stressed: for Foucault (as for Aristotle), the ethical field is a normative field, a field of obligations that impinge on the reflexive practice of freedom even as they logically and practically require it — otherwise they would not be obligations to be fulfilled (or cast off) but instead sentences or unilateral indentures merely to be served (or else). But there are obligations and there are obligations. Some are specific to one or another subject position — the physician is obligated to save lives, and the executioner obligated to take them. Others reign across occupations and statuses to encompass everyone capable of exercising reason or everything capable of suffering — or so, to many of us, it would seem. The ethical field is further a field of ideals, less obligatory than urged. Once again, some of these are relative to the subject one is or is in the process of becoming; the ideal man of honor, who would actively avenge every and any slight, is not the ideal Christian, who would, when struck, always turn the other cheek. Others are trans-subjective: the quest for excellence, for example, or saintly or heroic excess, whether of the ideal philanthropist or missionary or modern philosopher. Foucault's genealogical inquiries clearly reveal that he is aware of such modal complexities, of which the *Nicomachean Ethics* nevertheless continues to provide the more satisfying and perspicacious general synopsis.

Third, what work does a given ethical project demand? What *askēsis*, what "training," what plan or plans of exercise lead to the attainment of its imago, its version or vision of ethical "graduation," of ethical maturity? And fourth, what telos, what end does the project hold out for attainment? In what does its actualization consist? At first glance, the derivation of these last two questions appears to be straightforwardly Aristotelian. The *Nicomachean Ethics* is the *locus classicus* of the argument that ethical competence comes to us not by nature but through training, exercise, and practice (2.1. 3–8). It is also the *locus classicus* of the argument that the good is not, as Plato proposed, a singular *eidos*, one of the master forms of the cosmos, but is instead plural, distinct in its content from one species to another and—if only in its content—even from one human being to another. But Foucault's schema of the ethical field is not, in the end, Aristotelian, and its departure from Aristotelian precedent is twofold. Aristotle inaugurates a (weakly) pluralist analytics of ethics, but Foucault extends its scope, historically and culturally, far beyond its Aristotelian frontiers. The *Politics*—Aristotle's own version of an analytics of governmentality—could still be written in full confidence of the existence of what Weber called the ethically ordered cosmos, a real world that also embodied—or, at the very least, tended toward the realization of—the good (see M. Weber 1946: 351). It could still be written in full confidence that the Greek polis, especially the Athenian polis, condensed the real and the valuable into an integrated material whole. A thorough modern, Foucault could never share that confidence nor the metaphysics by which it was informed.

At this juncture, however, the *querelle des anciens et des modernes* still allows for mediation. If perhaps by oversight, the methodology that Aristotle espouses in the *Nicomachean Ethics* provides no more than attenuated support for the naturalistic premises from which his *Politics* is launched. Aristotle's methodological maxim that ethical inquiry must not be held to the more exacting demands of mathematical or logical proof is well known (1.3.1–4). It is worth repeating, however, that it rests on the more fundamental maxim that there are no other primary data relevant to ethical inquiry than the data of human opinion, except perhaps the "data" of logic (1.3–4). Aristotle could still presume that such data could be distributed into a natural hierarchy: the opinions of the young were never to be trusted; the opinions of the man who was "thriving"—as any member of the Greek elite of the time was likely to have understood the notion of thriving—were to be favored. We might *tentatively* support Aristotle's preference for the ethical opinions of social elders over those of social juniors. Even so, his philosophical elevation of the ethical opinions of ancient Greek elders over those of everyone else, of whatever place or time, must now appear methodologically naive (or "ideologically motivated," if one prefers). Abandon that elevation and the result is—or might be—a Foucauldean engagement with ethical opinion and ethical practice. Such an engagement would no longer be concerned with the general content of what is "good for man." It would instead be concerned with the coalescence, the entrenchment, and the dissolution of those diverse apparatuses that allow for and organize the reflexive practice of freedom. It would be concerned with the machinics of inescapably plural teleologies; with the generativity of that historical, cultural, and social array of "goods" that at once inspire and bring into being the subjects who are encouraged, exhorted, or duty-bound to aspire to them.

Foucault's second departure from Aristotle is perhaps of even greater consequence. In his discussion of the acquisition of the virtues, Aristotle is at pains to emphasize the importance of teaching, of pedagogy. He asserts: "Good builders become so through building well; bad ones become so through building badly. Were this not so, no one would have need of being taught [how to build]; instead, everyone would be born a good [builder] or a bad one. So, too, indeed it is with the virtues" (2.1.6–7). Plying a *tekhnē*, an "art" or "craft," demands the acquisition of those dispositions that underpin competency in it, and this comes in turn through practicing. So, too, with the acquiring of ethical competence; this, Aristotle writes, is why "it is of no small importance whether we become accustomed to doing one sort of thing or another from childhood, but of very great, or rather, supreme importance" (2.1.8). We might accordingly be invited to understand the *Nicomachean Ethics* as a sort of general manual for the pedagogue of ethics. Yet for all he has to say about the lineaments of the virtues and of virtuous conduct, Aristotle is remarkably silent about pedagogy itself—its procedures, strategies, and techniques, its scene. Plato would hardly have approved.

His silence on this count is, moreover, inextricable from his more telling silence on another. In the third book of the *Ethics*, Aristotle reviews those epistemic conditions that differentiate voluntary actions from their involuntary counterparts:

[A]ctions are said to be involuntary not because they are executed in ignorance of what is in one's best interest, nor because they are executed in a state of complete ignorance, but rather because they are executed in ignorance of their particular circumstances and consequences. . . .

These include knowledge of (1) the agent, (2) the act, (3) the thing that is affected by or is in the sphere of the act; and sometimes also (4) the instrument, for instance, a tool with which the act is done, (5) the effect, for instance, saving someone's life, and (6) the manner, for instance, gently or violently. (5–16)

He proceeds to provide a number of examples — from legend, the store of conventional wisdom, and common experience — of how such conditions might fail to hold. He examines the first of them, however — that of an agent knowing who it is who is performing a certain action — only to dismiss it. "No one," he says, "could be ignorant of all these conditions together unless he were mad, nor plainly could be ignorant of the agent — for how could he be ignorant of himself?" (17). Granted, Aristotle is not focusing here on that reflexive awareness of one's status, of the diacriticals of one's being in the world, which we have come to think of as "identity." His rhetorical impatience with the putatively simpler question of sheer sensory self-awareness should thus not lead us to ascribe to him a similar impatience with the more complex question that Foucault's second parameter of ethics underscores. Even so, whether in the *Ethics* or elsewhere, Aristotle is hardly inclined to explore the complexities and perplexities of identity with anything approaching the centrality or urgency that we moderns have come to think they demand.

In the *Ethics* at least, that disinclination might even lead to something vaguely resembling a mistake. There, Aristotle aims at codifying the abstract guidelines of that *arkhitektonikē* or "master craft" which is *hē politikē* — the designing and maintenance of the polis (1.1.4). The latter has as its end that unique object which is sought always for its own sake and never for the sake of anything else (1.7.1) — that is to say, the good for man, *eudaimonia*. The object of *hē politikē* must thus be an *energeia* or "activity," since it is evident that only among the class of activities, rather than the class of latent capacities or passive states, that one might locate an object perfect or complete enough to be sufficient for us, in and of itself. It is not until the sixth book of the *Ethics* that Aristotle argues explicitly that such an object must also be a *praxis*, a "practice," and never a *poiēsis*, a "creating" or "making." At issue in that book are the intellectual virtues, especially the cardinal intellectual virtue of the ethical actor — *fronēsis*, practical wisdom, skill at *proairesis*, deliberative choice. Assessing its genus, Aristotle concludes that practical wisdom cannot be a science, for it deals with the variable, not the fixed and determinate. "Nor," he continues, "can it be the same as 'art' (*tekhnē*) . . . [and] not art, because practicing and making are different in kind. The end of making is distinct from it; the end of practice is not: practicing well is itself the end" (6.5.3–4). Shortly before this, he will have declared that "all art deals with bringing something into existence; and to pursue an art means to study how to bring into existence a thing which may either exist or not exist, and the efficient cause (*hē arkhē*) of which *lies in the maker and not the thing made*" (6.4.4; my emphasis).

These distinctions have a number of striking implications. One of them amounts to a rejection of the Socratic analogy between ethical and "technical" virtuosity. Another is that *hē politikē* — qua *poiēsis*, in any case — is a technical enterprise, though one that aims at bringing ethical practice into existence. In this respect, it is "ethically relevant," a constant and indeed privileged component of the ethical field. The various activities to which Foucault refers as "practices of the self" or "techniques of the self" or "technologies of the self" are also technical enterprises, the ethical relevance of which seems obvious enough. They are vivid features of the Foucauldean ethical field. Yet here, Aristotle must differ — though how far is difficult to say. Taking him strictly at his word, he has no room for techniques and technologies of the self in the realm of "art," for all that is art manifests a causal fissure between maker and thing made. He would thus seem obliged to construe them as "doings," though done always for the sake of something else. He would not thus be guilty of paradox but could perhaps be accused of a certain classificatory awkwardness. He might be accused of oversight as well: for Aristotle, the "middle voice" of reflexive activity, of an agency in which the self is at once subject and object, doer and that to which something is done, is without its poetic pitch.[8]

Foucault restores its pitch and much of the genuine complexity of ethical subject–formation in doing so. He is not the first: one might look back to Nietzsche, Rousseau, or Montaigne. Matters of originality aside, though, the moderns (and near moderns) must be deemed to have won at least this stage or moment of the debate. Or to be more fair, we might judge the whole matter something of a red herring. Foucault has himself shown, after all, that practices and technologies of the self were altogether as integral to the ethical life of the ancient world as they were to its Christian successor. Yet we must still give Aristotle his due — and not simply because Foucault's analytics of ethics remains only a supplement to, and not a replacement of, his own. If he did not adequately· discern the distinctiveness or perhaps even the possibility of ethical "autodidacticism" (a term I introduce advisedly, since ethical subject formation can never be purely autodidactic, even at its most reflexive), he must still be given credit for discerning or reiterating (see *NE* 6.4.2: once again, matters of originality are irrelevant) the depth of the divide between making and doing, between creation and choice. It is regrettable that so few modern theorists of action have preserved this bit of his broader wisdom. Having slighted it, they tend to rush headlong toward dichotomization: either placing both creation and choice under the influence of a quasi-demonic psyche (or culture, or society); or releasing both into the Elysian expanses of sheer contingency. Hence, I would suggest, the decidedly modern quarrel between decisionists and determinists that continues to plague us. That antagonists on both sides of this quarrel have claimed Foucault as an ally is indicative less of his ambiguity than of his belonging no more to one side than to the other. With Aristotle, he sees in *poiēsis* an activity neither passively determined nor entirely "up to us" (3.3.6). Or to put it more positively: for Aristotle as for Foucault, *poiēsis* is an activity in which the peculiar dynamics of thought interposes itself between reaction and action. For Foucault, the indeterminate house of mirrors which thus permits access is the house of ethical maturation.[9]

The allusion to Lacanian imagery is intentional but not meant to suggest even ideal-typical affinity. Foucault could perhaps agree with some suitably diluted version of Aristotle's postulate that "the life of right conduct is pleasurable in itself" (1.8.10). He could at least agree that pleasure is an important epistemological index for ethical inquiry (Rabinow 1997: xxxvii). But he is not a theorist of desire ("libido"). He is a genealogist of "those practices by which individuals [have been] led to focus their attention on themselves, to decipher, recognize, and acknowledge themselves as subjects of desire, bringing into play between themselves and themselves a certain relationship that allows them to discover, in desire, the truth of their being" (1985 [1984]: 5). Nor is his analytics closed to other genealogies, other practices, other subjects. With its more generous scope, it provides a refreshing alternative to those automatic psychoanalyses too many contemporary cryptologists of subjectivity deploy in transferring—usually with dubious empirical warrant—the deep structures of the Lacanian psyche onto the social plane, the plane of interaction. It also provides us with the opportunity to reconsider the whole dialectics of internalization and objectification through which socialization itself transpires. It is especially striking that Foucault places within something like Husserlian brackets the prevailing tenet that our earliest, primary socialization bestows upon us our subsequent health or pathology, our subsequent psychic fate. He invites us to consider the possibility that technologies of the self might not always serve as the instruments of the reiteration and reinforcement of the cathexes and traumas, the defenses and disguises of our childhoods, but sometimes also as the instruments of their revision.

Such a possibility would not, however, exist were the ethical Imaginary simply the dark mirror of a given ethical Symbolic (and vice versa). It would not, in other words, exist were ethical *poiēsis* limited merely to mimesis, were its sole master trope the trope of simile. Foucault, for his part, does not develop an ethical semiology, a maker's guide to ethical creation; this is yet another lacuna in his address of modes of subjectivation. From the cases and commentaries he has left us, we can nevertheless say something about what such a guide would have to include. No less than *praxis* does *poiēsis* require reasoning about means and ends, so it, too, must rest on the logic of that intellectual capacity Aristotle regards as the signature of practical wisdom: the capacity for deliberation. Yet as figuration, it must further rest on a tropology, for which simile would be adequate only if the ethical life always and everywhere consisted in "living up to" a given exemplar or ideal. The Christian valorization of the *imitatio Christi* is an obvious case in point of the latter, but the case on which Foucault comments in *The Use of Pleasure* is not in tropological conformity with it. For the "practice-oriented" ethics of the classical Greek elite, an ethics that has its fulcrum in the *hiatus irrationalis* between the generality of precept and the particularity of situation, simile frequently cedes its place to irony, tragic or comic from one instance to the next. I have argued that metalepsis is the master trope of one prominent current of self-(re)formation in contemporary Greece (Faubion 1993). Or we could again visit the Hageners, for whom self-formation proceeds in an open-ended synecdoche Marilyn Strathern has deemed "cyborgic" (1991: part 2). Throughout a good stretch of North America, we could encounter a strange people whose ethical individualism has its tropological summum in Walt Whitman's grand metaphor: "I am everything." At the risk of advocating a formalism that would run counter to Foucault's methodological nominalism,[10] I cannot help but propose that tropology might in fact constitute the framework for a comparative hermeneutics of modes of subjectivation. But I leave a more substantial justification of that proposal for the future.[11]

To return, then, to what ethical *poiēsis* must in any event be, whatever its precise logic or semiology: *askēsis*, a labor, even if not always "disciplinary" labor. In *The Use of Pleasure* and *The Care of the Self* (1986 [1984]), Foucault collects the tool kit of the ancient ethical economy. It contains diaries, journals, the *hupomnēmata* or "memory books" Hellenistic Greeks kept as miscellanies for the conduct of life. It contains schedules of solitary reading, of the silent examination of the course of one's day, of such thought experiments as the *praemeditatio malorum* (a reflection on misfortunes that may occur in the future), of the interpretation of dreams. It contains an array of "calisthenics," from the restraint of sexual and other appetites to regular indulgence in walks in the countryside. Yet if ethics subsists in the relation of the self to itself, and if ethical *poiēsis* can (in part) be conducted alone and in private, Foucault grants pride of place to what we might think of as ethical exchange. In "Self-Writing," and again in "Technologies of the Self," for example, he focuses at length on one of Marcus Aurelius's intimate letters to his friend and confidant Cornelius Fronto; in *The Use of Pleasure*, on the management of the *oikos* and of pederastic affairs. Nor is the privilege an arbitrary one. Consider his remarks on the Greek ethics of the care of the self:

> [T]he care of the self is ethical in itself; but it implies complex relationships with others insofar as this *ethos* of freedom is also a way of caring for others. This is why it is important for a free man who conducts himself as he should to be able to govern his wife, his children, his household; it is also the art of governing. *Ethos* also implies a relationship with others insofar as the care of the self enables one to occupy his rightful position in the city, the community, or interpersonal relationships, whether as a magistrate or a friend. And the care of the self also implies a relationship with the other insofar as proper care of the self requires listening to the lessons of a master. One needs a guide, a counselor, a friend, someone who will be truthful with you. Thus, the problem of relationships with others is present throughout the development of the care of the self. (1997[1984]b: 287)

Most of these remarks reach little beyond the Greeks, or at least beyond antiquity. The last of them, however, is more wide-ranging. In fact, it suggests yet another basic parameter of an analytics of ethics, vaguely present already in Aristotle but, once again, better brought to the fore against the foil of Wittgenstein. Could there ever be a perfectly private ethics whose substance, mode of subjectivation, ascetics, and end only a single person might deem ethical as such? The legion of ethical subjectivists notwithstanding, the answer can only be no for many of the same reasons that Wittgenstein adduced in rejecting the possibility of a private language and to which I have already resorted in arguing against the possibility of a similarly private pedagogy. An ethics completely unmoored from public criteria of validity would simply be no ethics at all. It would be devoid of ethical sense (or, for that matter, of sense *tout court*). Nor does such a conclusion hinge on semantics alone. It is in fact pedagogical—for like language, as (in part) a part of language, ethics must itself be taught. Hence, if ethical *poiēsis* might sometimes occur in the remote isolation of a desert cave, its primal scene must also be a scene of instruction, the scene of that pedagogy, that interactive art which has as its overarching end the crafting of human beings into beings of ethical craft.

135

Hence, the programmatic (and decidedly nonsubjectivist) aspect of Foucault's insistence that the self *in its relation to others* is "the very stuff" of ethics, the groundwork for a comparative hermeneutics, a comparative anthropology, of pedagogies of autopoiesis. Precisely because it would have to delve into the devices, strategies, tactics, and tricks essential to any pedagogy, whatever its end, such an anthropology would also have to be an anthropology of power. There is no thinking of ethics without thinking of power, or rather of powers, whether those that suppress autopoiesis or allow it to flourish. I am uncertain whether Foucault's dictum that "the slave has no ethics" (1997[1984]b: 286) is an entirely accurate characterization of the condition of enslavement in ancient Greece, but it nevertheless has an ideal-typical justification. An individual under the unflinching control of another—whether completely dominated, exploited, or subjugated—would indeed be ethically abject. Even at best, he or she could function only as the ethical proxy of a master. Short of such abjection, autopoiesis emerges as a theoretical possibility, a historical potential. It is in need of what I might now more precisely identify as the social and cultural institutionalization of a practical pedagogy in order to be made animate.

And what of the politics of such a pedagogy, of its internal disposition of forces? Though Foucault speaks in the passage I have quoted of the ethical pedagogue as a "master," he certainly does not mean to imply that the ethical student is a slave. Short of performative inconsistency, any "ethical pedagogy" worthy of the name could neither maintain nor promote abjection. Its politics consequently cannot rest in permanent political asymmetries. The ethical master must devote himself (or herself) instead to the enhancement and refinement of the reflexive freedom of his students. He must devote himself to the production of other masters. His politics cannot ultimately be a politics of domination. It must instead rest in the maintenance and promotion of power relations. Is the ethical master thus forbidden to dictate, to seduce, to punish, to use coercion with those under his charge? Foucault does not say so, but his analytics does, I think, entail that such a prohibition must be in force, at least ultimately, insofar as the commands, the seductions, the punishments, and the coercion of which the ethical apprentice is the object would otherwise effectively cast him or her into a state of permanent obedience or irresistible manipulation. No disciplinary or pastoral (or other pedagogical) relationship can be (fully) ethical at its outset: this is Gramsci's point. Yet those relationships which, in spite of relatively permanent asymmetries, stop short of being purely authoritarian, of being nothing more than the play of subjugation and resistance, might still be counted as ethical—if only in small degree.

It is not, however, the issue of fluctuating ethical degrees that leads

Foucault beyond an analytics of ethical homeostasis to an analytics of ethical change. Problematization takes precedence. To reiterate, as that reflexive process through which one presents to oneself a certain way of acting or reacting, asks questions of it, examines its meaning and goals, problematization has nothing intrinsically ethical about it. Yet it has special interest to the genealogist (and the anthropologist) of ethics, not merely for its role in stylization or decision making but for its occasionally precipitating or inciting the parametric transformation of one ethical field into another, perhaps unprecedented one. Ethical pedagogies, ethical practices remain homeostatic so long as the contents of the Foucauldean ethical fourfold — substance, mode of subjectivation, work, and telos — remain stable. Yet by no means the least of Foucault's achievements as genealogist is his demonstration that each of these parameters can itself be (and in fact has been) the focus of problematization. In classical Greece, pleasures were rendered problematic as an ethical substance in light of the telos of *sōfrosunē*, self-mastery; the content of ethical work was rendered problematic in light of the antinomies of pederastic pleasure (Foucault 1986 [1984]: 49–50, 214–46). In the early Christian period, the received content of self-mastery was rendered problematic in light of substantive dualism of flesh and spirit; and so on. We are consequently not the Greeks, however much we fancy ourselves the beneficiaries of their legacy.

Between the Greeks and us, moreover, much else has passed besides the always limited dialectics of subjugation and resistance, with which Foucault's initial foray into the history of the present state of sexuality had virtually exclusively been concerned. The dynamics of subjectivation and problematization are much broader and far more various. Foucault in fact retrospectively declared them to encompass all he had previously treated, from *Madness and Civilization* forward (1994 [1984]b: 669). Yet they are not the same as, not merely the dynamics of, power knowledge and its driving "will to know." The motors of problematization are heterogeneous. The always vested will to know is one, but that less suspect urge Foucault came to call "the will to truth" is another (see Faubion 1998a: xxxvii–xxxviii). Sometimes problematization and its outcomes seem to conform closely to Weber's developmental model of rationalization. Foucault, however, was skeptical of the potential historical myopia of even that model and refused to recast the history of systems of thought exclusively in its terms. Problematization might lead away from what Weber had (antinomically) regarded as rationalization as often as toward it. It is quintessentially unpredictable, even if not arbitrary. Its background conditions are those in which any particular system (or subsystem) of thought, crisply coherent or cognitively bedraggled, rests at any given moment. Against them, it commences as an aporia, a paradox or puzzle, a surprise or anomaly, as just that sort of "problem" Foucault had found so compellingly articulated in the "transcendental empiricism" of Gilles Deleuze (1998 [1970]b). Against a given mental fabric of the expectable, it thus commences in the experience of the unexpected, the odd, the baffling. Cybernetically, problematization thus has its provocation in the encounter with what might (or might not) turn out to be "information" (cf. Luhmann 1990a: 30–31).

Yet, for all that it consequently stands apart from the prime Weberian hallmark of the history of the West, problematization also stands with it, not merely as antecedent but as consequence. If the dynamics of problematization do not entirely encompass the dynamics of rationalization, the former are at the very least an especially intimate correlate of the latter. They are operative across the same planes, the same ideational expanses; their repercussions affect the same universe. As Foucault's genealogy of ethics illustrates with particular acuity, they do not merely produce "elaborations" and "refinements." Problematization also constitutes the dynamic interface between one discourse and another, one discursive formation and another, one putative historical period and another. It is the specific mental catalyst of the brusque ideational disruptions that Foucault so diversely investigated. His investigations of the ethical field must be accorded anthropological pride of place—and not merely because of their illustrative clarity, nor even merely because of their greater attention to continuity through change. They earn it instead because they reveal that the ethical field, in which power is fluid and problematization capable of being the catalyst of revisionary resolution, is the primary site of the active transformation at once of the parameters of subjectivation and of given views of the world. They reveal, in short, that whether opening up at the banquet table, or in the streets, or even in the university, the ethical field is the primary site of cultural invention. Or to be more precise, the conditions that distinguish the ethical field from those of an ossified governmentality (dominating, exploiting, or subjugating as the case may be) would appear to be necessary conditions for anything we might properly designate as cultural invention. All that transpires elsewhere, in other situations, may well have to be deemed what many sociocultural diagnostics would have them be: reproduction or disruption; coercion or the feckless spontaneity of "resistance." For the later Foucault at least, resistance is one thing; the ethical field and the cultural invention it allows is another, not to be reduced to mere contrariness.[12]

To return, at long last, to Ms. Roden. Of her life before coming to Texas she has never been especially inclined toward great elaboration — at least not in her conversations with the anthropologist. Perhaps she has been reluctant to make too public the more troubling details of her "dysfunctional family." Even in her writings, her father and mother are present only by occasional allusion; her brother is not present at all. In her reading of a portion of the Book of Zechariah, her sisters and she are rendered antitypically as three cities — Sodom, Jerusalem, and Samaria. All are figures of waywardness or wantonness, though the latter two are also figures of cathartic redemption and godly service.[13]

She accordingly predicts that, in due time, she will not be the only Bishop sister to have converted to Branch Davidianism. The event has, however, not yet occurred, and other female figures loom far more importantly in her writings as a whole. Her son is not and never has been a Branch Davidian. Yet he and she are not at all estranged. She loves him deeply and is justifiably proud of his intelligence and educational success. She writes of him, ex cathedra, in the one lengthy biographical narrative in which she has no resort to biblical typology as frame or method. In the same text she also mentions his father. Neither her son nor his father find an antitypical place in her other texts. Only the daughter whom she bore with George Roden has such a place in them.

Perhaps her life before Texas lacked ethical clarity. If Luhmann is correct in arguing that the functional differentiation of our current social order leaves us without any single, overarching, all-encompassing source from which to derive our identities, then perhaps Ms. Roden's former life was simply as ethically scattered, or ethically complex, as those of the great majority of her contemporaries, as those of most of us (Luhmann 1990b: 431–32). Our common structural condition has not changed. Ms. Roden has changed — actively, if not by choice. She has continued to change. The ethical subject whom she conceived herself to be at the commencement of her conversations with the anthropologist is not precisely the same as the ethical subject she now conceives herself to be, or to be striving to be. Luhmann, it should be added, is willing to admit one possible institutional locus of the acquisition and cultivation of a "total" identity, even in so functionally differentiated order as our own, even if burdened with its own paradoxes, and even if not equally accessible (or palatable) to everyone. The locus — no surprise — is a religious one (1990b: 433–35; cf. Luhmann 1990a).

We have already met Ms. Roden's teachers. The woman who introduced her to a Pentecostal congregation in the aftermath of her dreams and visions was an "educator" in the etymological sense of the term. She "led" her friend and charge "out of" what had been her past and into what would become her future. Ms. Roden had her first introduction to apocalypticism and typological interpretation among the Pentecostals, but she did not remain with them for long. She turned to private and solitary studies. George Roden was the more sustained influence—but also passing. He was her converter, but not the converter of a biblical novice. George would inform her of the doctrines that he had himself inherited. She accepted them, but she did not accept those with which George sought to establish his own spiritual authority and spiritual legacy. The student was becoming her own master. The teacher would be reduced to a husband, though a husband upon whose spiritual authority as both son and sire Ms. Roden has always emphatically avowed. Her most enduring instructors have acted posthumously and indirectly through the volumes they have left behind. Of Ellen White's oeuvre, she knows primarily what Victor Houteff and the elder Rodens incorporated in their own writings through quotation. She owns a few of Mr. Houteff's various pamphlets; once again, the Rodens' quotations provide her with many of his other views and expositions. She follows almost all of the ritual prescriptions that Ben Roden enacted, but Lois is the more precious and prepossessing spiritual advisor. As she told me once: *It's kind of hard to get into Ben.* Among the living, she has few genuinely pedagogical interlocutors. She has become the master to whom others might listen. The woman who is her closest church friend is a partial exception. Though they live far apart, the two speak on the telephone. They engage in disputations and discussions through the mail. As Ms. Roden told me on another occasion: *Everything I write I write to [her].* Perhaps she imagines the relationship as a spiritual hierarchy, since she believes her friend to be the antitype of the seventh and final angel of Revelation. Intellectually, however, she is herself the more forceful of the two, though no means beyond being corrected. The relationship is thus teacherly, "intra-academic." It is a pedagogical *filia*, a "friendship," a "love."

The regime of subjectivation under which Ms. Roden now lives—or in any event that regime that now provides her with her primary ethical orientation—is of course Biblicist. The Bible has, however, been the canonical source of many such regimes. Though believers would beg to differ, its subjectivational determinacy is weak; it is always in need of a supplement—hermeneutical, pontifical, charismatic, or dogmatic from one instance to the next. So, for example, Ms. Roden lives as a Christian in her embrace of Jesus as the Christ. As a Branch Davidian, however, she does not see in Jesus' own conduct a model that all should strive to embody. In contrast to any number of others, hers is a church that does not elevate the *imitatio Christi* to a moral and ethical axiom. Or better, it does not elevate the imitation of the historical Jesus to such an axiom, because it does not regard him as the consummation of the Christ.

The ethical status of the Bible's other dramatis personae is even more ambiguous, and its disambiguation is largely dependent on the "tense" and the "tenor" of typological interpretation itself. Ranging over the past, operating retrodictively, the typologist is most often an ironist, who sees more in the suffering and the acts of any actor than the latter could possibly have seen himself or herself. The historical Jesus, for example, has left us with no evidence that he either knew himself nor strove to be the antitype of Adam, but that is the subject position that many a Branch Davidian (and many a non–Branch Davidian) typologist now assigns him. Operating retrodictively, in short, typological interpretation renders the personages of the Bible of theological and cosmological significance but not immediately of any ethical significance. Operating in the present, its outcomes might also lack immediate ethical significance — but not always. It can serve as a means of interpellation, of "hailing" — as it does in Ms. Roden's assignation of the antitypical role of the seventh angel to her friend, or as it did, reflexively, in David Koresh's apparent assignation of the same role to himself, or as it has, again reflexively, in Ms. Roden's assignation of a whole constellation of antitypical roles to herself, the role of the sixth angel among them. In all these instances, typology is the means to a mode of subjectivation that is "scriptural" in two senses of the term. It defines the self in light of a scriptural type or types; and it imposes upon the self that "script" in which such types have already had and played out their inscribed roles. Operating presentistically, typology can thus identify a personal past but also a personal future. Yet, this is not ethical being, the identification of an ethical project. It is the identification of fate, of necessity. This scriptural mode of subjectivation is a mode that collapses back into subjugation, into a kind of spiritual slavery. So Ms. Roden must be, and must continue to be, the Daughter of Zion, and the Wavesheaf, and the Sixth Angel, and George Roden's wife, and his daughter's mother, with all their attendant hardship, all their inevitable calamities, all their eventual blessings. She can neither choose to be or make herself into anyone else.

A.P.B.R.: *Although my work has not been particularly acceptable to the church, the very prophecies will cause them to refuse it . . . I don't know if you've ever had God put a hammer-lock on you.*

J.D.F.: Not that I know of.

A.P.B.R.: *But He's quite capable of doing exactly that. Slap you around and pin you around and put you down in exactly the direction He wants you to go in.*[14]

From Paul forward, typology has also been deployed normatively, precisely in order to identify in the past those "ensamples," negative and positive, that have been revealed as guides to conduct in the present and the future. The normative force of such ensamples would be moot were fate a mechanism rather than a Deleuzean machine, were its tuning so fine that it determined our every mood and our every move. Paul was not such a fatalist. True to her Branch Davidianism, neither is Ms. Roden. Following her parents-in-law, she attributes to the literal descendants of the Israelites a special proclivity for charismatic anointment, for spiritual grace or gifts. But descent is not a guarantee of giftedness, nor is giftedness a guarantee of entry into the Kingdom. Not even the divine appointment to a certain role or task comes with such a guarantee, not even if the role be fulfilled or the task completed. For the apocalyptic and millenarian believer, the Great Divide that separates the subjects of the world is the divide between the damned and the elect. For some, damnation, for others, election is itself fate. For the rest, is it an ethical telos. For the rest, for Ms. Roden herself, *the Kingdom must be earned*. Ethical problematization has its beginning just here. It is multistranded, but its guiding question can be stated simply enough: How?

In what is in many respects a radicalization of Seventh-day Adventist doctrines of practical conduct, especially a radicalization of the restorationism that the return to a Saturday Sabbath already suggested, the Branch Davidian looks to Jewish Orthodoxy, to the deuteronomic books of the Bible, to the Old much more frequently than to the New Testament. He or she looks to God's dicta and, if more critically or selectively, to the Abrahamic patriarchs, to their particular ensample. So, too, Ms. Roden. Yet she is an even more radical restorationist than the elder Rodens or Mr. Pace. If still recognizably the outcome of a Branch Davidian education, her outline of the ways proper to the holy, written in 1995, is also her own.

CHILDREN: *Have the right to be healthy and righteous. This implies a parental commitment to nutritious food and time spent teaching each child a Christian character. Do not have more children than you can raise as vigorous, intelligent, God-fearing neighbors. If you have to beat children with a rod, consider whether you are setting a Christian example for them to learn from in your doings. A loving communication of the values that you live by and a hard palm should be sufficient.*

DRUGS: *If God grew it you can use it, unprocessed. That means opium for the pains of childbed, coca leaves for childbirth, running, etc., and marijuana for relaxation. Both Christ and Paul gave you wine (Luke 22:17–20; Tim. 5:23). Drunkards damned (Isa. 5:11).*

HEALTH (MENTAL AND PHYSICAL): *Medical establishment, hospitals and poisonous drugs shunned. Woe unto the doctors! Meat only on feast days, i.e. Passover lamb. A high-protein organic vegetarian diet with plenty of fresh or home-canned vegetables, especially carrots and oranges, will minimize the need for herbs. Friends promote each other's mental health with sympathetic communication. To walk in God's law is mental health.*

JUSTICE SYSTEM: *God will provide (Isa. 32:1).*

LIFESTYLE: *Separate yourselves from the wicked.*

MARRIAGE: *Frankly, I would rather be the mother of harlots than give my daughter into Satan's version of marriage. Now that a woman alone has stood for seven months on Mount Carmel for the right of children to be safe in the church, I have a message which the daughter of Jepthah cried aloud on the mountains (Jud. 2:30–39), a message unheard of because of the Law of Coverture.*[15] *One person may not make a [marriage] contract for another to fulfill, nor interfere with another's right to contract. Men and women, both uncursed, stand equal in the Kingdom of the Righteous. If they desire, both may have more than one spouse; for the sake of their children they will not break wedlock unless there is unrelenting abuse. Youthful marriage and chaperones for unmarried young women are necessary to discourage fornication.*

MUSIC: *Elijah Worden wrote prophetic rock music heralding the Mount Carmel tragedy and the reemergence of the church. Any kind of music can praise God.*[16]

LAND, AGRICULTURE: *No more speculation in land and megafarms (Isa. 5:8). Every man to own a small acreage (Mic. 4:4). Feed the needy from the tithe. For the sake of health, organic farming only.*

POLITICS: *Stop supporting Satan, set up the Kingdom.*

RACIAL RELATIONS: *Racial purity emphasized but not enforced. Let those who love marry, lest they fornicate. Let the prophets keep to the prophets in the main; amidst a holy people is a race of prophets.*

SABBATH: *Do you think of doing good on the Sabbath? Do good six days and thank Yahweh the seventh that you have the means.*

SANCTITY OF LIFE: *Children have a right to be born free of physical defect. It's easier to rebuke women for the murder of children than it is to rebuke the wicked.*

TAXATION: *For the death decree, pay in bullets.*[17]

WOMEN: *See marriage.*

PREACHERS: *Hearken unto the prophets; they are the deliverance in the time of trouble. Let those who walk in God's Law speak at the meetings.*

The men who are trying to sustain their families and hold God's Law in their hearts are the only hope of mankind; nevertheless, the millennial Kingdom can't be sustained on an unrighteous law. It should be noted that I am not standing to judge you since I am a sinner myself. On the other hand, I've carried the burden while the strong men slept and the mighty men sat on their hands (Psa. 76:5). As you see from the

143

rest of the Psalm, God has risen to judgment to save the meek. At this time you need the wisdom of women.[18]

Ms. Roden's inventory is in fact a critical reply to a flyer distributed by the Israelite Assembly, an adamantly restorationist Protestant congregation located in Alba, Texas, a small town some one-hundred-twenty-five miles northeast of Waco.[19] She is more brief in her views on justice, more lenient in her views on the music and on the disciplining and rearing of children than they are. The Israelite Assembly declares rock music "Satanic."[20] She is more lenient in her attitude toward interracial marriages (which the Israelite Assembly strictly forbids) but recognizes a "race of prophets," the existence of which the Assembly would likely deny. She is considerably more lenient in her tolerance of "natural" drugs and wine. She has nothing to say about (but would probably agree with) the Assembly's condemnation of homosexuality, supports its condemnation of "fornication" and its declaration that marriage is a contract to which Yahweh, not the government, is the appropriate witness. The Assembly prescribes unqualified vegetarianism, which Ms. Roden has told the anthropologist that she thinks is most appropriate for prophets alone. The Assembly advocates the establishment of a "republic" in which (male) property owners would have exclusive suffrage.[21] Ms. Roden calls for the establishment of the Kingdom and every man's (here she almost certainly means every adult's) right to own land. The Assembly urges large families and homeschooling.[22] It embraces the Law of Coverture and thus both monogamy and the authority of the husband over his wife.[23] Ms. Roden is more qualified in her endorsement of the family, and, needless to say, she has little patience for proponents of either monogamy or conjugal (or gender) inequality.

As for many other Christian ethicists, so for Ms. Roden, the common and primary substance of ethical concern seems appropriately enough conceived as the will in its Augustinean sense: the seat of appetite and desire. In contrast to the ancient Greeks, but again like Saint Augustine, the most urgent ethical distinction is not that between will and *logos*, will and reason, but between the individual human will, with its inherent tendency toward *hamartia*, toward being "off the point," toward error and sin, and the will of God, revealed as dicta, as His Law and his ordinations. Hence, Ms. Roden's morality is predominantly a morality of the Law, of both prescriptions and proscriptions. Yet is does not imply an ethics merely of obedience. Or more carefully, it does not imply an ethics for which obedience would consist in the purging from the will of every need, every desire, that could pose even the risk of sin. What Paul was prepared to tolerate only in the average Christian, but not among such virtuosi as himself, what Augustine was prepared to tolerate among that common run of congregants who were likely damned in the first place, Ms. Roden deems appropriate among the elect themselves. Hers is a morality of *askēsis*, but not an asceticism. The body is not a prison from which the ethical actor must somehow design an escape. The fleshly is not inherently evil. Its appetites (some of them, in any case) permit accommodation, even a measured indulgence. Sexual desire demands its due. Even among the prophets, its righteousness does not reside merely in its compelling procreation. Ms. Roden might accept the good sense of the call for *moderatio in omnibus*, but here at least, she would understand the principle more in the manner of the ancient Greeks, far less in the manner of the English public schoolmaster. She is opposed to excess, to "addiction." But for the Greeks, so for her, the criteria of excess (and deficiency), of what is on the mark and what is wide of it, are situational; they are, beyond the explicit dictates of the Law, always spatio-temporally particular. So there is a time and a season for wine, for opium, for marijuana, for lamb, for eros. There is a time and a season for the wisdom of women. The Law is transcendent; the seasons and times of the reflexive practice of freedom further demand attention to the consequences of what one does, refrains from doing, fails to do.

So election is earned, for many of the common and the prophetic elect alike. The prophets, however, would be mistaken in believing that the limiting of the exercise of their wills to the confines of the divine Law should exhaust their ethical obligations, should be the end of their ethical formation, the telos of their ethical projects. They are burdened with a substance beyond the will, which could never be corrupted, never be made unvirtuous, but could still suffer ethically irresponsible neglect. Theirs is the burden of having a special gift, the gift of the spirit. The greatest part of Christian theology continues to cast both the soul and the spirit as immaterial, essentially different from and opposed to the bodily. Ms. Roden's prophets — and thus Ms. Roden herself — are instead the recipients and the bearers of the pneuma, as integral to the constitution of their corporeal selves as the more mundane air they breathe. The logic of their ethical condition is, no more than the logic of salvation, the logic of reciprocal exchange. Their being in possession — or being the possession of — the pneuma is no more a matter of their having responded appropriately to a gesture or an invitation, of having fulfilled an "obligation to receive," than is their breathing itself. It is simply "given"; it is another element, another dimension, of their personal fate. It is nevertheless a dimension that leaves them owing — if not obliged to settle accounts, as if that were possible, then obliged to pay tribute to the Sovereign who has seen fit to bless them with his largesse. For the prophets, the mode of obedience to the Law is consequently

145

only a part of the mode of their subjectivation. The rest is the mode of the debtor, of the taxed, whose remittance must come in the form of the cultivation of the body, of the will, of the pneuma itself—a triple self-nurturing. Its telos is not election; for that, the way of obedience is enough. Its telos is one of full disclosure: of the rescue of the pneuma from the long shadows of the frail and neglected body, of the errant will; of its epiphany in the full light of its proper truth.

Ask Ms. Roden how she spends her days. She will tell you of her work, of chores, of minding and tending. In the late summer of 1996, she described a typical day's agenda:

> *I get up. I mow. I always have work scheduled. I do the stuff that's out of doors and in the sunshine early, so I try to be done by ten or eleven, which means often I start at, uh, it takes five and a half hours to water the memoriam, and that's tomorrow's job, and that gets three gallons on each tree, because I have to do it by generator, and . . . so I try to start at six. . . . And then I am in a program of keeping signs out, little signs down at the end of the road, so I paint signs. And then various little projects. Yesterday we put up the white frames around the religious literature. That was Tom's idea. And every two or three days I cook. I don't cook a lot—whenever I run out of whatever it was that I cooked last time. And I talk to people a lot. And basically I just stay busy, and I find that is the best kind of therapy to keep my head on straight, is just to keep working, stay busy.*[24]

In the summer of 1996, Ms. Roden was still the most visible resident of Mount Carmel, but she was not alone. The security guards and the metal fences that had surrounded the ruins of the Koreshites' compound in the aftermath of the conflagration were gone. At some distance from Ms. Roden's encampment, however, Mr. Pace was constructing a house of worship. Her companion, Tom, had entered into a (polygamous) marriage contract with her first in 1989:

> *George Roden said* [that Tom would] *protect me, and he needed a place to live. And there were two houses at the farm—which there are, two houses—he moved into the other one. He came and asked me the same day that I discovered that the car had been tampered with. I had a problem. I assumed the problem was David Koresh, but anyway, I had a problem. So Tom, with eight years as a policeman, he could—he was a crack shot. I was very happy. I gave him George's .357; I let him take care of security. And indeed, he went after some people he heard whispering at two in the morning, and all the harassment stopped. He chased them, dressed solely in a .357.*

146

This crazy person with a gun. I asked him if he put his boots on; he said he didn't remember. Anyhow, my son went off to live with his father in Indonesia that summer, and on the way back from the airport, Tom said, "I'll protect you from everyone, but who's going to protect you from me?" . . . Tom had a drinking problem. So about February, Tom wanted to stop drinking, and he had seizures and visions, and he had several days of visions where he was in combat with Satan, who was trying to control him; and he was in an actual bout with Satan; it just lasted several days. He came out of it a sober man. Of course, we were always dear to each other. He came to visit. . . .

It makes me feel a lot safer. Last summer, I guess I put on about twenty pounds. The amount of poison — it seems to me that when you get too much toxicity in your body that your body encases it in fat and stashes it. And I became unable to control my weight, and I'm back in control now. What they were doing is they were coming into the building at night and poisoning all the food, since I only got to town once a week, I took in a lot of carcinogens. Some nasty stuff. But since Tom is here, I mean, we sleep in the Volvo, with the doors cabled shut, and we always put barrel locks on the doors. The back doors don't open at all, and the trunk is sealed with a couple of cables. It makes it a whole lot harder. They occasionally get my groceries, but they have to distract me. And they can do that. They're good. They get me talking religion, and. . . .[25]

She took it upon herself to maintain the memorial to the Branch Davidian dead. With Tom, she had labored to expand and polish her museum, which now had a proper building, crammed with photographs, the crosses that had once hung on the fence surrounding the ruined compound, and charred, twisted tricycles and other toys. Tom and she had posted signs throughout the ruins, which afforded visitors a self-guided tour of the traces of the buildings and interiors of the compound. Other signs bore quotations from the Bible, Ms. Roden's exegeses, welcomes to the more intrepid of the curious, warnings against the perpetration of further lies and falsehoods at Mount Carmel.

Several months later, while Ms. Roden was attending a family reunion in Florida, all their mutual work — and much more besides — would succumb to another fire. By early 1997, Tom would begin drinking again. Later in the same year, he secured George Roden's approval to collect donations from souvenirists even on the Sabbath; Ms. Roden left again for Florida over what she *regarded as a religious issue, returning only for emergencies or court appearances in the property lawsuit.*[26] Tom departed from Mount Carmel in February 1998; Ms. Roden returned in March. By the fall of 1999, they had reunited; Tom was busy helping Ms. Roden construct a more permanent shelter on the Mount Carmel property than the tiny tent in which she had been living, road-side, for the several preceding months, through the torrents that often drench the prairie in the early spring, through the oppressive brilliance of the sun, increasingly oppressive and brilliant with the turn to summer, fetching her drinking water, warm and algal, out of the same pond that kept the myrtles alive, always busy with her signs, her pamphlets, her greeting of strangers.

Whether or not she is *talking religion*, Ms. Roden often phrases her commitments instrumentally. So, she once spoke to the anthropologist of *honesty being the best policy*.[27] So she can speak as well of her daily labors as *therapy*, as the best way *to keep [her] head on straight*. So she speaks further of dietetics: *I have need in the way I live to be eating a very healthy diet. I also try to eat foods that provide all twenty-two amino acids to get the accelerated healing.* Alluding to her commentary, her profession, however, she speaks with the authority of a Biblicist, not a secular nutritionist:

> But what I preach is a little different from that. Now, the rest of the church is preaching vegetarianism. I'm preaching that there will be a time when we actually have a lamb at Passover, and cook it. Each family has their lamb, and we cook it exactly as the way the Bible says, even though Christ fulfilled the Passover lamb and ended the animal sacrifice, except as prophecy, because it does have its prophetic overtones. I preach that for Passover there will be a lamb, because it makes a lot of sense, first because God ordained it, but indeed, when we get back to an earth where every man owns his own property, and every man is under his own vine and his own fig tree, there will be farm animals, and young male farm animals, which are not economical to keep, because you don't need them. And you will eat them at Passover.
>
> Everything the Bible says you can eat is clean, and can be eaten. But if you look at the years before the Ark, before the flood, when they lived eight or nine hundred years, you will see that God gave them the herb of the ground, and right after the flood gave them all animals and the herb of the ground, and the difference in diet is particularly shown by Abraham, who lived to be a hundred and seventy-five. And Joseph, eating from the flesh-pots of Egypt, lived to be a hundred and ten. If you get away from animal foods, except perhaps for eating very young animals on ceremonial occasions, and that's your meat consumption, then you will live a lot longer.[28]

Within the Law, consequentialism has its entirely consistent place.

For the prophet, however, the means and methods of self-maintenance *make sense* not simply because of their role in facilitating obedience to the Law. They make sense above all because of their role in facilitating endurance, the health and well-being of a self whose responsibility to itself is inseparable from its responsibility to its mission, its calling from God. The prophet whom Ms. Roden understands herself to be is accordingly anxious, sensible to threat. Her anxiety permits psychomedical diagnosis, as all "deviations" inevitably do. It permits social-structural diagnosis as well. Yet, it is also the condition of a subject whose responsibilities to herself derive from a mission that others are fated to try to thwart, a calling that others are fated to try to cut short. Her task is in part simply to abide, to wait, because she cannot demand inspiration. She must instead be prepared to receive it, whenever and wherever it comes to her. Her labors would be easier were she able, like the cliff-dwelling hermits at Meteora, like Emily Dickinson or Marcel Proust in their beds, to cultivate what inspiration comes her way, to cultivate herself, as a work of art. The prophet's labors indeed include *aisthēsis* — "feeling," "experiencing." They include the stylization — indeed, the continuing formation and reformation — of the self. But they always reach beyond the "aesthetic" as we have come to employ the term. If Ms. Roden cannot resign herself to the life of an invalid, if she must always try to protect herself from what would debilitate her, this is because she has been called upon to do more than give objective form to her experience, her imagination. She has been called upon to speak and to live the truth, to make it word and flesh alike.

Among her labors, some are propaedeutic; they are preparatory exercises that have, since the early 1980s, become an increasing part of the techniques through which she preserves and further refines the self that she has already largely become. They include a physical regimen that, however often disrupted, she had always pursued as regularly as she could. She can no longer be a farmer; she has lost the right (and because her mission is what it is, the time) to return to the land on which she originally settled. Since 1998, she has ceased to tend to the upkeep of the Mount Carmel memorial; the Koreshites have come to claim that task as their own. She is left with her efforts as publicist. As she acquires the funds to purchase the materials for them, she continues to construct signboards and wooden frameworks to support them. When weather or some other adversary destroys them, she builds them again. Though she must always find a driver, she makes regular trips to one or another of the small towns in the Waco area to replenish her photocopies, to buy food. She is rigorous in following her diet. She bathes daily, not without awkwardness, at the edge of the pond from which she draws her drinking water. Thus, her calisthenics.

149

She studies the Bible, the elder Rodens' volumes of "field letters" and Sabbath School lessons, and Victor Houteff's surviving teachings. She writes. These, too, are propaedeutic activities, though perhaps less now than in the past. For this Biblicist, the Testaments have provided the primary avenue of self-knowledge, though a knowledge that would have remained incomplete without Houteff's and the elder Rodens' further instruction, further instructions. This textual and pedagogical legacy has of course served Ms. Roden as a *lecture de soi*, a "self-reading," just as her own texts have served her as an *écriture de soi*, a self-writing. Typology has been methodologically central to both, in all its tenses and tenors. Retrodictively, Ms. Roden has deployed it to distinguish, narratively to isolate and to highlight a fateful past from the merely ordinary events that always accompanied it. In the present, she has deployed it to define her place within and her relation to the tangle of forces — good, evil, merely neutral — in which she is caught, or from which she might extricate herself. Normatively, she has deployed it as a method not merely of moral estimation, of praise and condemnation, but also of the clarification of her own responsibilities to the self that has been given to her to become, to be, to continue to be. The great mythos of interiority, with all the psychoanalytic and psychological permutations it has fostered, would compel us to classify as "fantasy" much of what Ms. Roden would classify as facts — not least, as facts about herself. It would enforce a much more acute separation between the "self" — as the locus of feeling, experience, memory, fantasy — and its "world" than typology encourages, or indeed even permits. So once again, Ms. Roden is less of a dualist than most of the rest of us. Once again, her techniques, her ways, stand in violation of those that have come (however dubiously defended) to have the imprimatur of common sense. The typologist will not surrender her method, even so. She is capable of differentiating between her "private thoughts" and those that typology reveals to be of more public significance. She is equally capable of differentiating between those aspects of her personal character that are strictly personal and those that typology — which retains a license of externalization that the mythos of interiority has retracted — reveals to belong to the prophet within and beyond her. Enacted typologically, however, her self-reading and self-writing are also a reading and writing of the world. For ethical reasons among others, Ms. Roden is consequently no less devoted to the examination of her conscience than she is to following the news.

She is a witness. Propaedeutically, to make herself worthy of her summons to prophecy, she must bear witness. Practically, in the service of the mission she recognizes as her duty, and her due, she must continue to bear it, whatever the consequences might be. She writes of her *reputation for honesty*. She never overtly declares that her honesty might be that virtue — perhaps the sole virtue — which determined her election. *Hors de texte*, she is reluctant to speculate about divine intentions; she leaves her anointment always somewhat in the realm of mystery. In any event, as witness, she must exercise her virtue as the foremost of her obligations. Policy has nothing to do with it. *Marturia* — "witnessing" or "giving evidence" — would simply be error were it to stray from its mark; it would fall into sin were it anything less than exhaustive. This latter-day parrhesiast must tell the truth (the whole truth, nothing but what she believes to be the truth) whatever the risks. She must continue to tell it even in spite of herself, her safety, her welfare. Bound by legal strictures that she would herself reject, the anthropologist dare not reproduce many of the accusations she has leveled at government officials and her fellow religious. Visit her at Mount Carmel, and she will be happy to repeat them on her own.

Reflexively, the practice of bearing witness partakes of the tradition of confession, though not precisely of the ecclesiastical institution of the confessional. It can drift into a humbling of the self, even into self-humiliation. It can drift as often toward what the uncharitable reader would be all too eager to label pride but what could at least as accurately be called a respect of the self, whether or not it should also be called self-respect. It is Augustinean. It is also Rousseauvean. Negatively or positively, confession is for Ms. Roden an enterprise of self-estimation. Negatively, it is an accountancy of the self that does not leave — and dare not leave — any failing unnoted, any error or sin unremarked. It is a catalogue of unflattering admissions: *I always knew that I was too horny to be a saint; I was a backslider; I really should have asked God about [my fourth husband];*[29] *trying to stay righteous while living in a ditch is like standing on a banana peel in an ice rink.*[30] Positively, it is a catalog of "passions" in the ancient sense — of slights, physical pain, emotional anguish, disenfranchisement, oppression. Above all, it is a testament to what, in the name of witnessing, has been endured and thus a testament to endurance itself. Before her God, Ms. Roden confesses because it is her duty to confess, but also because it is a necessary step toward worthiness and with worthiness, perhaps toward absolution. In this respect, it is indeed also confessional. Before her human audience, it has more the character of a trial or a proof — of her being who she claims to be, of her being able to be no one other than who she is.

So she writes her typological tapestry of self and — with a seam apparent here and there — world at large. To be sure, she also speaks. For those who belong — or should belong — to her church, she has her *kēr-*

ugma, her "proclamation," her "preaching" to offer. She only asks that she be permitted to address them. To the rest of us, whose destiny is that of the outsider, she answers questions, elaborates her views, expounds with little circumspection even when her suspicions are aroused. Yet, writing is the technology she prefers, or if not that, to which she remains professionally most devoted. Her confessions, her responses to those questions she is asked most frequently, her views, and her expositions sooner or later find their way into typescript. Credit, twofold, her sense of economy. The woman who until 1998 was the only resident guide at Mount Carmel landed on a more efficient and less fatiguing means of repeating herself than the voice alone would afford her. She simultaneously landed on a means to take in a small but regular income — anthropologists are not alone in their willingness to purchase her writings. Credit her sense of scale: for all but the radio or television personality, the written word is far easier to disseminate and its potential audience far larger than the spoken word. Credit once again her sense of tradition. The spiritual legacy to which Ms. Roden attaches herself is of course a scriptural legacy of the most obvious sort; it is a legacy of authors, of words inscribed, in the recent and in the remote past. The Bible itself, however, offers little support for the elevation of writing over speech, the writer over the preacher. The scene of the prophet and of the proselyte was largely oral; the Books of Jeremiah and Revelation both note explicitly that their "authors" dictated their thoughts and visions to a scribe. Ms. Roden has accordingly never proffered her skills as a writer as evidence in itself of her spiritual authority, not even over David Koresh, who was by all accounts a rare and dazzling typological oralist but not a writer at all.[31] Nor does she emphasize such skills when she presents herself as a commentator rather than a charismatic. For Ms. Roden as for most of the rest of us, writing has become an indispensable aide-mémoire. For the witness, its special merit is still an instrumental merit but lies less in its serving the memory than in its serving memorialization. For the witness at Mount Carmel, writing was once part of an apparatus of memorialization that included the mowing of the grass, the watering of the myrtles, and cold nights chained inside a broken automobile. It remains of a piece with the vigil she continues to keep, which is a vigil of the memorialization of the future no less than of the past, of the truth of what will be no less than of the truth of what has already come to pass. *Marturia* drifts into "martyrdom" the more that the testamentary body itself attracts vengeance, the more that it is marked for reprisal or retribution, the more that it is threatened with the inscription of a counter-truth, a counter-testament. Writing displaces the locus of the testament from the body to the page and with it perhaps some measure of the risk of a corporeal counter-inscription, of the arena of torn flesh. It cannot, however, dissipate all such risk, nor entirely cancel the price that every witness, every martyr, must be prepared to pay for the truth to which he or she would testify, which is the price of the self itself, of its sacrifice.

In a brief and peculiarly heated passage in *The Savage Mind*, Lévi-Strauss declares sacrifice so much semiological confusion, a reductive serialization of substitutive signs that does away with any paradigmatic ordering and so lacks even the possibility of meaning (1966: 228). One can find similar remarks on serial music in the "Overture" to the *Mythologiques* (1969: 23–25). In *The Savage Mind* itself, however, the avant-guardist who provokes his contempt is less likely Pierre Boulez than Georges Bataille. In any event, Boulez is not widely known as an enthusiast of sacrifice. Bataille's fascination with it is linked to his (more notorious) fascination with the erotic and the pornographic. For this post-structuralist *avant l'heure*, sacrifice and lust harbor the same promise. Both are avenues of the transgression of the boundaries of the self, avenues of an *ekstasis*, a "stepping out of place," that would carry the self beyond itself, beyond its being as a subject, toward Dionysiac deindividuation (1976: 310–15, 317–18; cf. 1970: 130–45). Lévi-Strauss, the most uncompromising anthropological rationalist since Edmund Tylor, would understandably have little time or taste for Bataille's plot of escape from the prison house of the I, the prison house of the Kantian "I think." Whether or not wittingly, however, both bring to sacrifice (and perhaps to lust) much the same poetic regard. Both see it as transgressive — if the one a transgression of the conditions necessary for meaning, and the other a transgression of the conditions necessary for the exercise of rational subjectivity. Both see sacrifice as excessive, as an exceeding, which can be classified tropologically only as hyperbole and poetically only as sublime. Lévi-Strauss follows Kant's own poetics to the letter; for the former as for the latter, the sublime is strictly "transcendental" and so beyond making sense. Bataille would insist that ecstasy has a proper sense of its own, and perhaps he is even correct to posit that its sense (whatever that might be) is not the sense, the ratio, of the Kantian subject. It is not, however, a sense beyond subjectivation. The divine is not alone in its sublimity. It has its human counterparts. The saint — the subject of sublimation — and the martyr are among them. Like the divine, these sacral and sacrificial selves are Januses, their faces, their bodies, always a double epiphany of beatitude and the grotesque, of grace and humiliation, of a truth beyond reason and a flesh beyond saving from the fangs and claws of the arenas into which they are

153

thrown, from the flagellates, the shirts of hair, the cups of pus, the tepid yellow pond water, and the dessicating prairie sun of the arenas into which they throw themselves.

Is Ms. Roden's ethics an ethics of commitment? Or an ethics of responsibility? The immediate context of Weber's distinction is political. The distinction itself is meant to emphasize the rational and practical disparities between the ethical actor who is convinced that his values alone are of universal and supreme legitimacy and the actor who is prepared to recognize that his values belong to a mutually inconsistent and plural Kingdom of Ends, at least some of which might be as legitimate as his own. The committed actor is not an actor whose ends justify any and every means to their attainment any more than the responsible actor is an actor who recognizes his or her ends to be merely contingent, much less subjective.[32] To put it loftily, the distinction is instead between an actor whose ends preclude compromising even by the means that would attain them and an actor for whom the ethical life must always be a life of compromise, a pursuit constrained by the obligation to leave some room, some way for others to pursue their own goods, their own Good. To put it less loftily, the distinction is between an actor whose ends are dogmatic absolutes and an actor whose ends are strategic. Weber does not imply — and would be wrong to imply — that all religious ethics are — loftily or not — ethics of commitment. Many of them nevertheless lean much more toward commitment than toward the responsibility that Weber seems less to have favored than to have resigned himself as the ethics of modern politics (but cf. Roth and Schluchter 1979: 87–91). The Protestant ethic — or, rather, the Calvinist ethic — is merely one of these, though an especially noteworthy one for having been the harbinger, with its imperative to transform the world in accord with God's image, of the ethos of world mastery that had, in Weber's judgment, become so integral a part of the secular and modern West (Roth and Schluchter 1979: 45–59).

In one simple respect, Ms. Roden's ethics belongs on the side of responsibility. She does not think that all of the actual and potential elect are prophets. She does not expect those who have not been called to prophecy to meet the same standards or labor under all the same obligations as those she expects of herself. Even so, she attributes overriding and transcendent legitimacy to God's law. If she does not demand obedience to it, that would seem to be because she does not demand (and in any event, could not enforce the demand) that others render their comportment in conformity with that of the rightful subject of the Kingdom. What others do is thus their own business — yet any other business than conformity to the Law would seem in Ms. Roden's eyes (or, in any event, in her writings) to be illegitimate at best and positively evil at worst. If she is not tyrannical with others, if she refrains even from proselytizing to the strangers who have come and who continue to come to Mount Carmel, this would seem to be because she regards their fate as being not in her hands but in God's. She is not indifferent; she is willing, even eager to teach those who would listen. She is a messenger and a bearer of witness. She is not an inquisitor. She is not a judge. She leaves both of those roles to God as well. In the ultimate analysis, however, she seems no more prepared than her God to tolerate any veering from the straight, the narrow, the singular path of righteousness. Then again, in the ultimate analysis (or in the ultimate fulfillment of analysis), she would not need to tolerate it. It would have been purged. It would have vanished.

Like the rest of us, Ms. Roden nevertheless lives short of the ultimate fulfillment of analysis, short of what would confirm or invalidate its predictions, short of what would vindicate or undermine its teleological and eschatological projections. We are all passing; and if passing is a condition not altogether incompatible with that sort of confident subjective certainty that could galvanize ethical commitment, it is also a condition not unlikely to let loose those sorts of rude surprises and terrible ironies that could shatter it, dissolve it into embarrassment. Ms. Roden is certain of the presence of her God, certain of the persecutions that she has suffered in the past, certain that she will continue to act as witness in the future. She cannot be entirely certain that the future will unfold in accord with her current expectations, nor even certain that the normative principles she advocates, the very self she understands herself to be, will not give way to others as yet unforeseen. The sources of the doubts she must entertain, the doubts whose shadows must always dilute the clarity of the light that, as witness, she must give forth are in part internal, consequences of the epistemological and hermeneutical principles that have guided her from her conversion forward. This Biblicist knows very well what Matthew's Jesus proclaimed to his disciples: "Heaven and earth shall pass away, but my words shall not pass away. But of that day and hour knoweth no man, no, not the angels of heaven, but my Father only" (Matt. 24:35–36). The letter of the End will consequently always be beyond her deciphering; she will witness it, if she witnesses it, simply as witness, observer, perhaps mere bystander. Its spirit is the spirit of her gnosis, her light, as of the elder Rodens' light, of Houteff's, of White's, of Miller's. Perhaps she cannot even imagine that, like Descartes' "genius," it might be malign, or fickle, or elusive. She knows, however, that it cannot be goaded, cannot be tamed; she is its vessel, its mouthpiece, but not its mistress. She also knows that its light, if not inconstant, is nevertheless mutable and not as full as to one

155

or another of its vessels it might seem. Houteff figured himself the anti-typical Zerubbabel. The elder Rodens figured him the antitypical Moses, and Ms. Roden once did, too. Now she knows him to have been the second Christ and herself to be his belated baptizer. An overwhelming illumination, no doubt—but what it inescapably implies is not simply that one or another prophecy has failed, or might fail, but also that gnosis itself is defeasible, that spiritual knowledge comes not always as an accretion but sometimes as re-vision, that the light of present truth might sometimes cancel out the light of the past and the light of future truth cancel out that of the present.

The sources of her doubts are also in part external, or as much external as internal. She is a witness and, as witness, an ethical subject. But every ethical subject recognizable as such, interpretable as such, is an intersubject. It must always have features in common with other subjects; it must at the very least assert its individuality (if that is what it seeks to assert) as an intelligible recession from or transgression of the featural horizon of common subjects. A fortiori, the knowing subject, the subject who lays claim to having sense and to making it, to having the truth and to having warrant for it, is also an intersubject. The Wittgensteinean thesis is yet again applicable: the legitimation of belief, the proof of the justification and the truth of belief, is always an intersubjective process, always demands the marshaling of reasons to which others accord weight, always demands the following of methods that others take seriously, however crude or flexible or indeterminate such methods may be. One can at least conceive (as Durkheim did, as every lingering Romantic communitarian continues to do) of intersubjective collectivities so well insulated from the critiques, the skepticism, the alternatives lurking beyond their boundaries, collectivities so epistemologically and morally impermeable that their consensus alone might be enough to consecrate belief as truth, or an imperative as righteous. This was once among the stereotypical hallmarks of the anthropological primitive. It survives as a stereotypical hallmark of the religious fundamentalist, the religiously naive, the religiously zealous.

Even if her church were not riven with schism, Ms. Roden would hardly invite the stereotype of the primitive. She is not a religious fundamentalist (or is so only with what I presume to have shown to be baroque qualification). She is far from naive. Her religious energies and convictions are prodigious—the conviction that she is destined to be misunderstood, rejected, and mocked among them. Yet, not even that last conviction is enough to wall her away from the thought of the outside. She does not seek to erect any such wall. She does not seek, even symbolically, to declare herself a resident of "two worlds": the one, an inner world of devotion; the other, a corrupt wasteland that she would enter only when one or another practical necessity impelled her to do so. The erstwhile tour guide at Mount Carmel lives in one world, of which her God has said: *"I form the light, and create darkness: I make peace, and create evil: I the Lord do all these things"* (Isa. 45:7).[33] No doubts there, as far as she is concerned. From without, it would seem, they come instead from alterity itself, but an alterity to which she remains sensitive because it remains among her memories and inevitably within her body, for all that she has done to shed it, to leave it behind. It is the alterity of that self she used to be, that unconverted self who *had regular jobs and went to work and watched t.v.*, who was so *normal*, so much like the rest of us, *too horny to be a saint*, merely a *Sunday Christian*, a *backslider*, too distracted ever to have stopped even to consider that the world might soon be coming to its end. It is that self that quietly, almost inaudibly, continues to whisper to her — an evil self, perhaps, but if so, still an act of God.

So, speaking one day of her tending of the Mount Carmel memorial, Ms. Roden tells the anthropologist: *It's a lovely place. I'd like to see it made into a park. I'd like to see it all mowed and . . . not landscaped but cut down the thorn trees and emphasize the beautiful trees. Just make it beautiful.*[34] Sometime later, her comment gives him pause. The sentiment it expressed seems odd, the wish like a small unraveling of the fabric of her millennial tableau. Granted, she might have the Kingdom in mind, and perhaps there would be nothing more appropriate in that Kingdom than that Mount Carmel be made into a greenspace, serene and restful, a place of the leisure of the Sabbath. Yet, she did not make even a single allusion to the Kingdom. She was responding to an inquiry into how she spent a "typical day." Her idiom was the idiom of simple description. She would conclude her response with mention of therapy, of what she did to *keep her head on straight*. Not a word of the Bible.

Why, for that matter, bother talking to an anthropologist at all, especially one who, several months before, presented himself to her in a letter that concluded:

> I would . . . be very grateful to hear from you at some point in the near future — if not about the "need" for such a book as the one I have in mind (for I fear that you and your fellow congregants are all too modest to admit of any such "need") then at least about your willingness to participate with me in the writing of it. Let me emphasize again that I can certainly understand your exhaustion. I can certainly understand your thinking that you have better things to do with what time you have. I also recognize that you may have no particular reason to trust my intentions; after all, I am seeking not to join your church but instead to record its past and present situation

in the world. I am an "outsider." I cannot be your Matthew. At best, I can be your "translator," someone who tries to render your situation in terms that might do it proper justice and that even outsiders might understand. In any event, I would ask (though I grant that even this may be too much after all that you have endured) to be given the benefit of the doubt. I'm merely a scholar. Whatever else I may or may not be, I'm quite sure that I'm not evil.[35]

If no longer quite so sure that he is not evil, the anthropologist was in any event delighted to receive Ms. Roden's assurances that she was *happy to participate in [his] study*.[36] She did not remark on his own goals. She offered no explanation for her willingness to cooperate. Two general possibilities have subsequently (and frequently) come to the anthropologist's own (always suspicious) mind. One of these is that she has always seen him as the vehicle through which the message she was delivering to her church would find its way into the larger world (if a much smaller portion of that world than she might realize), that she saw him as her unwitting godsend. The other is that she thinks herself deserving of a scholar's attention, or is in any event willing to accommodate his thinking her worthy of his attention, and of the bound and dusty place in history that her convictions, her works and days, might thus occupy.

The anthropologist has come to be of the opinion that Ms. Roden entertains and maintains both visions, both of these possible worlds, and that both are also actual for her, even if their actualities are not similarly animate. If so, she would be guilty of no more egregious inconsistency than are those of us who begin our mornings with our astrological forecast and run off to preach secular humanism (or posthumanism) throughout the afternoon. She would not be guilty of inconsistency at all if, like many of the rest of us, she has accommodated herself to a world so shot through with epistemological and moral alternatives that none but the most perceptually or logically self-evident of beliefs — much less systems of belief, much less systems of morality — can be given full credit, accorded categorical certainty. Ideal-typically at least, neither epistemic nor ethical commitment would then ever be within even subjective reach. What would take its place, faute de mieux, would be a gamble, an investment of practical stakes, perhaps in a single outcome but far more often — far more "reasonably," one might say, or if not that, then at least more "responsibly" — in a plurality of always less than certain outcomes, any one of which might preclude the realization of any or all of the others.[37] This would not necessarily amount to a hedging of bets. If Ms. Roden is a wagerer, she is no Pascal. She has everything to gain if the Kingdom indeed comes. She will have almost everything to lose — has already lost almost everything — if it does not. Until the ultimate fulfillment of analysis, she must in any event live with that risk; and living with it, living in it, this countermodern restorationist is also, faute de mieux, living as a modern.

PART FOUR

A Colonization

In *The Eclipse of Biblical Narrative* (1974), Hans Frei scrutinizes the intellectual impetuses of the far-reaching transformation of the pedgagogy of biblical exegesis that began in Protestant Europe near the turn of the eighteenth century and began to have its impact in the United States soon afterward. Frei's focus is limited to pedagogues, to exegetical experts or authorities themselves. If thus narrow, it is also of especial consequence. Its institutional arena is one of universities and the most distinguished of academic divinity schools. Its scene is one of the instruction of those future generations of Protestant clerics who would preside over the religious education of the flocks of the mainstream of Protestant denominations from the nineteenth century to the present. Frei's historical foil, his backdrop, is the Reformation and, more particularly, the prevailing presumptions that Protestant exegetes — from Luther to Sir Isaac Newton — brought to the reading of the Bible during the late sixteenth and seventeenth centuries. His periodization is convenient, but the exegetical current, the "approach" he highlights, is much older than the Reformation itself. He characterizes it as "realistic" or "history-like" (1974: 10). It is at once literalist and realistic in presuming the events recorded or forecast in the Bible to be actual events in the past, the present, or the future of the world — of this world. It is, however, an approach that Frei characterizes as "extending naturally" into the figural (1974: 2). It is in fact the very approach that church fathers from Tertullian forward would term "figural" (see Brumm 1970: 25–27). It is the very approach that Auerbach describes as "'allegorical' in the widest sense" (Auerbach 1959: 53; cited in Brumm 1970: 23). It is Ms. Roden's approach, and William Miller's, and Saint Paul's. It is, as Frei is fully aware (1974; 2 passim), typology.

163

Nor does the approach come most immediately under assault for either its literalism or its realism. The opponents of typology, who would make up a nearly single professional mind by the 1850s, would attack it first — or most vociferously — for its referential imprecision, its insufficient referential determinacy. Among their earliest numbers, Frei emphasizes two: the English deist Anthony Collins, who in 1724 published a pamphlet denying that the "typical, or mystical, or allegorical, or enigmatic" sense of the Bible was any longer available to its living readers, and that its literal sense alone allowed for evaluation and analysis (Frei 1974: 66–85); and the anti-deist conservative Lutheran Sigmund Jakob Baumgarten, who from his chair at the University of Halle some quarter-century later would defend the Bible as a text of revelation at the cost of admitting that the historically specific words and languages in which it had been written were an often crude indication of its actual, literal "subject matter" (Frei 1974: 88–96). The Puritan divines of the United States — wedded to typology not simply as a methodology of the elucidation of the fulfillment of the Old Testament in the New but also as a methodology of the elucidation of the fulfillment of biblical prophecies in the world at hand or the world soon to come — were less tractable, but their official resistance was short-lived. At Yale, Harvard, and the great majority of the other leading seminaries of a country soon to drift into its Second Great Awakening, what was coming to be known as "new criticism" or "higher criticism" would earn official blessing as precipitously as typology was losing its former methodological dignity. Among theologians of the Old Denominations, it would have a modest twentieth-century recuperation, but largely as a means of elucidating what the New Testament authors read into and drew out of the Torah (see, for example, Goppelt 1982). In Great Britain, but especially in the United States, typology retained considerable popular appeal. As we have seen, the Second Great Awakening would have been much diminished — and Millerism nothing at all — without it. By the turn of the twentieth century, it had found renewed methodological favor in perhaps some fifty alternative institutional venues, Chicago's Moody Bible Institute and the Dallas Theological Seminary among them.[1] Yet, it can hardly be said that such a recuperation has restored to typological exegesis even a shadow of the epistemic authority or epistemological scope that it formerly commanded.

Seeking to account for its decline, Frei points to the rapid ascendance of a new philosophy of language, or at least a new theory of meaning. At its core is "ostensive definition." Linguistically, ostensive definition is usually understood to be that sort of definition or "sense" that is derived from a pointing to or picking out of a specific referent; in more current technical parlance, it is "deictic." Frei's usage, however, implies a much broader category and, both philosophically and linguistically, a weak one. Following his usage, ostensive definition has no single philosophical home; it is consistent with empiricist and Kantian theories of meaning alike. If it is "scientific," it is not merely the mode of definition appropriate for the terms of what an eighteenth- or nineteenth-century naturalist would have thought a properly scientific description. For "historical critics," whose theories of meaning Frei traces ultimately to Lockean empiricism, the sense of any term (and thus of any proposition) indeed depends on and is derivative of its "actual historical reference."[2] For the (largely German) "hermeneuticians," however, indebted less to Locke than to Christian Wolff, the sense of a term or a proposition derives not from its reference, *stricto sensu*, but instead from a double source: the linguistic environment, the semantic field to which it belongs; and the referential context in which it is deployed (1974: 99–101). The valorization of ostensive definition thus multiply construed is — so Frei would have it — what led the new critics (whether historical or hermeneutical) to insist that the sense of any term, any claim in the Bible, must come from the referential context, the referential universe, of the author who pronounced or inscribed it. So, for the more empirically minded, the "Babylon" of Revelation could only have been Rome; the sinners whom Jeremiah condemned could only have been the Baalworshippers of his own time; and so on. For the more hermeneutically minded, biblical terms and assertions might also give expression to "didactic ideas, whether dogmatic or those of natural religion" (1974: 103). Yet here as well, meaning was a matter of "ideal" reference, or in any event of an attempt at such reference, however historically clouded and linguistically limited it might be.

The triumph of ostensive definition dealt a triple blow to "pre-critical" exegesis (see Frei 1974: 17–41). By no means least, it would demote the Text of History to a place — if an important one — among the history of texts. Its substantive content, the history it seemed to tell, could no longer be taken for granted; it would instead have to be decrypted and corroborated archaeologically, iconographically, and "cross-referentially." Nor could the Bible any longer be read as having its literal reference in any future that lay beyond its actual inscription and compilation. By (ostensive) definition, its sense lay in and with the past in which it took form as a work — or rather, pasts: having been inscribed and compiled across some ten centuries, the Bible could only be a historical mélange, a hodgepodge of disparate contexts, of different styles and points of view, of internal revisions and rereadings that were never so "literal" as their authors might have considered them to be. For the pre-critical realists, the unity of the Bible was axiomatic. For the new critics, its unity was chimerical; whether empiricist or idealist, their methods would "effectively sunder the dogmatic unity and authority of the canon" (1974: 64–65). A second rupture is correlative of this first one. Frei characterizes it as a "great reversal": "[I]nterpretation [had become] a matter of fitting the biblical story into another world with another story rather than incorporating that world into the biblical story" (1974: 130). As a methodology of exegesis that was at once fundamentally transcontextual and fundamentally unitarian, typology would thus have to go.

What could legitimately take its place was an even more literalist and realistic "Bible history" than "pre-critical" typologists had ever thought to exercise. Frei plausibly sees in both its historical-critical and its hermeneutical expressions a common (and, one might add, anti-Catholic) rejection of the privileged exegetical authority of the theological specialist or adept (1974: 92–94). However learned it might become, the newer literalism is "populist" in just this respect. So it has continued to function rhetorically, not simply in fundamentalist discourse but also in the discourse of the typological revivalists from William Miller forward. What was left to transpire was far from a meeting of exegetical minds. Yet for all the debates among them, historical critics and hermeneuticians would not simply share a common hostility to esoterica — typological esoterica included. They would also come to fashion a new Christology, of which the ongoing cottage industry of portraits of the "historical Jesus" is simply one result. For the new Christologists

> [t]he events of Jesus' life are portrayed as a struggle against a really existing, personal, supernatural evil being; his death as a substitutionary blood atonement, appeasing the wrath of God against the guilty through the sacrifice of an innocent man; the eschatological cast of Jesus' own teaching, as well as the [biblical] writers' eschatological and Jewish-messianic description of his career and second coming — these are all . . . instances of . . . time-conditioned conceptions, explicable from cultural circumstances and views of the day, to which the writers had "accommodated" themselves. The genuine meaning of such passages, the authors' actual intention in them, is not identical with the words and descriptions of the text. (Frei 1974: 60–61)

Frei notes that Johann Salomo Semler — among the founders of the new criticism, the most eminent biblical scholar of the eighteenth century, and Baumgarten's successor at Halle — made precise appeal to accommodationism in emphasizing that the literal lesson of the Christ lay not in the miracles he reportedly worked but instead in the "character" he actually displayed (1974: 60–62; see also 109–11). Semler thus opened the way for homiletics that appropriated the ensamples of the Testaments as qualitative models of proper or saintly conduct, the present relevance or "applicability" of which the clever sermonizer would duly reveal to his audience. Though Frei does not address it in detail, what was further left to transpire was a doctrine that has become central to many of the more liberal denominations of our day. The doctrine is uncontroversially Christian in affirming that the Bible is a revelatory text. It is distinctly liberal in denying that the revelation contained in it is either infallible or complete. The Branch Davidian, the Seventh-day Adventist, awaits a more perfect light on the Bible itself. The liberal Christian is prepared to receive a light beyond its terms, its imperatives, its pages. No ardent restorationism here: in this respect at least, the liberal Christian is instead a believer in sacramental, ethical, and moral progress (see Reardon 1968: 60–62).

Frei's thesis is elegant and his defense of it immensely learned. However, both the thesis and its defense seem inadequate on several fronts. Most patently, both evade — to the point of begging — the question of the sources and the broader context of the triumph of ostensive definition itself. Perhaps the answer is obvious: ostensive definition owed its ascendance among theologians to the prestige it had already acquired among natural scientists; theologians were simply adopting the ways and means of their erstwhile adversaries. But, Frei makes little appeal to the burgeoning prestige of science, and for good reason. Even in England, the new critics appropriated their philosophies from more pious sources, even if the proto-scientistic (but still pious) Locke was paramount among them. In Germany, science (at least of the Baconian sort) had yet to turn learned heads, much less pious heads; there, the new critics would have primary resort to philosophies that led them not toward inductive generalization but instead toward idealism and empathy.

A supplemental — if equally historicist and still partial — answer to the question at hand can be found in Amos Funkenstein's *Theology and the Scientific Imagination* (1986). In some measure of partial accord with Frei (whom he does not cite), Funkenstein argues that a "profound revolution in historical thought in the sixteenth and seventeenth centuries" has its commencement in the "discovery" of history as "contextual reasoning" (1986: 206). He credits Giambattista Vico with giving the "first systematic expression" to the methodological fruit that the revolution bore. He traces its (perhaps largely unwitting) instigators to those humanist jurists of the sixteenth century who were reacting "against the elevation of the *Corpus iuris civilis* to the status of a universal, inexhaustible paradigm of legal wisdom, as if it were an ideal law valid for all times":

Th[is] historical school of interpretation explains the Roman institutions within their now obsolete circumstances. . . . The tedious dis-

pute between the adherents of the *Loi écrit* and the *coutumes* generated the insight that there could never be an ideal law valid for all
times. From the interpretation of Roman law, humanistic jurispru-
dence advanced to the historical reconstruction of non-Roman legal
institutions, the origins and career of "feudal" law. There was, it
seems, no real precedent for their work in the tradition they inherited.
(1986: 211)

There was, at least, no real precedent for their reconstructions. For their
contextualism, however, and so for Vico's contextualism, Funkenstein
finds an even earlier source in the medieval development of the doctrine
of accommodation — the doctrine that God always speaks in a language
that the persons and peoples to whom he reveals himself can understand (1986: 243–44). As we have seen, Frei is well aware of the doctrine itself, but he does not see it as the historical key to the "great
reversal" of which he writes. At least as venerable as Augustine, accommodationism would acquire in the later medieval period those distinctively holistic refinements — " 'harmony,' 'correspondence,' 'concordance'
within historical periods" — that Vico would acknowledge as his own
guidelines in his pursuit of a "new science" of the "providence" of the
gentes (1986: 213). In Vico's footsteps, anthropologists would long acknowledge as a similar guideline what Ruth Benedict was the first to
call the "integration" of "cultures" (1934: 45–56).

Funkenstein's excavations are at once plausible and provocative, but
they leave one aspect of the "great reversal" more obscure than Frei
does himself: its timing. If historical contextualism had already been
formulated by the fourteenth century, if the Renaissance humanists had
already carried it forward from texts to the world by the beginning of
the sixteenth century, why should the "revolution" it provoked not have
"triumphed" for another two hundred years? Funkenstein correctly — if
still vaguely — observes that propounders of "reason in history" from
Vico to Marx were indebted to the long labors of the secularizers who
had preceded them, especially to the labors of those secularizers who
had gradually found the grounds on which to effect the shift of both
accommodation and the evolution of providence from divine into other
hands. Yet, if the new critics shared this debt, few if any seem to have
worn it comfortably. For the most part, they refrained from championing secularism. Their hostility toward typological hermeneutics was not
an ardently secularist hostility. Most of them could still embrace what
Augustine may have been the first to propose and what their more secular successors from Arthur de Gobineau to Ernst Renan would repeat:
that the Jews (ancient and contemporary) were a relatively "primitive"
people to whom God had found it necessary and wise to communicate

largely in images and fiats (cf. Bernal 1987: 342–45). Many a typologist of the time, many a typologist still, would be happy to agree. To reiterate, what they uniformly rejected was that typology should or could serve as the methodology of either biblical or historical exegesis. Their rejection was all the more extreme when typology served to bolster apocalyptic and millenarian premonitions—textual or extra-textual. Their gesture and the juggernaut they captained consequently belong to the far broader history of the retraction, the restriction, of legitimate gnosis.

They belong as well to the more specific—but still broad—history of the pluralization of both the configurations and the processes of human history itself. Not until the middle of the nineteenth century would the emerging "human sciences"—anthropology included—begin definitively to contravert the time lines, the archaeologies of origin and dispersal, creation and miscegenation that Christian scholars had gleaned or extrapolated from the Bible itself (see Stocking 1987: 46–77). Funkenstein's retrieval of the career of the notion of divine accommodation clearly reveals that a great many of those scholars were more than prepared to grant that human history was a differential history, that it comprised a plethora of collectivities, some more advanced than others, some more blessed than others. Funkenstein's emphasis on the historical contextualism that accommodationism at once demanded and encouraged is entirely appropriate. Yet this formal, narrowly methodological dimension of accommodationist reasoning should not overshadow the substance to which such reasoning had long and regularly been applied. Here as well one might turn to Vico's project as a consummation. Funkenstein notes:

> Vico accepted a mild version of polygenetic theory—the "world of nations (*gentes*)" descends from those "giants" who, the Bible mentions, sometimes mixed with the "daughters of men" (Gen. 6:4). More important, Vico sought a better way to save the "history of the *gentes*" from being altogether devoid of divine providence. Direct providence, he maintained, governs the history of the chosen people, Jews and then Christians; but . . . indirect providence governs the affairs of nations by the very laws that govern the enfoldment of human societies. (1986: 278–79)

For Funkenstein, Vico's greatest—or, in any event, his most modern—achievement lies in his managing to insert the dynamics of human self-invention, human "autonomy," into the long course of both direct and indirect providence (1986: 288). No less noteworthy is his envisioning of the final stage of providence to have its culmination in a constellation of civilized and sovereign monarchies, each overseeing and preserving the equality of its citizen-subjects.

The anthropologist could dispute Funkenstein's characterization of contextualist history as a "discovery" only at the expense of performative paradox, for he, too, is a contextualist, epigone of Vico, and latter-day new critic. The symbiosis of contextualism and normative political theory, however, suggests that Frei's "great reversal," Funkenstein's "revolution," is more than a matter of the relentless force of truth alone. Whatever its relation to the truth, what is at issue is also a social fact, and it suggests that historical contextualism, carrying all the integrationist refinements with which medieval accommodationists had provided it in its train, also had a strategic value whose "timeliness" corresponded closely to theoretical and practical invention of new political forms in Europe itself. Here, Vico (who died in 1744) is less consummation than harbinger. The political summum he envisages is still that of the "commonwealth," though one far more similar to Locke's than to Hobbes's. If, as Funkenstein admits, Vico's personal "impact" was "negligible" (1986: 212), the political theory of the commonwealth was the intellectual pivot of the statecraft of an increasingly rebellious bourgeoisie. Against the special claims of the aristocracy, the bourgeoisie (who of course did not conceive of itself as "the bourgeoisie") was thus equipped to oppose the "natural" and "universal" rights of "man." Against the encroachments of outsiders, whether individual or collective, it was further equipped to oppose the pluralist and sovereigntist fiction of the "social contract" — or was so equipped, just as long as it was not relying on Vico: in contrast to its Hobbesian, Lockean, and (later) Rousseauvean counterparts, Vichian political theory is not a contractarian theory. Then again, bourgeois statecraft has never been an exclusively contractarian statecraft. The grounds on which it has sought to discriminate citizen from noncitizen, the grounds on which it has sought to establish the legitimate and equal sovereignty of a multitude of states, have never been those of man the contractor alone. They have always also made appeal to another person, another persona, which Vico might himself have conjured but for two reasons. He did not locate the "collective mentalities" of which he developed so refined and contextualist a conception within specific polities but instead within specific historical phases or "ages" (Funkenstein 1986: 285–87). He attached no specific rights to the *gentes*, only to the individuals who belonged to them. He had consequently yet to transform his polygenetic tribes into those entitled collectivities that modern political thought and modern political practice have enshrined as "nations."

Funkenstein has nothing to say about the nation, either as a political or philosophical category — a silence that even his self-imposed confinement to intellectual history would hardly seem to justify. He has almost as little to say about the Reformation and mentions its great instigator, Martin Luther, only twice and only in passing. Most surprising, he fails to remark what Ernst Breisach—a more comprehensive surveyor of the intellectual territory that Funkenstein charts—has underscored: that in a battle over "the validity of church tradition," Luther himself gave his imprimatur to the distinction between "sacred history (depicting God's design for human redemption, the *Heilsorder*) and human or profane history (God's design for an orderly human life on earth, the *Erhaltungsorder*)," the latter of which was initially devoted to the documentation of the Catholic "corruption" of the purity of the apostolic church (1994: 180–81). Luther's historical divide is not the precise equivalent of Vico's—the histories of the *Heilsorder* and of the *Erhaltungsorder* are for the Lutheran the histories of divine redemption and of the social life that precedes it, not the directly providential history of the chosen and the indirectly providential history of the rest. Yet, as Breisach has shown, the Lutheran conception, which precedes the Vichian one by more than a century, has an immediate and in the end the far more decisive impact on history as a discipline. In Germany, as Breisach notes, Luther's ally, Philip Melanchthon, oversaw a redirection of historical research at the Protestant universities of Marburg, Königsburg, and Jena that would soon lead to the institutional pursuit of "two entirely separate histories: one ecclesiastical, telling the story of Christ's church, and one mundane, concerned with the state as God's instrument." Breisach adds that "mundane" history would grow ever more distant from its godliness as historical research continued (1994: 166–67).

But then again, not altogether distant: in eighteenth-century France, the anticlerical and anti-Catholic philosophes were at the vanguard of the theoretical reformulation of the historical process as a progressive process; in Germany, however, the vanguard was of a different mind. Breisach locates it between two poles. At one "stood a group of historians at the University of Göttingen who, merging German erudition, English empiricism, and French rationalism, developed attitudes and methods which were to become most influential in the creation of nineteenth-century historical science." At the other was "the [Lutheran] theologian Johann Gottfried Herder's more theoretical response to the quest for a new order in history . . . modeled after the patterns of organic life, including the life cycle. It would become as influential an interpretation of the link between past, present, and future as the progress theory" (1994: 200–201). The professors at Göttingen were the more ardent particularists. Though not in the manner of the philosophes, they were also the greater historical optimists. In both these respects, they owe their greatest debt not to Vico but to Leibniz. The latter's monadology suggested what Breisach calls a "dialectical relationship between part and whole" that warranted the historian's approaching every historical phenomenon as "a complex and unique conjunction of forces" (1994: 204). Leibnizian teleology posited a world God-driven toward ever greater completeness and beauty, within which "religion . . . became once more a force in human life to be affirmed and not rejected" (204). No ardent secularism here. If still inchoately, both the Göttingen professors and Herder are at the cusp of those methods that Dilthey later declared distinctive of the *Geisteswissenschaften*, the "sciences of spirit."[3] They are among the founders of the historiographical turn toward the *Volk* as the spiritual embodiment, each of its own complex and necessarily unique morality, customs, laws, and course of collective life (cf. Breisach 1994: 230–31). With the *Volk*, the nation acquires at once its historical substance and its metaphysics.

Forming a productively inconsistent composite with the state, the nation is that novel political form whose triumphant and revolutionary sweep of the European continent coincides precisely with the more etherally intellectual mutations on which Frei and Funkenstein have concentrated. It is the ascendance of the nation — a quintessential creature of contextual reasoning — that inevitably imbues the new criticism with its extra-intellectual, strategic, and normative undertones. Perhaps the nation is not what it used to be. Contemporary federalism and globalism notwithstanding, epochal reports of its disappearance still seem premature (for example, Wallerstein 1999). To be sure, our political reason is no longer limited to either state reason or "national reason." Yet both endure heartily — the former now usually in the guise of the "interests" of "national [*sic*] security," the latter more nakedly, though also in the partially denatured offshoot we have come to call "ethnicity."

In lieu of any foolhardy attempt to summarize either the scholarship or the polemics that the nation has inspired over the past two hundred years, it is enough here simply to recall in abstract and by no means exhaustive outline the axioms longest entrenched in national discourse and national practice.[4]

1) Theoretically, every legitimate commonwealth might resemble every other. Every legitimate nation is necessarily distinct from every other, and the most salient features of its individuality of three kinds. i) Every legitimate nation (from the Latin *nascor*, "to be born") should display substantial genealogical continuity; it should be substantially "of one blood," in its past and in its present. ii) Every legitimate nation must have a localizable history of its own. The history of nations is consequently not — nor can be — a unitary history. On the

contrary, it is instead the primary source and means of the diacritical separation of one nation from another. iii) Ideally, every nation should have its own "genius" or "spirit," its own collective "mentality" or "character," whether due to innate "racial" peculiarities, to the influence of the environment, or (as cultural anthropologists would be fond of asserting from the 1920s through the 1960s) to the supra-individual integration of culture itself.

2) The nation is the bearer (and for the nationalist, the primary bearer) of the entitlement to exercise sovereignty over a particular geographical territory. Well into the twentieth century, its entitlement would still widely be understood to rest in two distinct grounds. i) One such ground (and the one that has normative priority today) is strictly historical. A truncated version of the right of first possession, it permits the nation to claim sovereignty over that territory (and just that territory) within which it has resided "from time immemorial" — or at least for a long time. Hence, the national politicization of history, conceived at once as the past and as contextual reason, but in need of far more "relevance" than the mere antiquarian could ever offer. The remnants of the past are of no political value simply for being old. Only when the archaeologist or historian can put them forward as evidence of a continuous local heritage, only when the expert can link them in a contextually coherent chain of evidence that attests to the longevity of "the same nation" do they assume the status of "national treasures." The national valorization of the past is a derivative of the value of sovereignty in the present and the future. ii) The other ground of legitimate national sovereignty — a necessary if not sufficient condition of it — is "advancement," or what the Victorians would come later to render as "maturity." It has become as incorrect in enlightened company as the imperialism that it was often used to justify. The nineteenth-century philosophers of the nation felt no need for euphemism; they could agree that only those nations who had advanced far enough up the ladder of enlightenment were proper rulers of themselves. For many (though not all), only the European nations (or some of the European nations) had attained such heights. The rest required protection, tutelage, overlordship — if they merited any benevolence at all. Yet, if such an evolutionist (and often racist) criterion of political investment leaves (allegedly) enlightened despots (despot nations included) to impose themselves in good conscience on the politically incapable or immature, it is far from restoring sovereignty to the person of the monarch. National reason is not incompatible with monarchy. It is, however, beyond countenancing the king or queen who would assert power over his or her fellow nationals by divine right, much less by sheer force. The sovereign national body is

173

a collective body, one of a universe of many other such bodies, who would dwell together in what has often been ideally conceived as "peaceful community."

Though by no means merely "negative," merely antithetical, national reason is vigorously contrarian, opposed as we have seen to moral and especially legal universalism. The largely Protestant child of the Thirty Years' War, it is opposed to "papism," and (so) to the counter-Reformation. Though the French would come soon enough to adopt it as their own (adapting it in the process), national reason is initially also the enemy of the later eighteenth century's greatest and most threatening warrior-saint of universalist and counter-Reformationist imperialism — Napoleon Bonaparte. Myriad historians have addressed the multiple antagonisms between an increasingly muscular Prussia and Bonapartist France, out of which Norbert Elias has distilled the dynamic and still evident horns of Europe's most enduring political, moral, and ethical dilemma: whether to champion the inward-looking specificity and the specific diversity of *Kultur* or champion the expansive (if still exclusionary) principles of *civilisation* (1978: 3–34). No solution has as yet proved satisfactory. The question of what constitutes Enlightenment — in Europe and elsewhere — burns as brightly now as it did two centuries ago.

For the original polemicists of national reason, Napoleon and his *civilisation* nevertheless constituted merely one battlefront. There was another army, scattered in pockets, some within Prussia, others throughout the continent, but particularly through the southeast. Materially, militarily, its threat was nonexistent; perhaps as a consequence, it is no longer the stuff of legend and its historiographers few and far between. Ideologically and spiritually, the anthropologist must suspect that its threat was much more imposing, even if he cannot call upon a historiography sufficiently rich or detailed to render his suspicions fully warranted. He can agree with Funkenstein and Breisach that the Renaissance humanists had already begun to undermine the presumption, so self-evident to early Christian and later medieval thought, that history was a unity, and that its unity was providential, of divine design (Breisach 1994: 166–67). The presumption would suffer further erosion as sixteenth-century explorers began to file their reports of previously unforeseen peoples and unforeseen expanses of the world (Breisach 1994: 176–77). As Breisach observes, the primary casualty of such reports was "Christian universal history in the manner of Eusebius and Jerome, marked by the subordination of all histories to sacred history" (1994: 177). Providential history did not, however, collapse along with it. If it was no longer self-evidently the history of the whole world, it could still be the history of the elect — of the Jews and the Christians, whoever they might ultimately turn out to be. If in potentially truncated form, history might thus continue to follow its preordained plan and typology thus continue to serve as one of several methods of the elucidation of its preordained details. What accordingly remained *dans le vrai*, in principle and in practice, was historiographical apocalypse, and within apocalypse, the historiographical documentation of the Return, of the imminence of the New Jerusalem.

By the latter half of the eighteenth century, British Protestants were more regularly inclined toward apocalypticism than their German counterparts, who had largely forsaken Luther's anti-papist premillennialism for his more sober pietism. Those who had not forsaken it frequently departed their homeland for the New World. The premillennialist agitants who remained were perhaps few, but their claims, their status, their very presence seem to have been uncommonly troubling to the pious and the secular alike. For the pious especially, their spiritual status was ambiguous but in poor accord with their social condition in any case. They were Jews — the first-chosen, in exile and under constraint not merely in Prussia but throughout the urban continent's archipelago of ghettos.

Some were members of what might properly be called a "messianic movement," if to what would prove to be something of its final chapter. Known now as Sabbatianism (or Sabbathianism), it was not the first such movement to have arisen in one or another diasporic outpost, but it was exceptional in three respects. Its most thorough investigator remains Gershom Scholem, and as he has pointed out, it was peculiarly popular, peculiarly widespread, and, though in derivative forms, peculiarly enduring (1971: 58; cf. Carlebach 1990). Sabbatianism takes its title from the name of its original figurehead, Sabbatai Zevi, a "rabbinically educated Jew" born in Smyrna in 1626 (1971: 59). Scholem cannot resist diagnosis: "[T]he sources suggest with almost absolute certainty that Sabbatai suffered from a manic-depressive psychosis, possibly combined with some paranoid traits — a constitutional disease, perhaps not a mental illness at all in the ordinary sense, though psychiatrists generally consider it as such" (126). In any event, he does resist condemning the patient to a second exile on the Ship of Fools. Instead, he places Sabbatai's not atypical religious career in the light of two collective forces. The first is pedagogical, has its scene in Safed, Palestine, has its sage in Isaac Luria, and has its paradigms in Luria's interpretations of the great texts of Kabbalistic mysticism. Luria taught during the sixteenth century, but as Scholem notes, his mysticism "had become a historical force within the rabbinic tradition, and to a large extent influenced and determined not only the thinking of those circles most affected by religion but, in its consequences, the entire Jewish community" a century later (59). Lurianic Kaballah was "in its whole design electric with messianism and pressing for its release; it was impelling a Messianic outburst which, as it turned out, came approximately one generation after" its pedagogical ascendance in the person of Sabbatai himself (59).

The second of these forces is for Scholem social-psychological: the appeal of the concrete promise of "restoration and utopia" (50–51) in the face of widespread and ineluctable "disappointment in the historical world" (61). Uniformly disenfranchised, culturally debased, Jewish enclaves "from Yemen and Persia to England, Holland, Russia, and Poland" rapidly embraced as their imminent savior a man who in Scholem's judgment was "highly unusual" only in one of his penchants: "in moments of religious exaltation he tended to commit bizarre acts which violated the law" (60). That his transgressions came to be seen as among the hallmarks of his election was all the more unusual because "the type of the 'holy sinner' did not belong to the stock of the Messianic tradition in Judaism" (60). Nor was Sabbatai even his own promoter. Having migrated from Smyrna to Palestine, he encountered his Elijah in Nathan of Gaza, who had seen him as Messiah in a vision. It was Nathan who became Sabbatai's publicist and who sparked the "fantastic wave of enthusiasm which swept up Jewish communities for an entire year [and] created a mental reality which had not been anticipated by the rabbis or considered in the ancient books" (61). At the end of that year came what Scholem characterizes as a "catastrophe": "[I]n September 1666 Sabbatai Zevi was brought before the Sultan in Adrianople and given the choice of upholding his Messianic claims and suffering martyrdom, or of converting to Islam." He chose conversion, and would die poor and alone in Albania a decade later. But, his "believers" would go on, understanding that most flamboyant of his transgressions as the consummate act of a savior who was necessarily an apostate, "required to complete his mission by passing or descending into the underworld" of the *gentes* (61). For Scholem, what Sabbatai thus personifies is the most severe of the historical Jewish "crises of tradition."

The crisis would continue, and spread, until the early nineteenth century, when the "Era of Emancipation" would begin. Scholem discusses the increasingly transgressive (and "libertine") doctrines of the "three most upsetting and astonishing" texts of the Sabbatian archive: Nathan's *Overthrow of the Tyrants* (ca. 1670), the Spanish Abraham Miguel Cardozo's *Shield of Abraham* (ca. 1668), and the Macedonian Israel Hazan's commentary on the Psalms (ca. 1678–79) (1971: 63–64). He notes the rise of long-sustained sects: emerging shortly after Sabbatai's death, in Thessalonike, the Dönmeh ("Apostates"), "whose members were ostensibly Muslim but in reality crypto-Jewish Sabbatians who felt themselves obliged to carry through in their lives the imitation" of their Messiah (63, 65, 142–66); and in Poland after 1756, the followers of Jacob Frank, who sought to gather together an army of spiritual soldiers who "were not allowed to have a religion" but nominally at least flirted with conversion to Catholicism (76, 77–93, 126–41). Throughout, Scholem is a partisan of rabbinic tradition. His primary concern is the danger Sabbatianism posed to the internal integrity of the "Jewish community" itself. He has far less to say about its reception among the Gentiles. One must nevertheless wonder what Protestants might have thought of the Frankists' solicitation of the Catholics. One must also wonder whether Protestants and Catholics alike were aware that Sabbatian doctrines of restoration and redemption were by no means merely national but world-historical (cf. Scholem 1971: 122–23). Zionism, an adaptation of Sabbatianism to the logic of national reason, would come later. Sabbatianism itself could hardly have been more opposed to nationalist pluralism. And, it must be added, vice versa.[5]

A more informative review of the interface between later eighteenth-century Jews and Gentiles appears in Julius Greenstone's *Messiah Idea in Jewish History*, a pro-Reformist study that the Jewish Publication Society of America saw fit to put into circulation in 1906, apparently unknown to Scholem. Greenstone sets the beginning of his chapter on the rise of Reformism in Germany, not least because the Berliner Moses Mendelsohn was the earliest and is still the most exemplary standard-bearer of the Jewish Enlightenment from which Reformism took its credentials. His introductory (and characteristically colorful) remarks are telling:

We can hardly appreciate the tremendous influence exerted upon the Jews of Germany by the Jewish Synod assembled by Napoleon, although it is true that in comparison with what was expected of it, the Synod accomplished very little. The mere fact, however, that the great Napoleon, the ruler of the civilized world, concerned himself with the Jewish question, was sufficient to intoxicate the crushed and degraded Jews with joy, and fill their hearts with extravagant hopes for the future. Christian poets, philosophers, and even churchmen began to advocate the cause of the Jews. . . . Monarchs and princes began to realize their duty to the ancient people. The Jews became the topic of conversation at the *salon*, the diet, the royal assembly, and little by little they were granted rights and privileges they had not enjoyed for many centuries. (1906: 243–44)

177

This is a somewhat sanguine (and *civilisée*) retrospective, but it implies clearly enough that Napoleon's revitalization of the Jewish question made it all the more perturbing for those monarchs and princes who happened to be Prussian, even though they had long been accustomed to keeping individual Jews at their courts and to granting special rights and privileges to individual Jewish families who had the (financial) means with which to give thanks for their elevation (cf. Poliakov 1965: 229–33).

Greenstone clarifies explicitly that in Prussia, the question of emancipation led immediately to the question of messianism in the minds of Jews as much as in the minds of their oppressors. The Sabbatians—among whose ranks, Scholem somewhat uneasily observes, were "eminent rabbis" in several Near Eastern and European cities, including Hamburg and Berlin—surely played a role in rendering it a controversial question, at least among the Jews themselves (1971: 80). Yet, the messianism of the period had nothing exclusively Sabbatian about it. Disburdened of its millenarian impatience, it was a central doctrinal element of rabbinic Orthodoxy of the most conservative and traditional sort. If for different reasons, traditionalist and reformist Jews recognized it to be what Greenstone describes as "a serious impediment to the acquistion of equal rights. Those unwilling to part with this hope were ready to forfeit their citizenship, and those who desired emancipation at any cost unhestitatingly gave up the cherished ideal of the Jewish people" (1906: 247–48). Among the latter was a certain David Friedländer, who published a pamphlet in 1812 urging his coreligionists to excise all messianic tendencies from their common prayer book, and even to abandon its Hebrew, thus demonstrating their "love for the land that would grant them citizenship" (Greenstone 1906: 246). The Prussian chancellor recommended the pamphlet to his king with a memorandum attached. In it, he observed reassuringly that once extended equal rights, the Jews could be expected to cease praying for their "renationalization in Palestine" and pray instead for "the peace and prosperity of the Prussian government"; to cease hoping for the coming of a messiah and pray instead "for the welfare of the king whom they love and respect with all their souls" (Bernfeld 1900: 67; cited in Greenstone 1906: 248). As Greenstone notes, the first edition of the prayer book of the Reform Temple of Hamburg retained the messianism of its Orthodox predecessors. Friedländer's position would not win the day until the publication of the second edition of the book in 1841, which nevertheless provoked widespread Orthodox protests (1906: 248–49). The Jews of Prussia would not gain emancipation for another seven years, in the aftermath of the revolution of 1848 (264). They would continue to debate the political implications of messianism in the decades beyond (253–63).

Greenstone leaves Prussia's late eighteenth- and early nineteenth-century historians beyond the scope of his observations. Scholem's contemporary Léon Poliakov is the first to address their views on Jews and Judaism systematically, though even his survey is far from complete. Poliakov is less hesitant than others in suggesting that such views continued to bear the impress of the extraordinarily bitter diatribes that the aging Luther himself directed against those Jews who had declined his earlier invitation to convert (Poliakov 1965: 216–26; 1975: 175–276). He further detects the impress of the English deists, perhaps especially at the University of Göttingen, which the Anglo-German house of Hanover had endowed in 1737 and which we have met with Breisach (Poliakov 1972: 177). Poliakov describes Göttingen as "a veritable hotbed of anti-Jewish propaganda" in the last half of the eighteenth century (1975: 177). Among its faculty, he mentions Johann David Michaelis (1717–1791), whom Frei (1974: 159) includes among the first rank of new critics. The "greatest Hebraicist of his time" was well known for his ardent rejection of the popular supposition that Hebrew was the original language of mankind (Poliakov 1972: 189). He was equally well known for his even more ardent rejection of Jewish emancipation on these grounds: Jews were "vicious and dishonest"; "without honor"; "worthless as soldiers because of their small stature and also because they refused to fight on the Sabbath"; and without any real religion, since Mosaic law merely "stipulated how to act and not what to believe" (Poliakov 1975: 177, summarizing Michaelis 1782). The latter criterion is unmistakably pietistic. In Michaelis's physiognomic allusions, Poliakov cannot help but detect the echo of the (ostensibly value-free) findings of another member of the Göttingen faculty, Johann Friedrich Blumenbach, father of physical anthropology and meticulous measurer of Jewish crania (1975: 138–39).

Herder favored emancipation. As Poliakov points out, he was certainly not "anti-Semitic" in the "modern" racialist sense of the term. He was far from being vehemently anti-Jewish. Yet, rather in the manner of the younger Luther, he favored the emancipation of the Jews primarily as the path to their assimilation into Gentile (and Christian) society. He evidently regarded them as redeemable. He did not, however, differ greatly from Michaelis in his estimation of their characterological condition. In one of the chapters of his most ambitious work, *Ideas for a Philosophy of the History of Mankind* (1784–1791), he remarks: "[T]he people of God, to whom Heaven itself once gave its homeland, has been for centuries, almost from its beginnings even, a parasitic growth on the trunks of other nations: a race of cunning dealers almost throughout the whole world, which despite oppression never yearns for its own honor and dwelling, never for its own homeland" (cf. Herder 1966; cited in Poliakov 1975: 162). Herder evidently knew next to nothing of Jewish messianism, Sabbatian or traditionalist.

Herder's judgments appear with little modification in turn in Kant's "minor" writings. Kant is also of the opinion that Judaism cannot be regarded as a true religion, but not simply because the Mosaic code is "purely political" rather than "moral." Evidently more aware than Herder of messianism and especially sensitive to its temporal finitism, this good pietist further faults Judaism — at least when "taken in its purity" — for lacking any conviction in an otherworldy "future life," a properly eternal redemption (cf. Kant 1960; cited in Poliakov 1975: 178). As Poliakov points out, Kant's low opinion of what is in his eyes a pseudoreligion would seem to be limited to the pseudoreligion itself, or at the very least in awkward accord with his personal relationships. As the saying goes, some of his best friends were Jews (Poliakov 1975: 179–80). Or perhaps not his best friends, if the passage that Poliakov cites from his *Anthropologie* is any indication:

> The Palestinians living amongst us are, since their exile, because of their usurious spirit not unjustifiably renowned for their deceitfulness, so far as the great majority is concerned. It does indeed seem disconcerting to conceive of a *nation* of usurers; but it is just as disconcerting to conceive of a nation of pure mercantilism, by far the largest part of which is bound together by a superstition recognized by the state in which they live [but in which they do not] seek any civic honor. But they try to compensate for this lack by outwitting the people amongst whom they find shelter and even by deceiving each other. Now this cannot be otherwise in a whole nation of pure merchants as non-productive members of society (e.g. the Jews in Poland). Thus, their constitution, sanctioned by ancient decrees and recognized also by us amongst whom they live (and with whom we have certain sacred writings in common), cannot be nullified without inconsistency even if they do make the slogan "Let the buyer beware" their highest principle in their intercourse with us. (cf. Kant 1974; cited in Poliakov 1975: 179)

It is hardly surprising that anti-Semitic propagandists would later seize upon these accusations — which they could also find repeated by Fichte and Hegel — with particular relish (Poliakov 1975: 179, 180–83).

Well below such philosophical heights, the anti-Jewish irritation of even so eminent a new critic as Semler sounds relatively harmless. Semler's petulance had its primary stimulus in what he perceived as the Jews' spiritual arrogance, their complaisant sense of spiritual privilege.

He was prepared to recognize them as God's elect. He was not prepared to attribute undue authority to "their" religious canon. He would ask: "[B]ecause the Jews regard these books as divine and holy, is it right to conclude that other people must also consider them divine, of a superior dignity to their own histories and annals?" (Poliakov 1975: 184). Or, a bit more malignantly: "[W]ill they therefore be eternally necessary, these foundations that the incompetent and untutored Jews we know, who cannot even be compared to many honest Greeks and Romans, have adopted under the name of holy Scripture as the true chronicles of their people?" (Poliakov 1975: 185). Frei estimates his "insistence that the Bible as such is not identical with the word of God" as nothing short of "epoch-making" (1974: 161).

One can only be struck in contrast by the relative serenity — post-epochal, perhaps, but in any case not to be conflated with charity — with which Semler's most celebrated student would write of Judaism in 1799, only some eight years after his teacher's death:

> Judaism is long since a dead religion, and those who at present still bear its colors are actually sitting and mourning beside the undecaying mummy and weeping over its demise and its sad legacy. . . . I speak of it, not because it was somehow the forerunner of Christianity; I hate that type of historical reference in religion. Its necessity is a far higher and eternal one, and every beginning in it is original. But Judaism has such a beautiful, childlike character, and this is so completely buried, and the whole constitutes such a remarkable example of the corruption and total disappearance of religion from a great body in which it was formerly found. Just take away everything political and, if God wills, everything moral by which it is commonly characterized; forget the whole experiment of joining the state to the religion (I shall not say "to the church"); forget that Judaism was to a certain extent simultaneously an order founded on an old family and preserved by priests; look merely to the properly religious element in it to which all this does not belong, and then tell me which is the idea of the universe that everywhere shines through. It is none other than that of a universal immediate retribution, of the infinite's own reaction against every individual finite form that proceeds from free choice by acting through another finite element that is not viewed as proceeding from free choice.

The writer, the lecturer in question, is Friedrich Schleiermacher (1988 [1799]: 114), the scholar to whom all subsequent "hermeneuts" must ultimately trace their title, in the fifth and final of his "speeches" to the "cultured despisers" of religion.

Departing from Kant, Schleiermacher has no desire to deny the Jews their sense of the infinite; and in the infinite's reaction against the errancy of the finite, he finds the "reason" for "the prominence of the dialogue that is in all [in Judaism] that is religious" (1988 [1799]: 114). The spiritual and practical matrix of dialogue was the gift of prophecy itself, which was developed in Judaism to such perfection as—here at least—to reduce Christians (especially pietistic Lutherans) to mere children by comparison (115). In its consummation, the gift demanded that "the imagination . . . anticipate the Almighty's word that he had just been about to speak, and from far away bring into view the second part of this same moment, while annihilating the intervening time and space" (115). Though Schleiermacher does not identify it as such, the imagination of which he writes is a typological imagination, if more proleptic than retrodictive. He is prepared in any case to pronounce upon its historical exhaustion:

> The belief in the messiah was its last fruit, engendered with great effort; a new ruler was supposed to come to restore the Zion in its splendor where the voice of the Lord had grown silent, and by the subjugation of peoples under the old law that simple course was again supposed to become universal in the events of the world, the simple path that was interrupted by their unpeaceful community, by their energies being directed against one another, and by the difference of their customs. It has long persevered, as a single fruit, after all the life force has vanished from the branch, often remains hanging until the bleakest season on a withered stem and dries up on it. (115)

This is the serenity of someone who is certain that, in the war of the gods, his god has won. This is the charity—if one dare call it that—of the good soldier for the defeated. It is the charity of the pietistic and naive soldier who was unable to imagine—beyond the survival of Judaism—the sustained vitality of those spiritual energies that fed the Second Great Awakening, much less their latter-day explosion, or implosion, at the outskirts of Waco nearly two centuries later.

So this is our history. It would be an exaggeration (if an exhilarating one) to say, with Frei, that it has "remained the same since the eighteenth century" (1974: 135). It is less of an exaggeration, however, to say that the reason—national, populist (many like to call it "democratic"), anti-Judaizing, by no means resolutely anti-apocalyptic but resolutely antimillenarian—that coalesced within the charged cloud of gas of revolutionary Europe is still expanding. It is "globalizing," in the going parlance. It meets resistance at its always somewhat tattered borders. Now as in the past, it suffers from external and internal parasites: internationalist, anarchist, theocratic, tyrannical, surrealist, irrealist, deconstructionist, genealogical, even the mutant anthropological. It has suffered through multiple diagnoses, a great lot of labwork. It has had its crises. For all this, it has yet to give way to any remotely credible, remotely as legitimate, remotely as normatively stable an alternative. Perhaps Deleuze and Guattari's nomadism (1987), or Foucault's declaration of the rights of the governed (1994 [1984]a), or the Greens' ecologism hint at the themes that the organic intellectuals of a new reason will hold dear in the future. But if such intellectuals are beginning to form a genuine league, this anthropologist has yet to be able to pick them out of the crowd.

So, then, our history—and with it, as one of its constitutive forces, among its stronger rather than its weaker forces, that push or pull whose manifestations are often grouped together under the generous rubric of "secularization." Sociologically, the latter has its most familiar characterization, its most familiar positivity, as an ebbing or withdrawal of the authority of a church. Culturologically, its description is more variable. Secularization sometimes appears as undermining or casting doubt on what was formerly taken for granted; as the ascendance of scientific or pragmatic perspectives over their transcendental or mystical counterparts; as the waning of devotion or conviction; as the collapse of belief. Sociologically and culturologically, it is a process that often poses a descriptive challenge to descriptive precision for what at first sight would seem to be its unusual empirical complexity. Authority, after all, is of manifold types. Churches are not everywhere the same. Ebbing or withdrawal is sometimes an all-or-nothing affair but more often a matter of degree. The substantive and perhaps formal constituents of scientific and other perspectives are historically and cross-culturally inconstant. Devotion takes many and mutually inconsistent forms. Belief and its object are not one but many different things. At second sight, however, the complexity of secularization is at least as much nominal as empirical, a matter of definitions as much as observation. Or to put it in more precise terms, secularization is an empirically indeterminate process, in part because it can neither be defined nor described independently of defining and describing (or, at the very least, assuming a definition and possible description of) its contraries. Its indeterminacy would be minimal were its contraries definitively and descriptively tractable. But they are not, and if secularization must consequently remain a thing of theory, this is above all because religion is a thing of theory itself.

Talal Asad has made just such a point in a trenchant genealogical overview of the constitution of religion as an anthropological category (1993: 37–39). Asad's provocation is what is in his view a catastrophically misguided "attempt to understand Muslim traditions by insisting that in them religion and politics (two essences that modern society tries to keep conceptually and practically apart) are coupled" (1993: 28). His historical foil is the medieval West or, in any event, a conventional view of the medieval West, which renders it as a society in which religion and politics were indeed so coupled but historically destined to come apart. Asad faults such a view for the presumptions on which it rests: that it is possible analytically to distinguish the medieval "religious" from the medieval "political" in spite of their entanglement; and more generally, that it is possible to distinguish the religious "in its essence" from the other institutional orders with which, at various places and times, it may or may not be conjoined. His position is that religion has no such essence, that there "cannot be a universal definition of [it], not only because its constituent elements and relationships are historically specific, but because that definition is itself the historical product of discursive processes" (1993: 29).

Neither the fact that religion is substantively and relationally variable nor the fact that its definition is the historical product of discursive processes entails that it will always defy the lexicographical or theoretical universalist. But no matter: Asad succeeds in distilling the translation, the drift of medieval "religion" into modern "religion" into incisive (one dare not say definitive) terms that among other things reveal the pietism that we have consistently encountered among the new critics to be very much of a piece with the reason they exercised. Of the broadest dimensions of that drift, he writes:

> [t]he Medieval Church was always clear about why there was a continuous need to distinguish knowledge from falsehood (religion from what sought to subvert it), as well as the sacred from the profane (religion from what was outside it), distinctions for which the authoritative discourses, the teachings and practices of the Church, not the convictions of the practitioner, were always the final test. Several times before the Reformation, the boundary between the religious and the secular was redrawn, but always the formal authority of the Church remained preeminent. In later centuries, with the triumphant rise of modern science, modern production, and the modern state, the churches would also be clear about the need to distinguish the religious from the secular, shifting, as they did so, the weight of religion more and more onto the moods and motivations of the individual believer. Discipline (intellectual and social) would, in this period, gradually abandon religious space, letting "belief," "conscience," and "sensibility" take its place. (1993: 39)

"But theory," he adds, "would still be needed to define religion." Indeed it would.

184

Asad's point of departure and return is the definition of religion Geertz puts forward in "Religion as a Cultural System" (1973: 87–125). His chart of its ancestry includes Talcott Parsons and Alfred Schutz. By implication if not by name, it includes Malinowski and Weber. It could well have included both Schleiermacher and Semler. We have in any event already become acquainted with its apical ancestors, from whom the new critics themselves descend, severally and jointly. One is the Locke of *The Reasonableness of Christianity* (1999 [1695]; cf. Asad 1993: 41–42). The other (not quite so apical) is Kant, who by 1795 could "produce a fully essentialized idea of religion which could be counterposed to its phenomenal forms" (Asad 1993: 42). Whether Geertz himself should properly be construed as producing a "fully essentialized" definition of religion that might be "counterposed to its phenomenal forms" *à la kantienne* is dubious, but not at the center of Asad's attention. Closer to its center is Geertz's assertion that religion serves to mollify our profound, and profoundly human need for a sense of order; that it is just that "cultural system" to which we appeal when, at the "limits" of either our "analytic capabilities" or our "powers of endurance" or our "moral insight," we face the threat of "chaos" (cf. Geertz 1973: 100; cited in Asad 1993: 45). Asad does not note that Geertz draws here directly from Weber's "Psychology of the World Religions" (1946: 267–301). He notes rather — and not altogether fairly — that the position amounts to "the bland suggestion that religion is ultimately a matter of having a positive attitude toward the problem of disorder, of affirming simply that in some sense or other the world as a whole is explicable, justifiable, bearable." He continues:

> This modest view of religion (which would have horrified the early Church Fathers or Medieval churchmen) is a product of the only legitimate space allowed to Christianity by post-Enlightenment society, the right to individual *belief*: the human condition is full of ignorance, pain, and suffering, and religious symbols are a means of coming positively to terms with that condition. . . . [It] is one indication of how marginal religion has become in modern industrial society as the site for producing disciplined knowledge and personal discipline. (45–46)

Asad suggests further that such a view comes close to that of religion as an opiate of the masses. It comes closer still to that of religion as subsisting in faith. This is in fact more narrow than Geertz's view (if not, perhaps, more narrow than his definition). It is, however, the view of every pietist, who would only add that the faith in which religion subsists is also its justification, and its sole justification, however much faith may be expected to manifest itself in the goodness of a character impelled to perform good works.

In and of itself, in the abstract, the contraction of religion into pietism would appear to leave the religious still with myriad opportunities of confession and profession — private and public, interior and exterior, otherworldly and this-worldly. In and of itself, in the abstract, it is indeed devoid of specific disciplinary implications. As the historical companion of a national, populist, anti-papist, anti-Judaizing, antimillenarian reason, its libertarian posture has been of considerable service. It has attracted a great many converts, Catholic and Jewish (and, for that matter, deist) among them. It has thus allowed a reason bred of religious conflict, of a particular war of the gods, to bury (or, in any event, to forget) at least some of its originary biases. But as the companion of that reason, as its elder but subservient squire, it has been conscripted to set an example of disciplined restraint to which its posture would otherwise give the lie. Epistemologically, it shows itself to be within its appropriate bounds so long as the faith it confesses and professes does not stray outside the "transcendental" into the "phenomenal." That, at least, is the specifically Kantian formula for the restriction of legitimate gnosis. Practically, pietism shows itself to be within its appropriate bounds so long as the faith in which and as which it is justified does not stray into the arenas of the competition between either partisan interests or sovereign powers. Definitions notwithstanding, this normative pietism is far from exhausting the actualities of either religiosity or religion, in the past or in the present. In the West(ernized), its standards are nevertheless those of the religious mainstream, but also those of the majority of those more peripatetic religious that belong to the "New Age" — an age the denominational and sectarian rhizomorphology of which that lance-breaking pietist, Luther himself, would not have wanted to dream.

In the West(ernized), the same standards are consequently the crossing guards of an epistemic and practical colonization whose gates are perhaps all the more effective for being more invisible than those of the ghettos of the (not long distant) past. They enclose more than pietists alone. They are not unbreachable. So, for example, Echo Fields has perceptively treated the New Christian Right as among the more recent gate-crashers of colonization, though she sees their rebellion as being against what Habermas deems the "technocratic" colonization "of the lifeworld" (1991: 182–87). Fields's analysis is less convincing in identifying conservative Christian activists as contrarians of the "hedonism and consumerism" of the technocratic apologetics of late capitalism (1991: 183–85). Such contrarians are and have long been more likely to make up the only occasionally politicized ranks of isolationist and utopian communities than those of the more regularly politicized battalions of (profitable) televangelism and the (often luxurious) subdivisions of fundamentalist suburbia. Her analysis is more convincing in identifying them as contrarians of the "juridification" of the private sphere, especially the juridification of the family (1991: 183–86). It would be misleading to stop here, however. The "family values" of the New Christian Right indeed run counter to the juridical formalism and individualism that liberal courts were busily reinforcing in the 1980s. Their strategies — which remain those of intervention in "the system," not those of its revolutionary overthrow — are nevertheless designed less with the technocratic formalist than with a more substantialist adversary in mind. That adversary is often enough both "liberal" and self-appointedly "secular." But he or she is no less often a liberal believer, a good pietist, who has long been prepared to favor juridical formalism and individualism as the best protection against having anyone else's gnosis impose itself on his or her own. One need only read de Tocqueville, moreover, to recognize that the synergy between an ever more abstract legalism and an ever more individualistic religiosity was already in place more than a century and a half ago (see de Tocqueville (1969 [1835–1840]: 61–98). The "system" was not yet technocratic. It was a national federation, for which increasing abstraction was one of the few means of preserving the unity of the first person of the increasingly plural "we" that its Declaration of Independence had enshrined as "the people" (cf. Lee 1997: 323–32).

The Habermasians are surely wrong if they presume that there was a time at which "the lifeworld" (if there ever was such a thing at all) was not yet colonized. They are right, however, to recognize the distinctiveness of technocratic colonization — or in any event, the distinctiveness of the restrictive effects of increasing technocratic domination. What must be added is that at least for the past one-hundred-fifty years, colonization — conceived precisely as a process of increasing restriction and domination — has been proceeding in the plural. There have been many colonizations — of epistemic authority, of practical wisdom, of poetic virtuosity — of which technocratic colonization has simply been the most vast. Yet, it has also been the least constraining. For all our putative alienation, we who are self-appointed secularists still roam freely through the marketplaces of vanity and, if begrudgingly, permit all but the murdering, the thieving, the "patently offensive" to join us. For us at least, the pietists are the latter-day successors of the "good Jews" who cut so fashionable a swath through the literature (and literary salons) of nascently national Germany (see Poliakov 1975: 163–75, 189–210). They join us — gatekeepers in their own turn — in monitoring the more orthodox and more "ortho-practical." They join us in raising the occasional warning flags: the black-and-white stripes of the social worker's report; the more finely grained stipple of the forms that might threaten revocation of tax-exempt status. On the whole, we allow the orthodox and ortho-practical to remain what they wish — to remain "in the system" but not "of" it, so long as they indeed agree to remain in it.

Even the orthodox are likely to prove our allies in tending the reinforced fences with which we seek to enclose the religious subversives in our midst, those true radicals who, like that latter-day avatar of Sabbatai Zevi, the self-proclaimed "sinful messiah" David Koresh, want nothing of the system more than its dissolution, its sacral banishment to Tartarus. Koresh does seem to have taken the law into his own hands; like Sabbatai before him, he does seem to have grown more transgressive as his term as Messiah lengthened. Sociologically speaking, that is the way of every charismatic who has little more than the ever more extraordinary character of his acts through which to demonstrate and maintain his authority. There is, after all, nothing so extraordinary as transgression; and if those miracles that would transgress the laws of nature are beyond the charismatic's power, nothing is left but those sins and crimes and torts that would transgress the laws at once of the religious canon and of merely ordinary women and men. Amo Paul Bishop Roden has followed, and has pursued, a more "Talmudic" path. Yet she shares with Koresh a (loudly cried) rejection of the dignity with which we have invested our collective, national sovereignty. She shares his contempt for our Laodicean and Sodomite laxities. Though she is far less inclined than Koresh to force it, she, too, awaits a revolution. And nothing could be crazier than that. Could it?

The anthropologist is at present inclined to repeat Frei's exhilarating exaggeration: nothing has changed since the eighteenth century. I, however, am a bit more cautious and a bit more hopeful — or must be, since I would otherwise have to wonder why I have spent so much time and energy and passion on a project that, if it gains any notice at all, is likely to gain the notice above all of polemicists to whose righteous bellicosity — on my behalf or against me — I can do nothing better than turn the other (if infidel) cheek. I would like to believe that I have at least succeeded in giving pause to those who would rather pathologize David Koresh or Ms. Roden than recognize them as the subversives they actually are. I am also not silly enough to let too much hinge on my having succeeded. I put more hope in the shadows that continue to be cast from Mount Carmel itself, shadows that are long and seem to have come to creep hauntingly into the lives of a far from negligible sector of a public that, something more than eight years ago, was at first inclined to find relief in, even to applaud their looming. Yet, one of the lessons I have learned from the inception of this project forward is that "we" are a forgetful "people."

I also have a lesson from Ms. Roden herself. Its light is feeble, but seemed never even to have dawned on those who orchestrated the assault on the Mount Carmel compound; for all I know, it never dawned on those inside the compound, either. It is not a new light. One might find it, for example, in John Stuart Mill's moral epistemology (1962 [1859]: 143–49) or in Georges Canguilhem's heuristic vitalism (1989 [1943] and 1952; cf. Foucault 1998 [1985]: 474–76), but with Ms. Roden, it is far less ethereal, far more ethically concrete. It is not likely to lead us to revolution, much less to the revolution that Ms. Roden herself thinks already underway. Still, it tempers the darkness of Mount Carmel and might be strong enough to temper at least a little of the darkness of those places where the rest of us dwell, and of our dwelling. It is the light of our ignorance; its revelation, the revelation that "we" — even we — might be in error.

Notes

Part One

1. Interview by William R. Dull, October 1995. Here and throughout, I include citations of archival sources as endnotes. Unless otherwise qualified, all references to interviews with Ms. Roden, to her writings, to the writings of Ben and of Lois Roden, and to those of Victor Houteff are drawn from sources I have accumulated as a personal archive through the course of my fieldwork.

2. See James 1985 (1859): 24. I share with James his experiential focus (cf. also Berger 1974; and Neitz and Spickard 1990) but not his "experientialism," on the limits of which see Proudfoot 1985 and the lucid and accessible discussion in Gallagher 1990: 11–24.

3. Interview by William R. Dull, October 1995.

4. Interview by the author, August 1996.

5. A.P.B. Roden, "The Book of Zechariah: The Seven Spirits of God," in *Babylon Is Fallen: The Legacy of David Koresh*, 112.

6. Interview by William R. Dull, October 1995.

7. A. Roden, "Zechariah," 111–12. Sociological and psychological elaborations of Anthony Wallace's conceptualization of "revitalization" (1956a, 1956b) have often emphasized such factors as transience or dislocation (Wilson 1973) and filial conflicts (Ullman 1982; Cushman 1984, 1986; Kirkpatrick and Shaver 1990) as distinctively productive of religious conversion (but cf. Heirich 1977). Ms. Roden's testimony offers partial support for such hypotheses, as well as partial disconfirmation of them.

8. Interview by William R. Dull, October 1995.

9. Ms. Roden's sister confirms the mathematics degree and the intelligence to which it was testament in her deposition for an investigative report Child Protective Services caseworker Suzi Colson filed in McClennan County, Texas, District Court on 20 June 1994 (#84–1963–1) on behalf of Ms. Roden's son.

10. Interview by William R. Dull, October 1995.

11. Interview by the author, August 1996.

12. A.P.B. Roden, *Cracking the Cover-up*, 18.

13. Interview by the author, August 1996.

14. Ibid.

15. A. Roden, *Cracking the Cover-up*, 17.

16. This is a reference to the month in which the attack occurred in her dream.

17. A. Roden, *Cracking the Cover-up*, 53–54.

18. Interview by the author, August 1996.

19. The mainstream denominations include Methodism, Lutheranism, Presbyterianism, Episcopalianism, and Catholicism. On the relative eschatological "temperance" of such denominations, cf. Boyer 1992: 116–17.

20. Boyer 1992: 4–7. Lindsey's other works include *There's a New World Coming* (1973) and *The 1980s: Countdown to Armageddon* (1981 [1980]).

21. The Southern Baptist Convention, for example, has a current membership of approximately fifteen million and is the single largest Protestant denomination in the United States. Add to this the membership of the Seventh-day Adventist Church, which virtually doubled in size between 1965 and 1990 and now has more than 700,000 members. Add to this the membership of several other churches inclined to emphasize the apocalyptic: the Assemblies of God, more than two million strong; the Jehovah's Witnesses, approaching one million; and the Church of the Nazarene, in excess of half a million. See Boyer 1993: 31. On the concomitant decline of such denominations as the United Methodist Church and the Presbyterian Church, cf. Boyer 1992: 3. Boyer draws his statistical information primarily from Gallup and Castelli 1989. For a comparable assessment, see Fowler and Hertzke 1995: 33–49.

22. A predecessor of many later televangelists, DeHaan enjoyed special prominence in the 1960s, when his radio program aired on some five hundred stations. See Boyer's review of his career and teachings (1992: 124–26).

23. Here and throughout, my treatment of millennialist poetics is deeply indebted to the "practical poetics" Harold Bloom has developed in such works as *The Anxiety of Influence* (1973) and *A Map of Misreading* (1975). On the poetics of the sublime and the countersublime, see esp. Bloom 1975: 98–100.

24. Timothy Weber offers a lucid formulation of the typology of millennialism (1979: 9–11), which like any such formulation runs the risk of an excess of formalization, of distinguishing at the level of the model what often blends together at the level of practice. So, for example, James West Davidson has argued persuasively that the distinction between premillennialism and postmillennialism coalesces logically and practically only in the thought of nineteenth-century America, but does not inform the thought of such eighteenth-century divines as Cotton Mather and Jonathan Edwards (Davidson 1977: 28–36 passim). A similar problem of applicability tends to emerge whenever one moves beyond the sphere of influence of the Abrahamic tradition — to the "cargo cults" of Oceania or the prophetic activism of sub-Saharan Africa. For this reason and a variety of others, scholarly usage is variable within and across disciplines. See Brummett 1991: 82–84 for an overview of such vicissitudes. See also Trompf 1990: 3–10.

"Millenarianism" (or "millenarism") often appears as a synonym of "premillennialism." Anthropologists and sociologists, however, tend to use it somewhat more abstractly, especially outside the context of Christian apocalyptic, and to treat it as a synonym of "millennialism" (of one or another kind: cf., e.g., Wallis 1982 and Trompf 1990; cf. also Barkun [1986: 2–5], who prefers to juxtapose "millenarianisn" with "utopianism"). In part 2 and thereafter, I will use "millenarianism" to designate the performative mapping of the climactic phase of millennialist narrative onto the here and now.

25. A. Roden, *Cracking the Cover-up*, 17.

26. Ibid. The court order to which Ms. Roden refers would have established her agreement to be committed.

27. A. Roden, *Cracking the Cover-up*, 18.

28. Ibid., 18–19.

29. Ibid., 19.

30. The record, an order of the dismissal of a request for Ms. Roden's "temporary-indefinite commitment" on the grounds of a failure to meet the necessary burden of proof, was filed with the McClennan County Court on 21 June 1984. Like many of the other official documents that have, for better or worse, pronounced upon Ms. Roden's status, this one, too, is included as an appendix to *Cracking the Cover-up*.

31. A. Roden, *Cracking the Cover-up*, 20.

32. A.P.B. Roden, "The Politics of Murder: The Why of the Branch Davidian Massacre," 5.

33. For example, the conflation of logical with social "necessity."

34. On the modern "functionalization" of theory, see Blumenberg 1983: 200. These distinctions derive from Blumenberg's discussion of the semantic divergence between modern "theory" and Aristotle's *theōria*.

35. For an expansive historical survey of something very like a semiotics of suspicion, see Foucault 1998 (1967).

36. There can be no question that millennialist movements outside the West have often been the inspiration, or the result, of "contact" with both Western missionaries and Western fortune hunters. But for one argument that the millennialist consciousness cannot always be supposed to derive from a Western predecessor, see Burridge 1960: 25–44.

37. See Thucydides 1980, 4:xxvii, 1–2.

38. These commentators include, among many others, Eva Keuls. In *The Reign of the Phallus* (1993: 381–403), Keuls writes of the "castration" of the Herms and, departing even further from Thucydides, postulates that the league of vandals was in fact made up of Athenian women.

39. Several of the points of this model have at least partial echoes in the work of several of the contributors to the aptly titled *Even the Paranoid Have Enemies* (Berke, Pierides, Sabbadini, and Schneider, 1998), especially that of Otto Kernberg (1998), John Jackson (1998), and Stanley Schneider (1998). It is likely, however, that most of these contributors would balk at the anthropologist's classification of all paranoia as sociocultural in its etiology. The anthropologist is prepared to admit as a theoretical possibility that a properly psychological modality of paranoia might exist, but must hasten to point out that neither

psychology nor psychiatry has yet to establish anything remotely resembling its etiology. So far, at least, the latter sort of paranoia is only a (presumptive) symptomatic syndrome without any identifiable cause.

40. On the concept of the regime of truth, see Foucault 1981: 305. For my rationale for enlarging it into the concept of the regime of signification, see Faubion 1993: 154–55.

41. The preceding eight paragraphs are a much modified version of a discussion in Faubion 1999: 378–82, 390–93. The thematic of embodiment has been central to anthropology and social theory alike for at least two decades. For a seminal overview, see Scheper-Hughes and Lock 1987. More recently, see Lyon and Barbalet 1994.

42. Erving Goffman's *Asylums* (1961) is seminal, but all these points now bear the stamp of Foucault (1965 [1961]; 1977 [1975]; 1997 [1972]; 1998 [1970]a).

43. So, for example, Judith Butler, who resorts to the term to identify what we reject or from what we "disidentify" ourselves when "confronted with a [subject-]position that seems too saturated with injury or aggression" (1993: 100) or with our own "failure to conform" (101).

44. The hypothesis that religion functions as a "compensatory mechanism" for individuals who have suffered insult to the self or suffered from a pattern of emotionally empty or "dissonant" relationships with figures of authority has proven to be of sustained interest to adherents to attachment theory (Allison 1968, 1969; Ullman 1982; Cushman 1986; Kirkpatrick and Shaver 1990) but also resonates strongly with John Lofland and Rodney Stark's "affectional" and "value-added" theory of conversion (1965).

45. Ludwig's analysis of the eternal patient (1971) is still the most comprehensive and acute. See also Estroff 1981: 200–205 and Basaglia 1987: 63–64.

46. Allan Young has amply illustrated this point in his recent study of the "invention" of posttraumatic stress disorder. See Young 1995: 169–70, 200–210.

47. Interview by William R. Dull, October 1995. The original sequence of these remarks has been slightly altered here.

48. A. Roden, *Cracking the Cover-up*, 20–21.

49. Ibid., 1.

50. Interview by William R. Dull, October 1995.

51. Ibid.

52. A.P.B. Roden, "The Excellency of Mount Carmel," 1.

53. See Lofland and Stark 1965. As Lofland and Skonovd note (1981: 377), most of "our contemporary definitions of mystical conversion are provided by psychoanalytically oriented scholars," not a few of whom have been ready to implicate the mystic among the mentally ill (for example, somewhat surprisingly, Greeley 1974: 81; and Spilka, Hood, and Gorsuch 1985: 292). For somewhat more cautious, more Jamesian approaches, see Schwab and Peterson 1990; and Stifler et al. 1993. Lofland and Skonovd, for their part, appear to prefer to hold such a diagnostic tradition at arm's length.

54. The authors cite Roger Straus's semi-autobiographical account of conversion to Scientology as a "protypical" case (see Straus 1976, 1979). Straus him-

self refers to such a mode of conversion as "active" (or "activist": see also Richardson 1980, 1985; Richardson and Kilbourne 1983; and Robbins 1984).

55. The authors note that this exploratory or imitative approach seems to mark much of the religious "New Age." Citing James Beckford's study of conversion to the Jehovah's Witnesses (1978), however, they offer at least one example of the approach among "old-time" churches. They hint only slightly at the economistic modeling of this and the "affectional" motif (see below), which has attracted a number of prominent analysts from the late 1980s forward. The model, appealing (but not exclusively) to scholars interested in "televangelism" in the contemporary United States, casts the religious arena as a competitive marketplace in which churches pitch their products to would-be spiritual consumers, whose purchases are grounded in the classically economistic assessment of costs and benefits. The model derives in part from the work of Gary Becker (1986) and other enthusiasts of "rational choice." It is a prominent component of the theory of religious dynamics developed by Rodney Stark with William Bainbridge (1985), but has more purist champions in Roger Finke (1990; cf. Finke and Stark 1992) and Laurence Iannaccone (1990; cf. also Fowler and Hertzke 1995). Critical responses include Wallis and Bruce 1984; Bruce 1993; and, more broadly, Bourdieu (1990).

56. See Lofland and Stark 1965; for a critique that anticipates Rambo, see Snow and Phillips 1980.

57. See the works cited in notes 7 and 44. To them should be added a number of treatments of the relationship between religious conversion or the intensification of religious commitment and such macrostructural conditions as economic recession (Sales 1972) and economic uncertainty (Fields 1991: 182–84).

58. Though Rambo does not cite them, C. Daniel Batson has sought in the past two decades to render "operational" a concept of religious quest as a distinctive "orientation," differing in particular from both the "extrinsic" and "intrinsic" orientations Gordon Allport earlier proposed. Batson's project has received considerable attention from psychologists and sociologists of religion who rely on statistical methods. See Batson 1976; Batson and Ventis 1982; Batson and Schoenrade 1991a, 1991b; cf. Allport 1950; Allport and Ross 1967; Hood and Morris 1985; Hilty, Morgan, and Hartman 1985; and McFarland and Warren 1992. For a balanced and engagingly idiographic intervention into the terrain of statistically oriented analyses of conversion, see Kwilecki 1999.

59. Gauri Viswanathan, for example, underscores the similarity between conversion and "cultural critique" in her study of Christianization in colonial India (1995). I would underscore the saliency of both critique and invention in Ms. Roden's conversion to Branch Davidianism here and will continue to underscore the saliency of both in her religious practice throughout.

60. Saint Perpetua, the first religious woman to write an autobiography, reports a similar self-interpellation. A native of Carthage, living at the end of the second century and the first years of the third century C.E., she refused to pay homage to the gods of her Roman conquerors. She was subsequently imprisoned. When her jailers demanded her name, she replied *Christiana sum*, "I am a Christian (woman)." See Dronke 1984: 1–4.

61. The analytical artificiality of the solitary reader is a central thematic of

the contributors to Jonathon Boyarin's volume, *The Ethnography of Reading* (1992).

62. Bloom 1975: 51; cf. H. Wheeler Robinson, *Inspiration and Revelation in the Old Testament* (Oxford: Clarendon, 1946).

63. Thomas Overholt's treatment of prophecy proceeds from just such a sociocultural triad, underscoring (as Weber also did) that charismatic authority allows for no psychologistic reduction. See Overholt 1989.

64. Stephen O'Leary (1994: 233–34n. 35) cites just these of Barkun's self-revisions as the point of departure for his rhetorical approach to millennialist commitment and conversion. Between O'Leary's model and my own, there is much in common with one crucial difference: the scene of persuasion is only one aspect of the scene of instruction. The former relegates objective conditions to the background, to the external; the latter does not and cannot. I address O'Leary's analysis at length in the second part of this monograph.

Part Two

1. Amo Roden, "What Branch Davidians Believe," 1.

2. Ibid., 1–2.

3. Ibid., 2–3.

4. Ibid., 3.

5. Amo Roden, "The Seven Angel Messengers of Revelation 14," in *Babylon Is Fallen*, 11.

6. Ibid., 11–12.

7. Ibid., 12.

8. Ibid., 12–13.

9. Ibid., 13.

10. On the establishment of SDA Church, see Damsteegt 1977: xv, and on the growth of the New Denominations generally, see part 1, n. 21 in this volume.

11. A. Roden, "The Seven Angel Messengers," 12.

12. This remains among the fundamental tenets (the sixteenth) in the most recent proclamations of the SDA credo, available through the Internet (General Conference of Seventh-day Adventists 2000).

13. As Damsteegt points out (1977: 154n. 297), the concept of "present truth" has been operative in SDA discourse since at least 1845. Ellen's husband, James White, found it in 2 Pet. 1:12 and offered the following scholium: "In Peter's time there was present truth, or truth applicable to that present time. The Church has ever had a present truth. The present truth now, is that which shows present duty, and the right position for us who are about to witness the time of trouble, such as there never was" (cited in Damsteegt 1977n. 297). The concept of such a successive — and potentially supercessive — truth remains fundamental to Davidian and Branch Davidian discourses as well.

14. By 1925, the SDA Church had a membership in excess of 245,000; by 1930, a membership of more than 314,000. See Land 1986, appendix 2, 253.

15. In his complaints against the excessive worldliness of the SDA Church of

his day, Houteff conforms tidily to what Stark and Bainbridge follow H. Richard Niebuhr in identifying as the "typical" Protestant sectarian (Stark and Bainbridge 1985: 99–101; cf. Niebuhr 1929). I have learned much about Victor Houteff's life from Ms. Roden's writings and from those of her Branch Davidian predecessors. I have also had the benefit of research at the Texas Collection at Baylor University and of conversations with William (Bill) Pitts, a professor at Baylor who has long been a specialist in the history of the Davidian and Branch Davidian churches. Among his published work, see especially Pitts 1993 and 1994: 34–36; see also Tabor and Gallagher 1995: 33–38. Houteff's own comments on the waywardness of the SDA Church are preserved in print in *The Shepherd's Rod* (Waco: Universal Publishing Association), 1:13.

16. Lois Roden, *Shekinah* 1(1): 2, 4.

17. "Miller's Rules," in Hale 1843: 103–6. Cited in Damsteegt 1977, appendix 1, 299–300. See also Damsteegt's commentary on Miller's hermeneutics (1977: 17–20). Cf. also O'Leary 1994: 116–20; and Judd 1987: 20–21.

18. Miller in fact found some fifteen numerological proofs that the Second Coming would occur in 1843. See Damsteegt 1977: 35–40.

19. One of the errors that Snow brought to light was that Miller's initial computation had presumed a zero year. See Damsteegt 1977: 90–100. See also Dick 1986: 25–26. There is some dispute over the degree to which Miller himself autonomously endorsed the revised date of the Advent, or instead had it urged upon him by his more ambitious promoters, especially Joshua Himes. See Rowe 1985: 135; and Arthur 1987: 50–54. Cf. Dick 1986: 20–22.

20. On the size of the Millerite movement, see Rowe 1987: 5–7. Dick cites a much higher estimate—though perhaps from a partisan source (1986: 34). On the afterlife of Millerite Adventism, see Damsteegt 1977: 113–64; and more briefly, Anderson 1986: esp. 36–46.

21. See Sandeen 1974: 110. Sandeen follows Francis D. Nichol (1945) in reporting that Miller had likely read the work of the British premillennialist George S. Faber, but adds that Miller's debt to the British is beyond determination. In Barkun's judgment, "independent invention rather than diffusion seems responsible for the similarities" between the views of Miller and his predecessors (Barkun 1986: 36).

22. Some of these were in fact quite venerable. The year-day principle, for example, already finds applications in the earliest Christian scholiasts. See Damsteegt 1977: 19.

23. These citations, from the King James Bible, indicate clearly enough that Elizabethan translators were already struggling to find a clear English equivalent of the Greek and Latin terms.

24. Typological interpretation does not appear overtly in the canonical Patristic distinction among the Bible's four senses: literal (or historical), moral (or tropological), allegorical, and anagogical (Brumm 1970: 24; cf. Farrar 1961 [1886]: 295–95). Here, typology is in fact a species of allegory, especially that species that has to do with the prefiguration of the New Testament in the Old. Protestants from Luther forward have registered their disgust with such hermeneutical pluralism, insisting that the Bible is a monosemic text. Those who have preserved typology have consequently reclassified it as a species not of

hated allegory but instead of respectable and respectably "literal" history. As Crapanzano has noted in his recent study of legal originalists and religious fundamentalists in the United States, "literalism" is often more a rhetorical figure than a sober description of hermenutical principle (2000: 33). It is curious that he does not care to belabor the point in his brief and somewhat nonplussed discussion of the fundamentalist deployment of typology (2000: 195–202). It is curious, too, that typology is so rarely mentioned in histories of hermeneutics written after Auerbach (for example, Bruns 1992; Grondin 1995; Ferraris 1996; but cf. Mazzeo 1978). The general sources that have proven most helpful in my research, beyond Auerbach, include Lampe and Woollcombe 1957; Brumm 1970; Goppelt 1982; and Johnson 1992.

25. Few contemporary academic rhetoricians preserve either Quintilian's or Tertullian's distinction between "figura" and "tropus," "figure" and "trope," and tend instead to use the two terms as synonyms. Genette (1982) is characteristic.

26. O'Leary 1994: 68–69. O'Leary's treatment of tragedy closely follows those of Susanne Langer (1953) and Kenneth Burke (1959).

27. In *Omens of Millennium* (1996: 1–2), Harold Bloom characterizes Gnosis (with the capital) as "an acquaintance with, or knowledge of, the God within," which (he rightly adds) "has been condemned as heretical by the institutional faiths." Gnosis thus defined is a Gnostic condition, or a Gnostic quest, which the Greeks call *apotheōsis*, "divination," and which the Orthodox Church still holds out for its contemplatives, who are thus permitted to live at a remove from the ordinary institutional life of their church. It is hardly surprising that Bloom, theorist of the poetic anxiety of influence (1973; 1975) and well aware of the centrality of the trope of metalepsis to prophetic discourse, should assert that our American, our "national Gnosis" (23), "our" preoccupation with "angels, telepathic and prophetic dreams, alien abductions, 'near-death experiences'" and the Second (or Next) Coming, testifies to "an expectation of release from the burdens of a society that is weary with its sense of belatedness, or 'aftering,' a malaise that hints to us that we have somehow arrived after the event" (226). Here, the anthropologist must insist that Bloom sees distinction in what is not distinctive at all: Americans are far from alone in suffering from the obsessions he lists. Culturologically, moreover, his thesis is of narrow applicability even within the United States (applying most tidily to such historically haunted spiritualist critics as Bloom himself). Sociologically, it is altogether empty (though Bloom would not care a whit about that). For all of this, however, Bloom's intuition is on the mark: there is indeed something infusive about the religiosity of which he writes, and its prevailing imagery is an imagery of taking or receiving the divine within. However, this imagery does not consistently imply that "God" is within; it implies somewhat more weakly that the divine is "present" — inside, in some respects, and outside but near in others. I use "gnosis" (without the capital) to refer to this less Gnostic (and more objectivistic) knowledge of the spiritual, to which the great majority of millenarians with whom I am acquainted, secondarily or face-to-face, would lay claim.

28. Crapanzano sees fit to devote an entire chapter to the topic of election in *Serving the Word* (2000: 45–107).

29. It should be said that O'Leary is well aware of the rhetorical consequences of the distinction between the elect and the damned; on that distinction, the reception of apocalyptic as ultimately tragic or comic crucially depends. It is a mistake, however, to relegate election to the domain of reception; though O'Leary prefers his topological approach to the generic approach that many other analysts favor, there is little doubt that election and its negative counterpart, the judgment of the damned, are the most constant motifs of the apocalyptic genre, at least in its Judeo-Christian expressions. See Schmithals 1975: 46–48; for an exceptionally rigorous and sensitive treatment, see Collins 1984.

30. The gnosis of the materiality of the Word is originally a Judaic gnosis and remains one; as Harold Bloom points out (by no means originally), "word, act, and thing are blent in the Hebrew for 'word'" (1989: 17–18; cf. McCartney and Clayton 1994: 115 [cited in Crapanzano 2000: 85]). Susan Harding notes a similar gnosis in the hermeneutical practices of the "fundamentalists" of her recent study, especially in their use of typology, "the reigning mode of reading the relationship between past and future events in many born-again Christian communities" (2000: 229). She reports that her subjects regard typological narratives as neither "allegorical" nor merely "representing history," but instead as *being* history (230). Hence, they understand such narratives to be "literally true" (110). As Harding appropriately notes, however, such literalism is in no sense "simple" (28). Crapanzano reports in contrast that his subjects "generally ignore" what he characterizes as "the performative features of language, its ability to evoke contexts, [and] to frame its subject matter"; he reports further that "they criticize those scholars in the first decades of this century who argued that as the Hebrew *dahar* can mean 'thing,' 'event,' or 'word,' the writers of the Old Testament thought of word and thing as the same thing" (2000: 85). Since his subjects, too, are typologists, their practices belie what would seem to be their testimony to the ethnographer.

31. Tabor and Gallagher report that the sum of the sale was $700,000 and that the prairie acreage was bought for $85,000 (1995: 38).

32. Ben Roden's writings indicate that the council delivered a public rejection of his claims on 9 November 1955.

33. Historians are largely silent on the details that lay behind the calculation of this date, perhaps because they are complex. Journalist Dick Reavis is in any case mistaken in his assertion that it was the result of adding the "forty and two months" of the Gentile trespass at the court of the temple of God mentioned in Revelation 11:2 to the date of Victor Houteff's death (Victor died 5 February 1955, nine months too early; see Reavis 1995: 61–62). Reporter Ann Badolati was also mistaken in asserting that (somehow) it was the result of adding the "thousand two hundred and threescore days" of the preaching of the "witnesses" referred to in Revelation 11:3 to 5 November 1955 (when, she seems to have been told, it was believed that the antitype of such witnessing had commenced; Ann Badolati, "Davidians Now to 'Watch,' 'Pray,'" *Waco News-Tribune* 1959, pp. 1, 4. [Texas Collection Archives]). The date is rather calculated from 22 October 1955, which was Atonement, the Jewish Yom Kippur.

34. Amo Roden, "The Seven Seals," 9.

35. Ibid., 10.

36. Ibid., 10–11.

37. Ibid., 11.

38. Mr. Roden argued for his position in a number of early tracts and letters from the field beginning in 1955 (*Branch Letters*, for example, letters dated 23 September 1955 and 18 October 1955; and epistles titled "Revival and Reformation" [25 January 1960] and "The Purification of the Sons of Levi" [21 March 1965]).

39. Duly reported in the *Waco News-Tribune*, 4 November 1965 (Texas Collection Archives). See also Tabor and Gallagher 1995: 39.

40. From a transcript of a telephone interview with radio talk-show host Paul Bryan on WFAA Dallas, 2:00 P.M., 4 November 1980. In *Shekinah* 1:1: 8 (Texas Collection Archives).

41. *Shekinah* 1(1): 8 (Bryan interview; Texas Collection Archives).

42. *Shekinah* 1(1): 1 (reprint of *Dallas Times Herald* report, 27 October 1980; Texas Collection Archives).

43. She explicitly says this in a letter dated 5 February 1980 (*Branch Letters*).

44. *Shekinah*, April 1981, p. 7 (reprint of Mary Lasovich, "Her Crusade: To Tell the World the Holy Spirit Is Feminine," *The Whig-Standard* [Kingston, Ontario], 28 February 1981) (Texas Collection Archives).

45. In *Naven*, Gregory Bateson defines schismogenesis as "a process of differentiation in the norms of individual behavior resulting from cumulative interaction between individuals" (1958 [1936]: 175). In *Naven* and elsewhere (1972 [1935]), Bateson sees schismogenetic processes as being the result of antagonistic, not amicable, interaction.

46. B. Roden, "The Man on the White Horse," 22 September 1965, p. 23; cf. "Behold, the Bridegroom Cometh," *Branch Sabbath School Lessons*, vol. 4:5–7, lesson 12, p. 71. This is a classic example of what Weber referred to as the routinization of charisma through heredity or blood (M. Weber 1946: 297).

47. B. Roden, "The Man on the White Horse" (*Branch Letters*).

48. L. Roden, *Branch Letters*, letter dated Passover 1980.

49. L. Roden, *Merkabah*, part 4, "The History of the Twelve Tribes of Israel," 1 December 1985.

50. From Ben Roden's obituary, *Waco Tribune-Herald*, 30 October 1978, evidently written by a church member, perhaps by Lois herself (Texas Collection Archives).

51. Lois Roden, "Numbering of the People," epistle dated 14 March 1979 (*Branch Letters*).

52. Robertson 1996: 96. Ms. Roden has never mentioned this explicitly to me, nor is there any explicit mention of it in her writings.

53. This delicate issue is a source of some controversy among Branch Davidians themselves. See, however, Tabor and Gallagher's judicious treatment (1995: 41).

54. Like all of Ms. Roden's marriages since her conversion to Branch Davidianism, her marriage to George was a "church marriage," formalized through a mutually negotiated contract, without the further blessing of civil authorities. Its civil status was (and is) contestable, though when involved with the courts, Ms. Roden insists on its legitimacy as a common-law union.

55. Tabor and Gallagher 1995: 43. In the aftermath of an escape, George was transferred to a higher-security facility, Big Spring State Hospital. He subsequently escaped from that institution but was reincarcerated there after a brief period as a fugitive. He attempted yet another escape in 1998. He managed to get beyond the institution's perimeters, but his body was found some hours afterward in a nearby field. He is sometimes reported to have died of a cardiac arrest; sometimes of a broken neck.

56. Weber's distinction between the emissary and the exemplary prophet is of particular pertinence here (M. Weber 1946: 285–92). Koresh did not present himself to his followers as an exemplar worthy of emulation (quite the contrary). His role was strictly that of messenger, though his message was partly revealed in his acts.

57. As an adult, Koresh took his message primarily to Seventh-day Adventist congregations, from which the great majority of his followers, whether from the United States or abroad, actually came (see Tabor and Gallagher 1995: 24–25). (Somewhat at odds with Tabor and Gallagher, Amo Roden has indicated to me that the membership of the community before Koresh arrived was of a more diverse religious background.)

58. Like the leaders who preceded him at Mount Carmel, Koresh had been formally removed from the rosters of the Seventh-day Adventist Church (Tabor and Gallagher 1995: 44).

59. On the location of Armageddon, literal and figurative, see Boyer 1992: 124–50.

60. On the belief that the United States and/or United Nations are Babylon, see Boyer 1992: 246–64.

61. Tabor and Gallagher 1995: 11. Agent Rodriguez was apparently unable to disguise his actual identity for any length of time. Koresh nevertheless permitted him to stay at Mount Carmel, and he was present the morning of 28 February. He had, however, departed from the compound before the raid, in part to inform his superiors that the residents expected their arrival. See Oliver 1994: 72–73.

62. These are the types of violations over which the BATF has jurisdiction.

63. In his affidavit requesting a warrant to search the Branch Davidian compound, filed with the Western Texas District Court on 26 February 1993 (author's archive), BATF Special Agent Davy Aguilera lingers at some length on his conversations with Joyce Sparks, the social worker who visited the Mount Carmel compound twice, first in February and again in April 1992. He reports Ms. Sparks's complaint that the tours she was provided seemed "staged" and that Koresh was minimally cooperative.

64. For a critique at once of the series and of its rapid proliferation in the national press, see Tabor and Gallagher 1995: 117–19.

65. For the official tally, see Scruggs et al. 1993: 313–28. Unofficial tallies vary widely. If not on the death toll, the government's report diverges in many other respects from such relatively rigorous journalistic accounts as that of Dick Reavis (1995). The preceding four paragraphs are a revised version of Faubion 1999: 376–78.

66. Interview by the author, August 1994.

67. Amo Roden, "Judges 17, Isaiah 27–32: The Graven and the Molten Image," in *Babylon Is Fallen*, 92.

68. Amo Roden, "Habakkuk: Judgment," 3.

69. A. Roden, "Judges 17," 92.

70. In the aftermath of the flight from Egypt, the priest Aaron fashioned a calf out of the melted gold jewelry of Israelite women to make the gods that had rescued them material to them. Through Moses, God issued his condemnation of Aaron's gesture and the idolatry it encouraged. See Exodus 32.

71. A. Roden, "Judges 17," 94.

72. Ibid., 98.

73. Ibid., 99.

74. A. Roden, "Habakkuk," 3–4.

75. Ibid., 4.

76. A. Roden, "Judges 17," 92–93.

77. Ibid., 93.

78. A. Roden, "Habakkuk," 4.

79. Amo Roden, "The Book of Nahum: A Call to Repentance," in *Babylon Is Fallen*, 71.

80. Amo Roden, "For the Law Shall Go Forth of Zion," 2.

81. Ms. Roden provides a reference here to V. T. Houteff's *Shepherd's Rod*, vol. 1, section 5, pp. 53–56.

82. Amo Roden, "Addendum on Polygamy," in *Christ and the Mosaic Law*, 13.

83. Ms. Roden is in fact doctrinally much closer than her mother-in-law to the position that has allowed women of the Judeo-Christian tradition to assume and cultivate leadership within the churches to which they belong. As Catherine Wessinger points out, such churches are far more likely to be "marginal" than mainstream and their relative eccentricity centered on the following: "1) a perception of the divine that deemphasizes the masculine either by means of a bisexual divinity or an impersonal, non-anthropomorphic divine principle; 2) a tempering or denial of the doctrine of the Fall; 3) a denial of the need for a traditional ordained clergy; and 4) a view of marriage that does not stress the married state and motherhood as the proper sphere for woman and her only means of fulfillment" (1993: 3).

84. In his public overview of the findings of the third investigative commission, of which he was the chair, Senator John Danforth took pains to stress that the Posse Comitatus Act had not been violated during the standoff.

85. The preceding three paragraphs are a revision of Faubion 1999: 384–85.

86. Though Durkheim did not specifically address the political in *The Division of Labor* (1938 [1895]), his judgment on the consequences of the "progress of organic solidarity" is still relevant here: a recession of the collective conscience and with its recession "the total, or almost total, disappearance of religious crimes" (159). Habermas develops his version of the thesis of separation most elaborately in the first volume of *The Theory of Communicative Action* (1984: esp. 43–101). Unlike Habermas, Arendt develops her own version of the thesis not on cognitive and evolutionary but instead on historical and particularistic grounds (1958). She nevertheless endows the history she recounts with

the unmistakable aura of the inevitable. As I will remark later, the early Weber seems to have been inclined (or at least can be read to have been inclined) to regard the Western diremption of the religious and political as something of a historical "accident," an irrational slip. By the time he writes his "intermediate reflections" on the results of his investigations of world religions, however, he is prepared to declare that "the rationalization and conscious sublimation of man's relation to various spheres of value, external and internal, as well as religious and secular, have . . . pressed towards making conscious the *internal and lawful autonomy* of the individual spheres; thereby letting them drift into those tensions which remain hidden to the originally naïve relation to the world" (1946: 328).

87. See M. Weber 1958 (1904–1905): esp. 167–83. Weber captures the "devolution" at issue most succinctly in a brief commentary on John Wesley's exhortation to Christians to "grow rich." "The full economic effect" of Wesley's and similar religious movements, he writes, "whose significance lay above all in their ascetic educative influence, generally came only after the peak of the purely religious enthusiasm was past. Then the intensity of the search for the Kingdom of God commenced gradually to pass over into sober economic virtue; the religious roots died out slowly, giving way to utilitarian worldliness" (1958 [1904–1905]: 176). Wolfgang Schluchter (see Roth and Schluchter 1979) and Malcolm MacKinnon (1993) provide particularly acute readings of Weber's thesis and of its place in his broader religious sociology.

88. Bruce Lincoln (1994: 103–13) has analyzed the religious tenor of such higher courts in other traditions, and his conclusions have stimulated my own. I am grateful to David Brent for providing me with Lincoln's study.

89. Both Robert Bellah (1972 [1964]) and Clifford Geertz (1973: 98–108) have construed religion as having to do with the "ultimate" (or the "really real"), whatever that might turn out to be. The definitional appeal to the supernatural is venerable. In anthropology, it is as old as Tylor. Almost a century after Tylor, Goody (1961) could still find no better hallmark of religion than the supernatural, even though he knew that he would likely be forced to conclude that religion was not a cultural universal. Less concerned about cultural universality than about what they see as the excessive inclusiveness of Bellah's and Geertz's own definitional predilections, Stark and Bainbridge have reasserted the supernatural as criterial (1985: 3–8), well aware that they are following Goody among others in doing so. The real cost of such a definitional position lies less in its potential failure of universality than in its taking for granted, or its taking as somehow "pre-cultural," the distinction between nature and supernature themselves. Definition, for that matter, may well be beside the point, at least if what is sought is a typification that fits all and only those cases or tokens that are "properly" religious. If I have resorted to the laborious locution of the "anthropologically adequate heuristic criterion" instead of the tidier "definition," this is because I think interpretation has no use for the latter. What it has need of instead are generalizations that permit connections to be drawn and comparisons to be made among what must always be understood as irreducibly particular phenomena.

90. Among scholars of early Judeo-Christian millennialism, Stephen Cook

(1995) is one of very few who has recognized and investigated at length the appeal of millennialist doctrines to powerful elites.

91. Amo Roden, "Mount Carmel Declaration of Independence" (circular).

92. In the Old Testament, the jubilee is a ceremonial year, occurring once every fifty years, marked by amnesties, the resting of tillage, and ceremonies of gratitude to God.

93. On suicide as a "genus" of sacrifice, see Halbwachs 1978 (1930). "Heaven's Gate" was the most recent name of a religious community that with much fluctuation of membership had persisted from the early 1970s under the early leadership of Marshall Herff Applewhite (known initially as Bo) and Bonnie Lu Nettles (known initially as Peep) and the later leadership of Applewhite alone. Settled in southern California, thirty-nine members of the community (including Mr. Applewhite) committed suicide in 1997, apparently convinced that the approaching Hale-Bopp comet was concealing a spaceship that would retrieve the souls that they had thus liberated from their bodies. For a thorough study of the first decades of the Applewhite-Nettles group, see Balch 1982.

94. The sources of such tallies tend to be unreliable. In the report of the FBI's Project Megiddo, the number of "doomsday cults" operating in the United States is estimated at "nearly one thousand." The author adds that "very few" of these "present credible threats of millennial violence." The report is accessible through the Apologetics Index at *http://www.gospelcom.net/apologetics-index/p00.html projection.*

95. A. Roden, "The Seven Seals," 11–12.

96. Ibid., 12.

97. Amo Roden, "Dear T'sa."

98. Amo Roden, "Ruth: The Wavesheaf," 2.

99. This identification is based on Ms. Roden's interpretation of the opening verses of the seventeenth chapter of Judges in a tract titled "The Graven and the Molten Image."

100. A. Roden, "Ruth," 2–3.

101. Ibid., 3.

102. A. Roden, *Cracking the Cover-up*, 12.

103. Amo Roden, "The Judgment of the Church," 18–19.

104. Ibid., 19. "Going after Baalim" — idolatry — is the figure that Ms. Roden interprets here as her own antitypical lack of faith.

105. One of the accused subsequently pleaded guilty to armed resistance of a federal officer and agreed to testify against the remaining eleven accused in exchange for having several of the other charges leveled against her dismissed. At the conclusion of their trial, on 18 June 1994, all of the latter were acquitted of charges of conspiracy and murder. Two were acquitted of all charges and freed. Two others were similarly acquitted but held for immigration violations. The rest were sentenced to between fifteen and forty years in prison and assessed fines ranging from $2,000 to $50,000. For a precise record of the indictments, see Scruggs et al. 1993: 341–47. For a review of the outcome, see Tabor and Gallagher 1995: 115–16, 234nn. 36, 38, 39. Five others were sentenced to forty years in prison.

106. Douglas Doe, *Waco Tribune-Herald*, 8 July 1994, p. 1C (Texas Collec-

tion Archives). Ms. Roden subsequently confirmed Mr. Doe's recounting of the events.

107. Interview with William R. Dull, October 1995.

108. A. Roden, "The Judgment of the Church," 19–20.

109. Ibid., 20.

110. Ibid., 21.

111. In *Cracking the Cover-up*, for example, Ms. Roden reports that attorney Linda Thompson had suspected that David Koresh was running a safe house for the CIA and points to other evidence that she believes to strengthen the suspicion: "The autopsies of 49 Branch Davidians showed lethal levels of cyanide in their blood. CS gas [the tear-gas used to try to force the Koreshites from the compound] breaks down into hydrogen cyanide under high heat. According to TNRCC [Texas Natural Resources Conservation Commission] Cleanup Coordinator Don Fawn, cyanide-specific gas mask filters were found on the site as well as syringes of a type to penetrate clothing. In addition to suggesting that the government set the fire, this also suggests that they expected to be inside the building during the fire and to need to treat persons for cyanide exposure" (47). The causes of death listed in the government's report make no mention of cyanide poisoning (see Scruggs et al. 1993: 313–28).

112. A. Roden, "The Judgment of the Church," 22.

113. Ms. Roden appends a footnote naming her daughter at this juncture in her narrative.

114. A. Roden, "The Judgment of the Church," 24.

115. Rumors that Dallas hospitals had been warned to prepare for burn victims in advance of the 19 April fire did indeed circulate informally in the weeks that followed it, but I have been unable to confirm their veracity.

116. A. Roden, "The Judgment of the Church," 25.

117. Ibid., 28.

118. Ibid., 29.

119. "That which is crushed breaketh out into a viper (Isa. 59:5)" (Amo Roden's footnote).

120. See Haggai 2:20–23 (Amo Roden's footnote).

121. A. Roden, "The Book of Zechariah," 107–8.

122. Ibid., 108. (See Matt. 21:42 [Amo Roden's footnote].)

123. See Revelation 18:1–3 (Amo Roden's footnote).

124. Amo Roden, "Houteff and the Holocaust," 1–8, abridged.

125. Amo Roden, "Messiah and Elijah, the Second Coming," 1.

126. On my use of the term "millenarianism" and its relation to more standard usage, see part 1, note 24.

127. Not all members of the ancient aristocracy were wealthy (Ober 1989: 252), and not all the wealthy were aristocrats. Yet such "irregularities" seem not to have challenged the customary association between wealth and aristocratic standing until the period of Roman dominion, and even then, not until the third century C.E., when Christianity began to flourish. Even in democratic Athens, as Austin and Vidal-Naquet have observed, no alternative to the aristocratic worldview ever emerged (1977: 15–17); and still in 200 C.E., as Peter Brown succinctly puts it, "the Roman empire . . . was held together by the illusion that

it was still a very small world" and "ruled by an aristocracy of amazingly uniform culture, taste, and language" (1989 [1971]: 14).

128. The classic study of the Ghost Dance movement is James Mooney's (1896). Mooney's primary subject was the Wanapum visionary Smohalla, but he provides comparative notes on the Shawnee prophets as well. The sources on the Xhosa prophets, Makanna included, are collected in Wilson (1973: 236–40). Worsley (1968), Wilson (1973: 309–48), and, even more comprehensively, Lindstrom (1993) review the extensive scholarship on cargoism throughout Oceania. See also Trompf, ed. 1990. On the Mahdiya, see L. Brown 1970; and Dekmejian and Wyszomirski 1972; on the Ahmadiyah, see Ahmed 1976; and cf. Smith 1982. For a particularly thorough treatment of one Quaker millennial community, see Schrauwers 1993; on the Rastafarians, see Faith 1990. A Trinidadian millennialist community, led by the visionary Mother Earth, is the subject of a rich and judicious inquiry by psychiatrist-turned-anthropologist Roland Littlewood (1992); on the Tupinamba, see Métraux 1948; and cf. Wilson 1973: 207–10. Of all these sources (which merely scratch the scholarly surface), Wilson's is the most compendious. His thesis — that millenarian movements have in common their attempts to marshall "magic" in the quest for salvation (70–195) — is a development of Weber's analysis of charisma and charismatic authority but does not altogether leave behind a "Marxist" penchant, evident in Worsely's work as in Hobsbawm's (1959), to render the millenarian consciousness false, or at least severely misguided. Lindstrom, for his part, is more interested in why "we" remain so fascinated by (what we call) cargoism than in why cargoists believe as they do. His answer — that cargoism serves us as a modern picaresque, a bittersweet, farcical narrative of "unrequited desire" that echoes back to us our own fetishized consumerism — is intriguing but comes at the cost of ignoring even the poetic dimensions internal to cargoist discourses themselves.

129. Little is known with certainty about the The Solar Temple other than that several of its members, living in secretive communion in Switzerland, France, and Canada, committed suicide in what appears to have been a quest for corporeal liberation not unlike that of the members of Heaven's Gate.

130. Wilson's "revolutionists" expect or hope for a radical transformation of the world but see themselves as having little if any agency in the process. See Wilson 1973: 23.

131. Blumenberg specifically treats the modern infinitalization of progress. I should note that the characterization of infinite progress as a "fetish" is not Blumenberg's but my own.

132. Early in his critique of Karl Löwith's construal of many modern philosophies of history as Christian eschatology in secular disguise (1949), Blumenberg argues that the (millenarian) "contraction" of the denouement of the historical process to the "lifetime of the generation that is told of the final events" diminishes historical consciousness to a zero degree (1983: 41). In an ideal-typical construal, the argument is sound. Empirically, however, it postulates what would seem to be an almost empty category (though perhaps those Millerites who gathered in the autumn of 1844 to greet the returned Christ come close to filling it).

133. Davidson 1977: 30–35. Davidson restricts this point to the first half of the eighteenth century, after which he thinks more "coherent" postmillennialist theologies appear. But I think the point stands generally; the later developments are largely substantive and "internal" developments, though they do mark an emerging distinction between catastrophist and gradualist understandings of the historical process. Too much gradualism, however, spells the end of millenarianism, whether premillennial or postmillennial.

Part Three

1. There is some controversy over whether 2 Thessalonians should be ascribed to Paul. Cf. Hayes 1971: 390.

2. Such dispossessions of ordinary life were common among the people who sought to be near William Miller in 1843 and again in 1844; they were common again among the migrants to Florence Houteff's New Mount Carmel in 1959. The rejection or reversal of customary routine has been widely attested among cargoists. See, for example, Worsley 1968: 135–39, 242–45.

3. The most condensed of Weber's ethical portraits come in his "Intermediate Reflections" (known in English as "Religious Rejections of the World and Their Directions" [1946: 323–59]). He undertakes a more extended, more normative sketch of the scientist in "Science as a Vocation" (1946: 129–56) and of the politician in "Politics as a Vocation" (1946: 77–128). It is in the last essay that he makes the distinction between an ethics of commitment and an ethics of responsibility most explicitly and at greatest length.

4. For a broad-ranging discussion of this issue, see Hatch 1983.

5. A few anthropologists have recently begun to explore the domain of bioethics. Little research has, however, appeared in print. For an important exception, see Rabinow 1999.

6. For a subjectivist position, see Mackie 1977; for a conventionalist position, see Harman 1977.

7. My citations of Aristotle rely on Aristotle 1975, but I have taken the occasional liberty of altering the English translation for greater accuracy and clarity.

8. On the middle voice, cf. Tyler 1998.

9. A much truncated version of this treatment of the relation between Foucault and Aristotle appears in Faubion 2000.

10. It should be noted that Foucault's "nominalism" was a methodological posture of less than universal scope.

11. I should at least add that this is a more limited assertion than it might appear, since modes of subjectivation constitute only one of the several parameters of the ethical field.

12. It is under the rubric of possible and actual "cultural invention" that Foucault spoke on several occasions about the gay movements in Holland and the United States. See, for example, "The Social Triumph of the Sexual Will" (1997 [1981]). "Resistance," for its part, has had much diagnostic prominence in the past two decades. In Foucault's own work, the term tends to refer to the mechanical byproduct of the ossification of power relations. De Certeau's treat-

ment of "resistance" in *The Practice of Everyday Life* (1984 [1974]) begins to approach Foucault's construal of the ethical but remains a category of far less historical dynamism, even potentially. Gramscian "resistance" also bears some comparison to the Foucauldean ethical field, but it always remains a moment in a transcendent dialectic of liberation that Foucault's skepticism could hardly endorse.

13. Amo Roden, "The Book of Zechariah," 109–13.

14. Interview by the author, August 1996.

15. Ms. Roden refers here to any of various laws enforcing monogamy and defining a woman as under the authority and protection of her husband. The biblical source of the law is often taken to be the thirtieth chapter of the Book of Numbers.

16. Mr. Worden was not a Branch Davidian but was apparently a friend of David Koresh and several of his followers.

17. It is unclear whether this is a call to arms or a summons to gather the means of self-defense. I have never known Ms. Roden, whether in her writing or in our conversations, to advocate taking "offensive action" against what she regards as the forces of evil. One must note in any case that the pronouncement is far from conforming to the Nazarene's advice to "turn the other cheek."

18. Amo Roden, "Commentary on the Law as Presented in Christians on Point," 2–4.

19. Israelite Assembly, "Christians on Point" (author's archive).

20. Ibid., 4.

21. Ibid.

22. "Christians on Point," 2.

23. "bid., 4, 6.

24. Interview by the author, August 1996.

25. Ibid.

26. Amo Roden, "Crime and Coverup," 20.

27. Interview by the author, October 1995.

28. Ibid.

29. Amo Roden, *Cracking the Cover-up*, 32.

30. Ibid., 35.

31. What remains of David Koresh in writing is either the result of what he dictated to his follower Ruth Riddle (who survived the fire with an electronic transcript in hand) in the days immediately preceding the fire, or what has subsequently been transcribed from audiotapes of his sermons and lessons.

32. I am grateful to Robert Bellah for disabusing me of the erroneous impression that Weber understood the ethics of commitment precisely as an ethics for which the ends justify the means.

33. Cited in Amo Roden, "The Seven Seals," 7.

34. Interview by the author, August 1996.

35. From the author's letter to Ms. Roden, 17 July 1995.

36. Letter to the author from Amo Roden, 1 September 1995.

37. At least one of Crapanzano's interlocutors, theologian Robert Brumley,

was of a similar mind. His faith, he said, "rested on his 'staking his eternal destiny on what [Jesus] taught'" (Crapanzano 2000: 98).

Part Four

1. Boyer (1992: 92) notes that more than fifty such institutions were actively promoting premillennialist theologies at the time. He makes no precise mention of their methodological commitments, but typology would surely have been at the forefront of most of them.

2. Frei 1974: 77; on the Lockean sources of historical criticism more broadly, see Frei 1974: 66–85.

3. Breisach (1994: 205) speaks not of Geisteswissenschaften but instead of the methodology of Verstehen and of "historicism."

4. It would be foolhardy as well to attempt a bibliographic catalog of such polemics and scholarship. To my knowledge, the notion of "national reason" has not been formulated as such. My primary inspirations for the locution nevertheless come from Anderson 1991, Gellner 1983, and Herzfeld 1987. My broader project in this concluding section has a further debt to Cornell West's (1982), Louis Dumont's (1986 [1983]), and Martin Bernal's (1987) genealogical investigations of the constitution of modern racism. I would nevertheless assert that anti-Semitism is more central to an account of the historicist and nationalist turn against millennialist reason than either Dumont or Bernal seems to recognize, and more central than the anti-African racism on which West and Bernal primarily focus.

5. The antagonism between millenarian and national reason I am underscoring here might at first sight appear incompatible with the argument that James Holston has recently developed in a fascinating essay on the Brazilian Valley of the Dawn. Holston's central thesis is that the "millenarian and messianic" members of the Valley of the Dawn espouse and enact doctrines that are homologous with those of the Brazilian nation-state, and that the tension between the former and the latter is thus not one of alternative rationalisms but instead of alternative visions of modernity (Holston 1999: 606–7). Were the Valley of the Dawn a genuine New World analogue of the Sabbatians, it would indeed constitute a counterexample to my own thesis. Yet, Holston clarifies that the Brazilian community is not millenarian and messianic alone. Indeed, he attributes its initially imperiled persistence to its having "combined the millenarian tradition of rupture based on revelation with the non-millenarian tradition of spirit-possession cure." He continues:

> As exemplified by Candomblé, Umbanda, and Spiritism, among others, cults in the latter tradition are far more accommodating to the existing structures of authority and social difference. Their conflicts are not about establishing a new kind of consensus concerning the basic institutions of social life. They do not usurp the authority inherent in existing relations of property, labor, or hierarchy to establish new ones based on a revealed destiny. Rather, and

above all, they seek gains in this world, not in the next, by protecting their initiates from spiritual and human malevolence and by syncretizing their symbols with those of other religions to garner more universal powers. In recent decades, these strategies have crystallized into a broad-based and non-sectarian recruitment of affiliates as they harmonize different social and religious orders. (610)

This is far from Sabbatianism and indeed far from what I am calling "millenarianism proper." Though still an analytical stretch, the Valley of the Dawn is in fact a nearer homologue of Jewish Zionism than of Sabbatianism or "millenarianism proper" themselves.

References

Agamben, Giorgio. 1998. *Homo Sacer: Sovereign Power and Bare Life*. Trans. Daniel Heller-Roazen. Stanford: Stanford University Press.

Ahmed, Akbar S. 1976. *Millennium and Charisma among the Pathans: A Critical Essay in Social Anthropology*. London: Routledge.

Allison, Joel. 1968. Adaptive Regression and Intense Religious Experience. *Journal of Nervous and Mental Disease* 145:452–63.

———. 1969. Religious Conversion: Regression and Progression in an Adolescent Experience. *Journal for the Scientific Study of Religion* 8 (1): 23–38.

Allport, Gordon. 1950. *The Individual and His Religion*. New York: Macmillan.

Allport, Gordon, and Michael Ross. 1967. Personal Religious Orientation and Prejudice. *Journal of Personality and Social Psychology* 5 (4): 423–43.

Anderson, Benedict R. 1991. *Imagined Communities: Reflections on the Origin and Spread of Nationalism*. Rev. ed. New York: Verso.

Anderson, Godfrey T. 1986. Sectarianism and Organization, 1846–1864. In *Adventism in America: A History*, ed. Gary G. Land, 36–65. Grand Rapids, MI: William B. Eerdmans.

Arendt, Hannah. 1958. What Was Authority? In *Authority*. Vol. 1, *Nomos*. Ed. Carl J. Friedrich. Cambridge, MA: Harvard University Press.

Aristotle. 1975. *Nicomachean Ethics*. Vol. 19. Trans. H. Rackham. Cambridge, MA: Harvard University Press.

Arthur, David T. 1987. Joshua V. Himes and the Cause of Adventism. In *The Disappointed: Millerism and Millenarianism in the Nineteenth Century*, ed. Ronald L. Numbers and Jonathon M. Butler, 36–58. Bloomington: Indiana University Press.

Asad, Talal. 1993. *Genealogies of Religion: Discipline and Reasons of Power in Christianity and Islam*. Baltimore: Johns Hopkins University Press.

Auerbach, Erich. 1953. *Mimesis: The Representation of Reality in Western Literature*. Trans. W. R. Trask. Princeton: Princeton University Press.

REFERENCES

Auerbach, Erich. 1959. *Scenes from the Drama of European Literature: Six Essays*. Trans. Ralph Manheim. New York: Meridian Press.

Augustine of Hippo. 1952 (413–426). *The City of God*. Vol. 18, *Great Books of the Western World*. Ed. Robert M. Hutchins. Trans. Marcus Dods. Chicago: Encyclopedia Britannica Inc.

Austin, Michael M., and Pierre Vidal-Naquet. 1977. *Economic and Social History of Ancient Greece: An Introduction*. Trans. and rev. Michael M. Austin. Berkeley: University of California Press.

Balch, Robert W. 1982. Bo and Peep: A Case Study of the Origins of Messianic Leadership. In *Millennialism and Charisma*, ed. Roy Wallis, 13–72. Belfast: Queen's University.

Barkun, Michael. 1974. *Disaster and the Millennium*. New Haven: Yale University Press.

―――. 1985. Nuclear War and Millenarian Symbols: Premillennialists Confront the Bomb. Paper presented before the Society for the Scientific Study of Religion.

―――. 1986. *The Crucible of the Millennium*. Syracuse: Syracuse University Press.

Basaglia, Franco. 1987. *Psychiatry Inside Out: Selected Writings of Franco Basaglia*. Ed. Nancy Scheper-Hughes and Anne M. Lovell. New York: Columbia University Press.

Bataille, Georges. 1970. *La Somme athéologique*. Vol. 1, L'Experience intérieure. In *Oeuvres complètes*, vol. 5. Paris: Gallimard.

―――. 1976. *Théorie de la religion*. In *Oeuvres complètes*, vol. 7. Paris: Gallimard.

Bateson, Gregory. 1958 (1936). *Naven*. Stanford: Stanford University Press.

―――. 1972 (1935). Culture Contact and Schismogenesis. In *Steps to an Ecology of Mind*, 61–87. New York: Ballantine Books.

Batson, C. Daniel. 1976. Religion as Prosocial: Agent or Double Agent? *Journal for the Scientific Study of Religion* 15 (1): 29–45.

Batson, C. Daniel, and Patricia A. Schoenrade. 1991a. Measuring Religion as Quest: 1) Validity Concerns. *Journal for the Scientific Study of Religion* 30 (4): 416–29.

―――. 1991b. Measuring Religion as Quest: 2) Reliability Concerns. *Journal for the Scientific Study of Religion* 30 (4): 430–47.

Batson, C. Daniel, and W. Larry Ventis. 1982. *The Religious Experience: A Social-psychological Perspective*. New York: Oxford University Press.

Becker, Gary. 1986. The Economic Approach to Human Behavior. In *Rational Choice*, ed. John Elster, 108–22. Oxford: Blackwell.

Beckford, James A. 1978. Accounting for Conversion. *British Journal of Sociology* 29: 249–62.

Beidelman, Thomas O. 1982. *Colonial Evangelism*. Bloomington: Indiana University Press.

Bellah, Robert. 1970. *Beyond Belief: Essays on Religion in a Post-traditional World*. New York: Harper and Row.

―――. 1972 (1964). Religious Evolution. In *Readings on Premodern Societies*, ed. Victor Lidz and Talcott Parsons, 30–51. Englewood Cliffs, NJ: Prentice-Hall.

Benedict, Ruth. 1934. *Patterns of Culture*. Boston: Houghton Mifflin.

Berger, Peter. 1974. Some Second Thoughts on Substantive versus Functional Definitions of Religion. *Journal for the Scientific Study of Religion* 13 (2): 125–33.

Berke, Joseph H., Stella Pierides, Andrea Sabbadini, and Stanley Schneider, eds. 1998. *Even Paranoids Have Enemies: New Perspectives in Paranoia and Persecution*. New York: Routledge.

Bernal, Martin. 1987. *Black Athena: The Afroasiatic Roots of Classical Civilization*. Vol. 1, *The Fabrication of Ancient Greece, 1785–1985*. New Brunswick, NJ: Rutgers University Press.

Bernfeld, Simon. 1900. *Toledoth Hareformation Hadathith B'Israel*. Krakow: Ahiasaf.

Bloom, Harold. 1973. *The Anxiety of Influence*. New York: Oxford University Press.

———. 1975. *A Map of Misreading*. New York: Oxford University Press.

———. 1989. *Ruin the Sacred Truths: Poetry and Belief from the Bible to the Present*. Cambridge, MA: Harvard University Press.

———. 1996. *Omens of Millennium: The Gnosis of Angels, Dreams, and Resurrection*. New York: Riverhead Books.

Blumenberg, Hans. 1983. *The Legitimacy of the Modern Age*. Trans. R. M. Wallace. Cambridge, MA: MIT Press.

Bourdieu, Pierre. 1977. *Outline of a Theory of Practice*. Trans. Richard Nice. Cambridge: Cambridge University Press.

———. 1990. *The Logic of Practice*. Trans. Richard Nice. Stanford: Stanford University Press.

Boyarin, Jonathon, ed. 1992. *The Ethnography of Reading*. Berkeley: University of California Press.

Boyer, Paul. 1992. *When Time Shall Be No More: Prophecy Belief in Modern American Culture*. Cambridge, MA: Belknap Press.

———. 1993. A Brief History of the End of Time. *The New Republic* 208 (20): 30–33.

Brandt, Richard B. 1954. *Hopi Ethics: A Theoretical Analysis*. Chicago: University of Chicago Press.

Breisach, Ernst. 1994. *Historiography: Ancient, Medieval, and Modern*. 2nd ed. Chicago: University of Chicago Press.

Brown, Donald E. 1988. *Hierarchy, History, and Human Nature: The Social Origins of Historical Consciousness*. Tucson: University of Arizona Press.

Brown, L. Carl. 1970. The Sudanese Mahdiya. In *Protest and Power in Black Africa*, ed. R. I. Rotberg and A. A. Mazrui, 145–68. New York: Oxford University Press.

Brown, Peter. 1980. *The Cult of the Saints: Its Rise and Function in Latin Christianity*. Chicago: University of Chicago Press.

———. 1989 (1971). *The World of Late Antiquity,* A.D. 150–750. New York: W. W. Norton.

Bruce, Steve. 1993. Religion and Rational Choice: A Critique of Economic Explanations of Religious Behavior. *Journal for the Scientific Study of Religion* 54 (2): 193–205.

Brumm, Ursula. 1970. *American Thought and Religious Typology*. New Brunswick, NJ: Rutgers University Press.

Brummett, Barry. 1991. *Contemporary Apocalyptic Rhetoric*. New York: Praeger.

Bruns, Gerald L. 1992. *Hermeneutics Ancient and Modern*. New Haven: Yale University Press.

Burke, Kenneth. 1959. *Attitudes toward History*. Los Altos, CA: Hermes Publications.

———. 1966. *Language as Symbolic Action*. Berkeley: University of California Press.

Burridge, Kenelm. 1960. *Mambu: A Melanesian Millennium*. Princeton: Princeton University Press.

———. 1969. *New Heaven, New Earth: A Study of Millenarian Activities*. New York: Schocken.

Butler, Judith. 1993. *Bodies That Matter: On the Discursive Limits of "Sex."* New York: Routledge.

———. 1997. *The Psychic Life of Power: Theories in Subjection*. Stanford: Stanford University Press.

Canguilhem, Georges. 1952. *La Connaissance de la vie*. Paris: Vrin.

———. 1989 (1943). *The Normal and the Pathological*. Trans. Carolyn R. Fawcett, with Robert S. Cohen. New York: Zone Books.

Carlebach, Elisheva. 1990. *The Pursuit of Heresy: Rabbi Moses Hagiz and the Sabbatian Controversies*. New York: Columbia University Press.

Carpenter, Stanford. 2001. What We Bring to the Table: The Means of Imagination in an African-American Family. In *The Ethics of Kinship: Ethnographic Inquiries*, ed. James D. Faubion, 194–214. Lanham, MD: Rowman and Littlefield.

Cohn, Norman. 1970. *The Pursuit of the Millennium: Revolutionary Millenarians and Mystical Anarchists of the Middle Ages*. Rev. ed. New York: Oxford University Press.

Collins, John J. 1984. *The Apocalyptic Imagination: An Introduction to the Jewish Matrix of Christianity*. New York: Crossroad.

Cook, Stephen L. 1995. *Prophecy and Apocalypticism: The Post-Exilic Setting*. Minneapolis: Fortress Press.

Crapanzano, Vincent. 2000. *Serving the Word: Literalism in America from the Pulpit to the Bank*. New York: The New Press.

Cross, Whitney R. 1965. *The Burned-Over District: The Social and Intellectual History of Enthusiastic Religion in Western New York, 1800–1850*. New York: Harper and Row.

Cushman, Philip. 1984. The Politics of Vulnerability: Youth in Religious Cults. *Psychohistory Review* 12 (4): 5–17.

———. 1986. The Self Besieged: Recruitment-Indoctrination Processes in Restrictive Groups. *Journal for the Theory of Social Behaviour* 16 (1): 1–32.

Damsteegt, P. Gerard. 1977. *Foundations of the Seventh-day Adventist Message and Mission*. Grand Rapids, MI: William B. Eerdmans.

Davidson, James W. 1977. *The Logic of Millennial Thought: Eighteenth-century New England*. New Haven: Yale University Press.

214

De Certeau, Michel. 1984 (1974). *The Practice of Everyday Life*. Trans. Steven Rendall. Berkeley: University of California Press.

De Tocqueville, Alexis. 1969 (1835–1840). *Democracy in America*. Ed. J. P. Mayer. Trans. George Lawrence. New York: Harper Perennial Library.

Dekmejian, Richard H., and Margaret J. Wyszomirski. 1972. Charismatic Leadership in Sudan: The Mahd of Sudan. *Comparative Studies in Society and History* 14 (1): 193–214.

Deleuze, Gilles, and Félix Guattari. 1987. *A Thousand Plateaus*. Vol. 2, *Capitalism and Schizophrenia*. Trans. Brian Massumi. Minneapolis: University of Minnesota Press.

Desroche, Henri. 1969. *Dieux d'hommes, dictionnaire des messianismes et millénarismes de l'ère chrétienne*. Paris: Mouton.

Dick, Everett N. 1986. The Millerite Movement, 1830–1845. In *Adventism in America: A History*, ed. Gary G. Land, 1–35. Grand Rapids, MI: William B. Eerdmans.

Doan, Ruth Alden. 1987a. *The Miller Heresy, Millennialism, and American Culture*. Philadelphia: Temple University Press.

———. 1987b. Millerism and Evangelical Culture. In *The Disappointed: Millerism and Millenarianism in the Nineteenth Century*, ed. Ronald L. Numbers and Jonathon M. Butler, 118–38. Bloomington: Indiana University Press.

Dronke, Peter. 1984. *Women Writers of the Middle Ages*. New York: Press Syndicate of the University of Cambridge.

Dumont, Louis. 1986 (1983), trans. *Essays on Individualism: An Anthropological Perspective on Modern Ideology*. Chicago: University of Chicago Press.

Durkheim, Emile. 1938 (1895). *The Rules of Sociological Method*. Ed. G.E.G. Catlin. Trans. S. A. Solovay and J. H. Mueller. Glencoe, IL: The Free Press.

———. 1995 (1912). *The Elementary Forms of the Religious Life*. Trans. K. E. Fields. New York: Free Press.

Elias, Norbert. 1978. *The History of Manners*. Vol. 1, *The Civilizing Process*. Trans. Edmund Jephcott. New York: Pantheon.

Estroff, Sue E. 1981. *Making It Crazy: An Ethnography of Psychiatric Clients in an American Community*. Berkeley: University of California Press.

Faith, Karlene. 1990. One Love—One Heart—One Destiny: The Ras Tafarian Movement in Jamaica. In *Cargo Cults and Millennial Movements: Transoceanic Comparisons of New Religious Movements*, ed. Garry W. Trompf, 295–341. Berlin: Mouton de Gruyter.

Farrar, Frederic William. 1961 (1886). *History of Interpretation*. Grand Rapids, MI: Baker Book House.

Faubion, James D. 1993. *Modern Greek Lessons: A Primer in Historical Constructivism*. Princeton: Princeton University Press.

———. 1998a. Introduction to *Essential Works of Michel Foucault*. Vol. 2, *Aesthetics, Method, and Epistemology*. Ed. James D. Faubion. New York: The New Press.

———. 1998b. Outline for and Anthropology of Religion and Violence. In *Philosophical Designs for a Socio-Cultural Transformation: Beyond Violence and the Modern Era*, ed. Tetsuji Yamamoto, Edward G. Andrew, Roger Chartier, and Paul Rabinow, 675–82. Toyko: Ecole des Haute Etudes en Sciences Culturelles and Rowman and Littlefield.

———. 1999. Deus Absconditus: Conspiracy (Theory), Millennialism, and (the End of) the Twentieth Century. In *Late Editions 6. Paranoia within Reason: A Casebook on Conspiracy as Explanation,* ed. George E. Marcus, 375–404. Chicago: University of Chicago Press.

———. 2000. Hieros Gamos: Typology and the Fate of Passion. *Postmodern Culture* 10 (May) *http://jhu.edu/journals/postmodernculture/toc/pmc10.3 html.*

Ferraris, Maurizio. 1996. *History of Hermeneutics.* Trans. Luca Somigli. Atlantic Highlands, NJ: Humanities Press.

Festinger, Leon, Henry W. Riecken, and Stanley Schachter. 1964. *When Prophecy Fails.* New York: Harper Torchbooks.

Fields, Echo E. 1991. Understanding Activist Fundamentalism: Capitalist Crisis and the "Colonization of the Lifeworld." *Sociological Analysis* 52 (2): 175–90.

Finke, Roger. 1990. Religious De-regulation: Origins and Consequences. *Journal of Church and State* 32: 609–26.

Finke, Roger, and Rodney Stark. 1992. *The Churching of America, 1776–1990: Winners and Losers in our Religious Economy.* New Brunswick, NJ: Rutgers University Press.

Foucault, Michel. 1965 (1961). *Madness and Civilization: A History of Insanity in the Age of Reason.* Trans. Richard Howard. New York: Pantheon.

———. 1977 (1975). *Discipline and Punish: The Birth of the Prison.* Trans. Alan Sheridan. New York: Pantheon.

———. 1978 (1976). *The History of Sexuality.* Vol. 1, *An Introduction.* Trans. Robert Hurley. New York: Pantheon.

———. 1981. Truth and Power. In *French Sociology: Rupture and Renewal since 1968,* ed. Charles C. Lemert, 293–307. New York: Columbia University Press.

———. 1985 (1984). *The History of Sexuality.* Vol. 2, *The Use of Pleasure.* Trans. Robert Hurley. New York: Pantheon.

———. 1986 (1984). *The History of Sexuality.* Vol. 3, *The Care of the Self.* Trans. Robert Hurley. New York: Vintage Books.

———. 1994 (1984)a. Face aux gouvernements, les droits de l'homme. In *Dits et écrits, 1954–1988* vol. 4, ed. Daniel Defert and François Ewald, 707–8. Paris: Gallimard.

———. 1994 (1984)b. Le Souci de la vérité. In *Dits et écrits, 1954–1988,* vol. 4, ed. Daniel Defert and François Ewald, 668–78. Paris: Gallimard.

———. 1997 (1972). Psychiatric Power. In *Essential Works of Michel Foucault,* vol. 1, *Ethics: Subjectivity and Truth,* ed. Paul Rabinow, 39–50. New York: The New Press.

———. 1997 (1975). The Abnormals. In *Essential Works of Michel Foucault,* vol. 1, *Ethics: Subjectivity and Truth,* ed. Paul Rabinow, 51–57. New York: The New Press.

———. 1997 (1981). The Social Triumph of the Sexual Will. In *Essential Works of Michel Foucault*, vol. 1, *Ethics: Subjectivity and Truth*, ed. Paul Rabinow, 157–62. New York: The New Press.

———. 1997 (1984)a. On the Genealogy of Ethics: An Overview of Work in Progress. In *Essential Works of Michel Foucault*, vol. 1, *Ethics: Subjectivity and Truth*, ed. Paul Rabinow, 253–80. New York: The New Press.

———. 1997 (1984)b. The Ethics of the Concern for Self as a Practice of Freedom. In *Essential Works of Michel Foucault*, vol. 1, *Ethics: Subjectivity and Truth*, ed. Paul Rabinow, 281–301. New York: The New Press.

———. 1997 (1984)c. Polemics, Politics and Problematizations. In *Essential Works of Michel Foucault*, vol. 1, *Ethics: Subjectivity and Truth*, ed. Paul Rabinow, 111–19. New York: The New Press.

———. 1997 (1984)d. What Is Enlightenment? In *Essential Works of Michel Foucault*, vol. 1, *Ethics: Subjectivity and Truth*, ed. Paul Rabinow, 303–19. New York: The New Press.

———. 1998 (1966). The Thought of the Outside. In *Essential Works of Michel Foucault*, vol. 2, *Aesthetics, Method, Epistemology*, ed. James D. Faubion, 147–69. New York: The New Press.

———. 1998 (1967). Nietzsche, Freud, Marx. In *Essential Works of Michel Foucault*, vol. 2, *Aesthetics, Method, Epistemology*, ed. James D. Faubion, 269–78. New York: The New Press.

———. 1998 (1970)a. Madness and Society. In *Essential Works of Michel Foucault*, vol. 2, *Aesthetics, Methodology, and Epistemology*, ed. James D. Faubion, 335–42. New York: The New Press.

———. 1998 (1970)b. Theatrum Philosophicum. In *Essential Works of Michel Foucault*, vol. 2, *Aesthetics, Methodology, and Epistemology*, ed. James D. Faubion, 343–68. New York: The New Press.

———. 1998 (1985). Life: Experience and Science. In *Essential Works of Michel Foucault*, vol. 2, *Aesthetics, Methodology, and Epistemology*, ed. James D. Faubion, 465–78. New York: The New Press.

Fowler, Robert B., and Allen D. Hertzke. 1995. *Religion and Politics in America: Faith, Culture, and Strategic Choices*. Boulder, CO: Westview Press.

Frei, Hans. 1974. *The Eclipse of Biblical Narrative: A Study in Eighteenth and Nineteenth Century Hermeneutics*. New Haven: Yale University Press.

Funkenstein, Amos. 1986. *Theology and the Scientific Imagination from the Middle Ages to the Seventeenth Century*. Princeton: Princeton University Press.

Gallagher, Eugene. 1990. *Expectation and Experience: Explaining Religious Conversion*. Atlanta: Scholars Press.

Gallup, George, Jr., and Jim Castelli. 1989. *The People's Religion: American Faith in the Nineties*. New York: Macmillan.

Geertz, Clifford. 1960. *The Religion of Java*. Chicago: University of Chicago Press.

———. 1973. *The Interpretation of Cultures*. New York: Basic Books.

———. 1992. *Local Knowledge: Further Essays in Interpretive Anthropology*. New York: Basic Books.

Gellner, Ernest. 1983. *Nations and Nationalism*. Ithaca: Cornell University Press.

General Conference of Seventh-day Adventists. 2000. What We Believe. *http:// www.adventist.org/beliefs/index.html*

Genette, Gérard. 1982. *Figures of Literary Discourse.* Trans. Alan Sheridan. New York: Columbia University Press.

Goffman, Erving. 1961. *Asylums: Essays on the Social Situation of Mental Patients and Other Inmates.* Garden City, NY: Anchor Books.

———. 1963. *Stigma: Notes on the Management of Spoiled Identity.* Englewood Cliffs, NJ: Prentice-Hall.

Goody, Jack. 1961. Religion and Ritual: The Definition Problem. *British Journal of Psychology* 12:143–64.

Goppelt, Leonhard. 1982. *Typos: The Typological Interpretation of the Old Testament in the New.* Trans. Donald H. Madvig. Grand Rapids, MI: William B. Eerdmans.

Gramsci, Antonio. 1971. *Selections from the Prison Notebooks of Antonio Gramsci.* Ed. and trans. Quentin Hoare and Geoffey Nowell Smith. New York: International Publishers.

Greeley, Andrew M. 1974. *Ecstasy: A Way of Knowing.* Englewood Cliffs, NJ: Prentice-Hall.

Greenstone, Julius H. 1906. *The Messiah Idea in Jewish History.* Philadelphia: Jewish Publication Society of America.

Greer, Bruce A., and Wade Clark Roof. 1992. "Desperately Seeking Sheila": Locating Religious Privatism in American Society. *Journal for the Scientific Study of Religion* 31 (3): 346–52.

Grondin, Jean. 1995. *Sources of Hermeneutics.* Albany: State University of New York Press.

Habermas, Jürgen. 1984. *The Theory of Communicative Action.* Vol. 1, *Reason and the Rationalization of Society.* Trans. Thomas McCarthy. Boston: Beacon Press.

Hacking, Ian. 1999. *The Social Construction of What?* Cambridge, MA: Harvard University Press.

Halbwachs, Maurice. 1978 (1930). *The Causes of Suicide.* Trans. Harold Goldblatt. London: Routledge.

Hale, Apollos. 1843. *The Second Advent Manual: In Which the Objections to Calculating the Prophetic Times Are Considered; the Difficulties Connected with the Calculation Explained; and the Facts and Arguments on Which Mr. Miller's Calculations Rest, Are Briefly Stated and Sustained.* Boston: J. V. Himes.

Halsell, Grace. 1986. *Prophecy and Politics.* Westport, CT: Lawrence Hill.

Harding, Susan Friend. 2000. *The Book of Jerry Falwell: Fundamentalist Language and Politics.* Princeton: Princeton University Press.

Harman, Gilbert. 1977. *The Nature of Morality: An Introduction to Ethics.* New York: Oxford University Press.

Hatch, Elvin. 1983. *Culture and Morality: The Relativity of Values in Anthropology.* New York: Columbia University Press.

Hayes, John H. 1971. *Introduction to the Bible.* Philadelphia: Westminster Press.

Heirich, Max. 1977. Change of Heart: A Test of Some Widely Held Theories about Religious Conversion. *American Journal of Sociology* 83 (3): 653–80.

Herder, Johann Gottfried. 1966. *Outlines of a Philosophy of the History of Man*. Trans. T. Churchill. New York: Bergman Publishers.

Herzfeld, Michael. 1987. *Anthropology through the Looking-glass: Critical Ethnography in the Margins of Europe*. Cambridge: Cambridge University Press.

———. 1991. *A Place in History: Social and Monumental Time in a Cretan Town*. Princeton: Princeton University Press.

Hilty, Dale M., Rick Morgan, and Wilmer Hartman. 1985. A Structural Equation Modeling Analysis of the Means, End, and Quest Dimensions. *Journal for the Scientific Study of Religion* 24 (4): 426–36.

Hobsbawm, Eric J. 1959. *Primitive Rebels*. Manchester: Manchester University Press.

Holston, James. 1999. Alternative Modernities: Statecraft and Religious Imagination in the Valley of the Dawn. *American Ethnologist* 26 (3): 605–31.

Hood, Ralph W., Jr., and Ronald J. Morris. 1985. Conceptualization of Quest: A Critical Rejoinder to Batson. *Review of Religious Research* 26 (4): 391–97.

Hubert, Henri, and Marcel Mauss. 1964 (1899). *Sacrifice: Its Nature and Function*. Trans. W. D. Halls. Chicago: University of Chicago Press.

Iannaccone, Laurence. 1990. Religious Practice: A Human Capital Approach. *Journal for the Scientific Study of Religion* 29 (3): 297–314.

Jackson, John. 1998. Bureaucracies at Work. In *Even Paranoids Have Enemies: New Perspectives in Paranoia and Persecution*, ed. Joseph H. Berke, Stella Pierides, Andrea Sabbadini, and Stanley Schneider, 125–38. New York: Routledge.

James, William. 1985 (1859). *The Varieties of Religious Experience: A Study in Human Nature*. Cambridge, MA: Harvard University Press.

Johnson, Elliott E. 1992. Premillennialism Introduced: Hermeneutics. In *A Case for Premillennialism: A New Consensus*, ed. Donald K. Campbell and Jeffrey L. Townsend, 15–34. Chicago: Moody Press.

Judd, Wayne R. 1987. William Miller: Disappointed Prophet. In *The Disappointed: Millerism and Millenarianism in the Nineteenth Century*, ed. Ronald L. Numbers and Jonathon M. Butler, 17–35. Bloomington: Indiana University Press.

Kant, Immanuel. 1960. *Religion within the Limits of Reason Alone*. Trans. Theodore M. Greene and Hoyt H. Hudson. New York: Harper.

———. 1974. *Anthropology from a Pragmatic Point of View*. Trans. Mary J. Gregor. The Hague: Nijhoff.

Kernberg, Otto F. 1998. Paranoid Social Developments as a Consequence of Ideological and Bureaucratic Regression. In *Even Paranoids Have Enemies: New Perspectives in Paranoia and Persecution*, ed. Joseph H. Berke, Stella Pierides, Andrea Sabbadini, and Stanley Schneider, 87–99. New York: Routledge.

Keuls, Eva. 1993. *The Reign of the Phallus: Sexual Politics in Ancient Athens*. Berkeley: University of California Press.

Kierulff, Stephen. 1991. Belief in "Armageddon Theology" and Willingness to Risk Nuclear War. *Journal for the Scientific Study of Religion* 30 (1): 81–93.

Kirkpatrick, Lee A., and Phillip R. Shaver. 1990. Attachment Theory and Religion: Childhood Attachments, Religious Beliefs, and Conversion. *Journal for the Scientific Study of Religion* 29 (3): 315–34.

Koselleck, Reinhart. 1985. *Futures Past: The Semantics of Historical Time.* Trans. Keith Tribe. Cambridge, MA: MIT Press.

Kwilecki, Susan. 1999. *Becoming Religious: Understanding Devotion to the Unseen.* Lewisburg, PA: Bucknell University Press.

Lambropoulos, Vassilis. 1993. *The Rise of Eurocentrism: Anatomy of Interpretation.* Princeton: Princeton University Press.

Lampe, G.W.H., and K. J. Woollcombe. 1957. *Essays on Typology.* London: SCM Press.

Land, Gary G., ed. 1986. *Adventism in America: A History.* Grand Rapids, MI: William B. Eerdmans.

Langer, Susanne K. 1953. *Feeling and Form.* New York: Charles Scribner's Sons.

Lee, Benjamin. 1997. *Talking Heads: Language, Metalanguage, and the Semiotics of Subjectivity.* Durham: Duke University Press.

Lévi-Strauss, Claude. 1966. *The Savage Mind.* Chicago: University of Chicago Press.

———. 1969. *The Raw and the Cooked.* Introduction to *A Science of Mythology,* vol. 1. Trans. John and Doreen Weightman. New York: Harper Torchbooks.

Lincoln, Bruce. 1994. *Authority: Construction and Corrosion.* Chicago: University of Chicago Press.

Lindsey, Hal. 1970. *The Late, Great Planet Earth.* New York: Bantam Books.

———. 1973. *There's a New World Coming.* Santa Ana, CA: Vision House Publishers.

———. 1981 (1980). *The 1980's: Countdown to Armageddon.* New York: Bantam Books.

Lindstrom, Lamonte. 1993. *Cargo Cult: Strange Stories of Desire from Melanesia and Beyond.* Honolulu: University of Hawaii Press.

Littlewood, Roland. 1992. *Pathology and Identity: The Work of Mother Earth in Trinidad.* New York: Cambridge University Press.

Locke, John. 1999 (1695). *The Reasonableness of Christianity: As Delivered in the Scriptures.* Ed. John C. Higgins-Biddle. Oxford: Clarendon Press.

Lofland, John. 1966. *Doomsday Cult: A Study of Conversion, Proselytization, and Maintenance of Faith.* Englewood Cliffs, NJ: Prentice-Hall.

Lofland, John, and Norman Skonovd. 1981. Conversion Motifs. *Journal for the Scientific Study of Religion* 20 (4): 373–85.

Lofland, John, and Rodney Stark. 1965. Becoming a World-Saver: A Theory of Conversion to a Deviant Perspective. *American Sociological Review* 30: 862–74.

Löwith, Karl. 1949. *Meaning in History. The Theological Presuppositions of the Philosophy of History.* Chicago: University of Chicago Press.

Ludwig, Arnold M. 1971. *Treating the Treatment Failures: The Challenge of Chronic Schizophrenia.* New York: Grune and Stratton.

Luhmann, Niklas. 1990a. *Essays on Self-Reference.* New York: Columbia University Press.

———. 1990b. The Paradox of System Differentiation and the Evolution of Society. In *Differentiation Theory and Social Change: Comparative and His-*

torical Perspectives, ed. Jeffrey C. Alexander and Paul Colomy, 409–40. New York: Columbia University Press.

Lyon, Margot L., and Jack M. Barbalet. 1994. Society's Body: Emotion and the "Somatization" of Social Theory. In *Embodiment and Experience: The Existential Ground of Culture and Self*, ed. Thomas J. Csordas, 48–66. Cambridge: Cambridge University Press.

Mackie, John L. 1977. *Ethics: Inventing Right and Wrong*. Harmondsworth: Penguin.

MacKinnon, Malcolm H. 1993. The Longevity of the Thesis: A Critique of the Critics. In *Weber's Protestant Ethic: Origins, Evidence, Contexts*, ed. Hartmut Lehmann and Guenther Roth, 211–43. Washington, DC: German Historical Institute and Cambridge University Press.

Mauss, Marcel. 1973 (1934). Techniques of the Body. Trans. Ben Brewster. *Economy and Society* 2 (1): 70–88.

———. 1990 (1925). *The Gift: The Form and Reason for Exchange in Archaic Societies*. Trans. W. D. Halls. New York: W. W. Norton.

Mazzeo, Joseph Anthony. 1978. *Varieties of Interpretation*. Notre Dame: University of Notre Dame Press.

McCartney, Don, and C. Clayton. 1994. *Let the Reader Understand: A Guide to Interpreting and Applying the Bible*. Wheaton, IL: Victor Books (Bridge Point).

McFarland, Sam G., and James C. Warren, Jr. 1992. Religious Orientations and Selective Exposure among Fundamentalist Christians. *Journal for the Scientific Study of Religion* 31 (2): 163–74.

Métraux, Alfred. 1948. The Tupinamba. In *Handbook of South American Indians*, ed. Julian H. Steward. Bureau of American Ethnography, bulletin 143, vol. 3. Washington, DC: Smithsonian Institution.

Michaelis, Johann David. 1782. *Orientalische und exegetische Bibliotek XIX*. Frankfurt am Main.

Mill, John Stuart.1962 (1859). On Liberty. In *Utilitarianism, On Liberty, Essay on Bentham*, ed. Mary Warnock, 126–250. New York: Meridian Books.

Miller, William. 1833. *Evidences from Scripture and History of the Second Coming of Christ about the Year 1843, and of His Personal Reign of 1000 Years*. Brandon, VT: Vermont Telegraph Office.

Mooney, James. 1896. *The Ghost Dance Religion and the Sioux Outbreak of 1890*. Washington, DC: GPO.

Neitz, Mary Jo, and James V. Spickard. 1990. Steps toward a Sociology of Religious Experience: The Theories of Mihaly Csikszentmihalyi and Alfred Schutz. *Sociological Analysis* 51 (1): 15–33.

Nichol, Francis D. 1945. *The Midnight Cry*. Washington, DC: Review and Herald Publishing Association.

Niebuhr, H. Richard. 1929. *The Social Sources of Denominationalism*. New York: Henry Holt.

Ober, Josiah. 1989. *Mass and Elite in Democratic Athens: Rhetoric, Ideology, and the Power of the People*. Princeton: Princeton University Press.

O'Leary, Stephen D. 1994. *Arguing the Apocalypse: A Theory of Millennial Rhetoric*. New York: Oxford University Press.

221

Oliver, Jr., Moorman. 1994. Killed by Semantics: Or Was It a Keystone Cop Kaleidoscope Kaper? In *After the Ashes: Making Sense of Waco*, ed. James R. Lewis, 71–86. Lanham, MD: Rowman and Littlefield.

Overholt, Thomas. 1989. *Channels of Prophecy: The Social Dynamics of Prophetic Activity*. Minneapolis: Fortress Press.

Peirce, Charles S. 1961. *The Collected Papers of Charles Sanders Peirce*. Vol. 1. Ed. Charles Hartshorne and Paul Weiss. Cambridge, MA: Belknap Press.

———. 1982. *Writings of Charles S. Peirce: A Chronological Edition*. Vol. 5, 1884–1886. Ed. Christian J. W. Kloesel. Bloomington: Indiana University Press.

Pitts, William. 1993. The Mount Carmel Davidians: Adventist Reformers, 1935–1959. *Syzygy: Journal of Alternative Religion and Culture* 2 (1–2): 39–54.

———. 1994. The Davidian Tradition. In *From the Ashes: Making Sense of Waco*, ed. James R. Lewis, 33–39. Lanham, MD: Rowman and Littlefield.

Pizzorno, Alessandro. 1987. Politics Unbound. In *The Changing Boundaries of the Political: Essays on the Evolving Balance between the State and Society, Public and Private in Europe*, ed. Charles S. Maier, 27–62. Cambridge: Cambridge University Press.

Poliakov, Léon. 1965. *The History of Anti-semitism*. Vol. 1, *From the Time of Christ to the Court Jews*. Trans. Richard Howard. New York: Vanguard Press.

———. 1972. *Le mythe Aryen: essai sur les sources du racisme et des nationalismes*. Paris: Calmann-Lévy.

———. 1975. *The History of Anti-semitism*. Vol. 3, *From Voltaire to Wagner*. Trans. Miriam Kochan. New York: Vanguard Press.

Price, Richard. 1983. *First-Time: The Historical Vision of an Afro-American People*. Baltimore: Johns Hopkins University Press.

Privitera, Walter. 1995. *Problems of Style: Michel Foucault's Epistemology*. Trans. Jean Keller. Albany: State University of New York Press.

Proudfoot, Wayne. 1985. *Religious Experience*. Berkeley: University of California Press.

Quintilian (Quintilien). 1978. *Institution oratoire*. Vol. 5, books 8, 9. Ed. and trans. Jean Cousin. Paris: Collection des Universités de France.

Rabinow, Paul. 1997. Introduction to *Essential Works of Michel Foucault*. Vol, 1, *Ethics: Subjectivity and Truth*, ed. Paul Rabinow. New York: The New Press.

———. 1999. *French DNA: Trouble in Purgatory*. Chicago: University of Chicago Press.

Rambo, Lewis R. 1993. *Understanding Religious Conversion*. New Haven: Yale University Press.

Rawls, John. 1971. *A Theory of Justice*. Cambridge, MA: Harvard University Press.

Reardon, Bernard M. G., ed. 1968. *Liberal Protestantism*. Stanford: Stanford University Press.

Reavis, Dick J. 1995. *The Ashes of Waco: An Investigation*. New York: Simon and Schuster.

Richardson, James T. 1980. Conversion Careers. *Society* 17: 47–50.

———. 1985. The Active vs. the Passive Convert: Paradigm Conflict in Conversion/Recruitment Research. *Journal for the Scientific Study of Religion* 24 (2): 163–179.

Richardson, James T., and Brock K. Kilbourne. 1983. Classical and Contemporary Brainwashing Models: A Comparison and Critique. In *The Brainwashing/Deprogramming Controversy*, ed. David G. Bromley and James T. Richardson, 29–45. Toronto: Edwin Mellon Press.

Richman, Michèle. 1990. Anthropology and Modernism in France: From Durkheim to the *Collège de sociologie*. In *Modernist Anthropology: From Fieldwork to Text*, ed. Marc Manganaro, 183–214. Princeton: Princeton University Press.

Robbins, Thomas. 1984. Constructing Cultist "Mind Control." *Social Analysis* 45 (3): 241–56.

Robertson, J. J. 1996. *Beyond the Flames: The Trials of the Branch Davidians*. San Diego: Promotion Publishing.

Robinson, H. Wheeler. 1946. *Inspiration and Revelation in the Old Testament*. Oxford: Clarendon Press.

Rosaldo, Renato. 1980. *Ilongot Headhunting, 1883–1974: A Study in Society and History*. Stanford: Stanford University Press.

Roth, Guenther, and Wolfgang Schluchter. 1979. *Max Weber's Vision of History: Ethics and Methods*. Berkeley: University of California Press.

Rowe, David L. 1985. *Thunders and Trumpets: Millerites and Dissenting Religion in Upstate New York, 1800–1850*. Chico, CA: Scholars Press.

———. 1987. Millerites: A Shadow Portrait. In *The Disappointed: Millerism and Millenarianism in the Nineteenth Century*, ed. Ronald L. Numbers and Jonathon M. Butler, 1–17. Bloomington: Indiana University Press.

Sahlins, Marshall. 1985. *Islands of History*. Chicago: University of Chicago Press.

Sales, Stephen M. 1972. Economic Threat as a Determinant of Conversion in Authoritarian and Nonauthoritarian Churches. *Journal of Personality and Social Psychology* 23 (3): 420–28.

Sandeen, Ernest R. 1970. *The Roots of Fundamentalism: British and American Millenarianism, 1800–1930*. Chicago: University of Chicago Press.

———. 1974. Millennialism. In *The Rise of Adventism: Religion in Mid-Nineteenth-Century America*, ed. Edwin S. Gaustad, 104–18. New York: Harper and Row.

Scheper-Hughes, Nancy, and Margaret Lock. 1987. The Mindful Body: A Prolegomenon to Future Work in Medical Anthropology. *Medical Anthropology Quarterly* 1:6–41.

Schiller, Friedrich. 1965 (1794–95). *Notes on the Aesthetic Education of Man, In a Series of Lectures*. Trans. R. Snell. New York: Frederick Ungar.

Schleiermacher, Friedrich. 1988 (1799). *On Religion: Speeches to Its Cultured Despisers*. Trans. Richard Crouter. Cambridge: Cambridge University Press.

Schmithals, Walter. 1975. *The Apocalyptic Movement: Introduction and Interpretation*. Trans. John E. Steely. Nashville: Abingdon Press.

Schneider, Stanley. 1998. Peace and Paranoia. In *Even Paranoids Have Enemies: New Perspectives in Paranoia and Persecution*, ed. Joseph H. Berke, Stella

Pierides, Andrea Sabbadini, and Stanley Schneider, 203–18. New York: Routledge.

Scholem, Gershom. 1971. *The Messianic Idea in Judaism and Other Essays on Jewish Spirituality*. New York: Schocken.

Schrauwers, Albert. 1993. *Awaiting the Millennium: The Children of Peace and the Village of Hope, 1812–1889*. Toronto: University of Toronto Press.

Schwab, Reinhold, and Kay Uwe Peterson. 1990. Religiousness: Its Relation to Loneliness, Neuroticism, and Subjective Well-Being. *Journal for the Scientific Study of Religion* 29 (3): 335–45.

Scruggs, Richard, Steven Zipperstein, Robert Lyon, Victor Gonzalez, Herbert Cousins, and Roderick Beverly. 1993. *Report to the Deputy Attorney General on the Events at Waco, Texas, February 28 to April 19, 1993*. Redacted version. Washington, DC: GPO.

Smith, Peter. 1982. Millenarianism in the Babi and Baha'i Religions. In *Millennialism and Charisma*, ed. Roy Wallis, 231–83. Belfast: Queen's University.

Snow, David A., and Cynthia L. Phillips. 1980. The Lofland-Stark Conversion Model: A Critical Reassessment. *Social Problems* 27 (4): 430–47.

Spicer, Edward H. 1971. Persistent Cultural Systems: A Comparative Study of Identity Systems That Can Adapt to Contrasting Environments. *Science* 174 (19 November): 795–800.

Spilka, Bernard, Ralph W. Hood, and Richard Gorsuch. 1985. *The Psychology of Religion: An Empirical Approach*. Englewood Cliffs, NJ: Prentice-Hall.

Stark, Rodney, and William Sims Bainbridge. 1985. *The Future of Religion: Secularization, Revival, and Cult Formation*. Berkeley: University of California Press.

Stifler, Kenneth, Joanne Greer, William Sneck, and Robert Dovenmuehle.1993. An Empirical Investigation of the Discriminability of Reported Mystical Experiences among Religious Contemplatives, Psychotic Inpatients, and Normal Adults. *Journal for the Scientific Study of Religion* 32 (4): 366–72.

Stocking, George W. 1987. *Victorian Anthropology*. New York: The Free Press.

Strathern, Marilyn. 1991. *Partial Connections*. Savage, MD: Rowman and Littlefield.

Straus, Roger. 1976. Changing Oneself: Seekers and the Creative Transformation of Experience. In *Doing Social Life*, ed. John Lofland, 252–72. New York: Wiley.

———. 1979. Religious Conversion as a Personal and Collective Accomplishment. *Sociological Analysis* 40:158–65.

Tabor, James D., and Eugene V. Gallagher. 1995. *Why Waco? Cults and the Battle for Religious Freedom in America*. Berkeley: University of California Press.

Thucydides. 1980. *History of the Peloponnesian War*. 4 vols. Trans. Charles F. Smith. Cambridge, MA: Harvard University Press.

Trompf, Garry W. 1979. *The Idea of Historical Recurrence in Western Thought: From Antiquity to the Reformation*. Berkeley: University of California Press.

———. 1990. Introduction to *Cargo Cults and Millenarian Movements*. Ed. G. W. Trompf. New York: Mouton de Gruyter.

———, ed. 1990. *Cargo Cults and Millenarian Movements*. New York: Mouton de Gruyter.

Turner, Victor W. 1969. *The Ritual Process: Structure and Anti-Structure*. Ithaca: Cornell University Press.

Tyler, Stephen. 1998. Them Others — Voices without Mirrors. *Paideuma* 44: 31–50.

Ullman, Chana. 1982. Cognitive and Emotional Antecedents of Religious Conversion. *Journal of Personality and Social Psychology* 43 (1): 183–92.

Van Gennep, Arnold. 1960 (1909). *The Rites of Passage*. Trans. Monika B. Vizedom and Gabrielle L. Caffe. Chicago: University of Chicago Press.

Van Zandt, David E. 1991. *Living in the Children of God*. Princeton: Princeton University Press.

Viswanathan, Gauri. 1995. *Coping with (Civil) Death: The Christian Convert's Rights of Passage in Colonial India*. Princeton: Princeton University Press.

Wallace, Anthony C. 1956a. Mazeway Resynthesis: A Biocultural Theory of Religious Inspiration. *Transactions of the New York Academy of Sciences*, 2nd ser., 18: 626–38.

———. 1956b. Revitalization Movements. *American Anthropologist* 58: 264–81.

Wallerstein, Immanuel. 1999. *The End of the World as We Know It: Social Science for the Twenty-first Century*. Minneapolis: University of Minnesota Press.

Wallis, Roy. 1982. Charisma, Commitment and Control in a New Religious Movement. In *Millennialism and Charisma*, ed. Roy Wallis, 73–140. Belfast: Queen's University.

———, ed. 1982. *Millennialism and Charisma*. Belfast: Queen's University.

Wallis, Roy, and Steve Bruce. 1984. The Stark-Bainbridge Theory of Religion: A Critical Analysis and Counter-proposals. *Sociological Analysis* 45 (1): 11–28.

Weber, Max. 1946. *From Max Weber: Essays in Sociology*. Ed. and trans. Hans Gerth and C. Wright Mills. New York: Oxford University Press.

———. 1958 (1904–1905). *The Protestant Ethic and the Spirit of Capitalism*. Trans. Talcott Parsons. New York: Charles Scribner's Sons.

Weber, Timothy. 1979. *Living in the Shadow of the Second Coming: American Premillennialism, 1875–1925*. New York: Oxford University Press.

Wessinger, Catherine. 1993. Going Beyond and Retaining Charisma: Women's Leadership in Marginal Religions. In *Women's Leadership in Marginal Religions: Explorations Outside the Mainstream*, ed. Catherine Wessinger, 1–19. Urbana: University of Illinois Press.

West, Cornell. 1982. *Prophesy Deliverance: An Afro-American Revolutionary Christianity*. Philadelphia: Westminster Press.

Wilson, Bryan. 1973. *Magic and the Millennium*. London: Heinemann.

Worsley, Peter. 1968. *The Trumpet Shall Sound: A Study of "Cargo Cults" in Melanesia*. 2nd ed. New York: Schocken.

Young, Allan. 1995. *The Harmony of Illusions: Inventing Post-traumatic Stress Disorder*. Princeton: Princeton University Press.

Index